Dracula and
Philosophy

Popular Culture and Philosophy® Series Editor: George A. Reisch

For full details of all Popular Culture and Philosophy® books, visit www.opencourtbooks.com.

Popular Culture and Philosophy®

Dracula and Philosophy

Dying to Know

Edited by
NICOLAS MICHAUD
and
JANELLE PÖTZSCH

OPEN COURT
Chicago

Volume 90 in the series, Popular Culture and Philosophy ®, edited by George A. Reisch

To order books from Open Court, call toll-free 1-800-815-2280, or visit our website at www.opencourtbooks.com.

Open Court Publishing Company is a division of Carus Publishing Company, dba Cricket Media.

Copyright © 2015 by Carus Publishing Company, dba Cricket Media.

First printing 2015

ISBN: 978-0-8126-9890-9

Library of Congress Control Number: 2015937872

Contents

Death Becomes Him— Finally

$\mathbf{M}$any writers have tried their luck with the vampire genre, among them literary giants like Tolstoy and Goethe. But all of them were trumped by an Irish civil servant and freelance journalist—Abraham Stoker, just another guy trying to make a living. The most disturbing and lasting image we have of vampires was created by a man who tried to make a tiny bit more out of his chance meeting with a Hungarian professor who liked to tell scary stories.

Bram Stoker's version of the age-old vampire myth radically changed our view of the Undead. That creepy withered thing, which used to lie sucking and smacking in its grave, was given a title and a castle, and the ability to travel the world. *Count* Dracula's powers increased still further when the movie business leaned in: Dracula now frequents fashionable salons and is a real lady's man.

Let's face it: Van Helsing and consorts may have done their very best, but in the long run, Dracula just can't be killed. He has been haunting the world for more than a hundred years and still hasn't lost his morbid appeal. We continue to enter his world freely and of our own free will . . .

But is it, or has it ever been, truly Dracula's world? Dracula has become such a well-known phenomenon of our culture, and in a fairly short time, that our hero worship of him says a great deal about *us*. Which made us wonder: Why would we willingly seek out an evening of nightmares because of browsing Stoker's novel or watching the latest Dracula movie? Why are we so fascinated by this guy with his outdated clothes and the funny accent?

We left no coffin unopened in our effort to shed light on these issues. We've undertaken the task of exposing what Stoker's scary masterpiece, as well as its numerous spin-offs, tells us about ourselves (because that's just what a classic is about, right?).

In our quest for truth, we'll ponder questions like: Is Dracula truly evil? What's wrong with dressing a bit . . . differently? And if we take offense at the Count's consumption of blood, shouldn't we equally stop eating meat?

We'll enter not only the twisted mind of the Count but also the best-hidden corners of our own subconscious to reveal why we are so awkwardly in love with the most powerful of all vampires. One thing's for certain, like any encounter with Dracula, expect to leave changed . . . and not necessarily for the better.

Sit back, take another savory bite of whatever dish heats your blood and then get ready to sink your teeth into *Dracula and Philosophy.*

I

The Downside
of Undeath

1
The Curse of Living Forever

JAMES EDWIN MAHON

The Un-Dead. That was almost the title of *Dracula*. The original manuscript, the publisher's contract, even the five-act play version of the story, all had "Un-Dead" in the title. Thankfully, Bram Stoker decided to change the title at the very last minute. But Stoker uses "Un-Dead" throughout the book to refer to vampires, and he changed the meaning of these words forever.

Before *Dracula*, to be "undead" simply meant to be *not dead*. To be "undead" meant to be *alive*, or *living*. This older meaning is apparent in another title Stoker considered, *The Dead Un-Dead*, which translates as "The Dead Living" (like the classic zombie movie *Night of the Living Dead* (1968). All of this changed with *Dracula*. After *Dracula*, "undead" would never again simply mean living or alive.

With the publication of *Dracula*, to be "undead" meant to be *dead-but-alive*, or to be *living dead*. Of course, it is possible to kill the undead, including vampires. A vampire can be killed by driving a stake through its heart, or by decapitating it. But vampires need to be killed, and need to be killed in a particular way. As Van Helsing says, they do "not die by the passing of time." If a vampire is not killed, it will simply go on living, *forever*. Although vampires come into existence at a certain point in history, and are not eternal, like gods, there is no natural death for vampires. They are immortal.

Although Stoker had vampires in mind when he coined the term "undead," it also covers zombies, ghouls, ghosts, and animated mummies. All of them are immortal. Nevertheless, vampires are different from the rest of the undead in at least two ways. First, they are suave and sophisticated. Second, they are highly intelligent. It is this second difference that makes their immortality different from that of the other undead, because vampires are immortal creatures who *know* that they are immortal. The question is whether this knowledge of their own immortality—this knowledge that their lives will never end—makes their lives a "curse," or whether it causes something else, something much worse.

From Rags to Riches

Originally, the vampire, or *"nosferatu,"* was a hideous, misshapen, nasty creature you mostly came across in folk tales and ghost stories. All of this changed at the beginning of the nineteenth century after a ghost-story competition. A group of Romantic authors—Lord Byron, his young personal physician John William Polidori, Percy Bysshe Shelley, Shelley's soon-to-be wife, Mary Wollstonecraft Godwin, and Mary's step-sister (and Byron's lover) Jane "Claire" Clairmont—were holidaying near Lake Geneva. Bored by bad weather, Byron proposed, "We will each write a ghost story." This competition not only gave us Mary Godwin's masterpiece *Frankenstein*. It also changed vampires forever, thanks to Byron's unfinished story "The Burial: A Fragment," inspiring Polidori to write the novella *The Vampyre*, which introduced "Lord Ruthven."

Unlike the *nosferatu* of old, Polidori's vampire is a suave, sophisticated nobleman. He is powerfully attractive to women, who are his primary victims. He moves through high society, keeping his true identity secret. Lord Ruthven was in fact modeled on Lord Byron himself. Stoker's own vampire, Count Dracula, is in this Byronic tradition of the upper-class vampire. He is a Transylvanian aristocrat, a nobleman descended from an old family.

Before becoming a vampire he was a military leader who led troops against the Turks. He speaks German, Hungarian, Slovak, Serbian, Wallachian, and Romany, as well as English. He is a learned individual, and studied diabolical secrets at the legendary school of black magic, Scholomance, at Lake Hermannstadt in Transylvania, where he became a vampire.

Although he is not as young as Lord Ruthven, he is tall, and thin, and has a sensual face, which is admittedly hard and cruel. Dracula has it all: he's aristocratic, highly educated, and far from being unattractive. All of this makes him not only hugely popular with the ladies, it also sets him apart from the rest of the undead, such as zombies and ghouls, who are just ugly and brutish monsters. None of this seems so awful, though, as to make being "undead" such a bad thing. In fact, so far it sounds like he's got a pretty good unlife.

Existential Undead

Despite his good looks, Dracula has an extremely complicated life. He has many goals in addition to consuming people's blood, and he makes elaborate plans to satisfy these goals. He arranges, through the law firm that Jonathan Harker works for, to buy an estate in Purfleet, East London, because he plans to move there and dine on Londoners. He later decides to track down Wilhemina "Mina" Murray, the fiancée of Jonathan Harker, and her friend Lucy Westenra, the fiancée of the Honorable Arthur Holmwood (later Lord Godalming). Had it not been for the intervention of his nemesis, Van Helsing, Dracula would have outsmarted them all.

Dracula, and vampires in general, are highly intelligent beings. They are much more intelligent than zombies and ghouls and the rest of the undead. But they're not just the most intelligent members of the undead family. They're the only members of the undead family who *know* that they are undead. Vampires are immortal beings who *know* that they are immortal beings.

To paraphrase Martin Heidegger (1889–1976) vampires have *being-toward-undeath*. Their knowledge of their own immortality gives them their peculiar status within existence. To have a "being-toward-death" means that a person has a kind of authentic awareness of their finite existence. So to have a "being-toward-*undeath*" would mean to have a full and authentic awareness of being undead. It may be why Van Helsing refers to the vampire's immortality as a "curse." But what precisely makes such an appealing idea like immortality a curse?

Immortal Senior Citizens?

It may seem strange to say that immortality is, or can be, annoying. Immortality seems to be something that all people desire. The promise of immortality is a hugely important part of most religions—especially Christianity, which forms the background to the modern vampire tradition. In his satirical masterpiece, *Gulliver's Travels* (1726), Jonathan Swift presented bodily immortality in a miserable light. When Gulliver visits the kingdom of Luggnagg, and hears about the small number of "*Struldbruggs*, or *Immortals*," that live in the kingdom, his response is typical. He reports, "Happiest beyond all comparison, are those excellent *Struldbruggs*" because he assumes immortality brings happiness.

Gulliver's favorable opinion of immortality is quickly dispelled. He is told that in Luggnagg, "the Appetite for living was not so eager, from the continual Example of the *Struldbruggs*." These immortal individuals are not young and healthy, but rather have "a perpetual Life under all the usual Disadvantages which old Age brings along with it." They suffer from infirmities and diseases, and lose their teeth and hair at the comparatively early age of ninety. They have no memory of anything beyond their middle age, they commonly forget the names for things and people, and they cannot read because "their Memory will not serve to carry them from the beginning of a Sentence to the end," and they cannot keep up with changes in the language. They cease to be legal persons when they reach the age of eighty, and although they are granted a pittance of an allowance by the state, they have no occupation other than begging. As a result, "they lye under the Disadvantage of living like Foreigners in their own Country" and are "despised and hated by all sorts of People; when one of them is born, it is reckoned ominous." After Gulliver meets with some of them, he declares that the reader will no longer think of immortality as such a gift.

The bodily immortality of the Struldbruggs is certainly a curse. But this is a bodily immortality of being weak, disease-ridden, toothless, hairless, incapable of remembering things, incapable of communicating with others, incapable of affection, and unable to earn a living. It is a bodily immortality of *old age*. Even though Dracula is an "old man," he is nothing like the

Struldbruggs. He suffers from none of their deformities or weaknesses. On the contrary: his memory and intellectual abilities surpass those of most other people. He is amazingly strong, and he can read, write, and converse in at least seven languages. He is also wealthy and able to buy property in London.

Although Dracula is old, vampires don't have to be old. They can be young and handsome. The three vampire "sisters," otherwise known as the Brides of Dracula, are a case in point. Jonathan Harker describes them as young and exceedingly beautiful:

> In the moonlight opposite me were three young women, ladies by their dress and manner. . . . Two were dark, and had high aquiline noses, like the Count, and great dark, piercing eyes, that seemed to be almost red when contrasted with the pale yellow moon. The other was fair, as fair as can be, with great, wavy masses of golden hair and eyes like pale sapphires. . . . All three had brilliant white teeth, that shone like pearls against the ruby of their voluptuous lips.

Unlike the Struldbruggs, vampires can be young, beautiful, strong, charming, intelligent, educated, aristocratic, and wealthy. Their kind of immortality is—or can be—an eternal youth kind of immortality. So if immortality is indeed a curse for vampires, as Van Helsing claims, it's definitely not because they become wrinkled. There must be a different reason.

Bored to Death (and Beyond)

One argument for the cursed nature of immortality, even of the eternal youth variety, is given by the English philosopher Bernard Williams (1929–2003). Williams argued that there is nothing we can imagine in the afterlife that will prevent the inevitability of boredom. There is no state of activity, according to Williams, that would not eventually become boring to someone who has particular interests, tastes, and dislikes. For such a person, "boredom . . . would be . . . a reaction almost perceptual in character to the poverty of one's relation to the environment." That is, anyone who is immortal will eventually become bored with life.

Williams's argument is taken up by the American philosopher Shelly Kagan, who says that immortality doesn't just mean living a very long time, but living *forever.* And is there anything that we can think of that we want to do forever? Even if we contemplate a life going through different careers, "fifty or a hundred years pursuing philosophy . . . fifty or a hundred years traveling around the world . . . fifty or a hundred years being an artist," and so on, still, there's no life we would take on that would prevent it from becoming boring.

If we contemplate a life spent in a "pleasure-making machine," then we also contemplate growing tired of such a life. This certainly seems to apply to Dracula. Eventually, he becomes bored with his life in Transylvania and wants to move to London. Think about what this means, though. He has become bored with his three beautiful brides. He is bored of his gorgeous castle and all of the things in it, he is bored of having an entire town of people to amuse him as his slaves, he has exhausted all he can do there, and that is only after a few hundred years. We can assume the same thing would eventually happen in London, and then perhaps in New York, and then Tokyo, and *everywhere.* After just a few thousand years, Dracula would have exhausted all of the pleasures offered in the world. Being stuck in Transylvania is like being stuck in a pleasure-making machine.

Despite living in a place where his every wish is granted, he decided to leave, to endanger his immortality for something *new.* We would eventually become bored with the pleasure-giving machine. This is because we have the ability to reflect on our experiences and can step back and assess them. Anyone having such experiences forever would wonder, "Is this all that there is to life?" He or she would eventually "become horrified" at being stuck in this life.

The only way to endure such an everlasting life would be to lobotomize ourselves—and living forever as a lobotomized human being is surely repugnant, since it is the life of a zombie; surely nobody wants to be a zombie. All in all, Kagan says, immortality would become a nightmare, something we would desperately seek to free ourselves from. Perhaps that's why Dracula took on the seemingly suicidal trip to London. That's why Kagan claims that dying is in fact a good thing, because it spares us this increasingly dull nightmare.

Killing Time

If Williams and Kagan are correct, the life of a vampire must be horrible. Just imagine: they live a life that will inevitably become a terrible bore, and yet they must continue to live, bored, forever. And since vampires are quite smart, they must have figured this out. Even before they actually become bored with life, they *know* that they will become bored with it. Unbearable and endless tedium awaits them, and they *know* it. For vampires, becoming bored *takes the place* of death. But becoming bored is far worse than death, because being bored is a painful experience. Death would be the experience of nothingness, but boredom for Dracula would be an unloving hell, the experience of suffering *forever*. The normal cure for boredom is to switch your hobbies, or (if you really have absolutely nothing else to do), to kill yourself. But there's no cure for being bored with life, other than death, and this is precisely what is out of reach for an undead being.

There is no cure for the boredom vampires face: it's a painful experience without end. And since vampires are intelligent creatures, they *know* this. Not only do vampires, because they are immortal, inevitably suffer from endless pain, they also *know*, because they are intelligent, that they *will* inevitably suffer from endless pain. So, if Williams and Kagan are correct, not only do vampires have *being-toward-undeath*, they also have *being-toward-endless-pain*. They have an authentic and full awareness of the inevitability of their suffering. This could be the "curse of immortality" that Van Helsing is talking about. Seen in this light, you'd do vampires *a favor* by killing them. Skewering their hearts simply frees them from their curse, giving them the "death that should have come centuries agone."

But hang on. If immortality is a curse, and if vampires know this, why the hell do they do everything in their power to remain immortal? After all, Dracula does take on that unnecessarily dangerous trip to London, but it's not like he just rolls over in his grave when Van Helsing comes to kill him. He does everything he can to live. Why do vampires resist being killed by vampire hunters? Do they simply not understand that immortality is a curse? Perhaps. But it's also possible that Williams and Kagan are wrong, and that inevitable boredom is not the "curse of immortality" that Van Helsing has in mind. Both Williams and Kagan imagine endless lives in which you pursue various projects, such as doing philosophy and traveling the world.

But this is still to imagine immortality as largely self-engrossed. What if immortality were imagined as a life devoted to helping others, similar to the endlessly looping life that the bad-turned-good character Phil Connors eventually leads in the movie *Groundhog Day*? And what if that endless life was shared with other, equally altruistic, immortal (and, of course, interesting) friends? Such a life would be similar to the life of a good divinity, surrounded by other good divinities, engaged in helping mortals.

Would immortal humanitarians get tired of ending wars, curing the sick, feeding the hungry, repairing the damage of tsunamis, and the like? This is a way of engaging with others that likely will never end, without being totally self-absorbed. So the problem of becoming bored with the realization that you are just indulging yourself *forever* would not be as much of a concern. Would that life, also, eventually, become tedious? Well, whatever the answer to that question might be, we should keep in mind that this kind of immortal life isn't available to vampires. Or at least, not to the vampires of *Dracula*.

Immortal Psychopaths

Van Helsing says that vampires "cannot die, but must go on age after age adding new victims and multiplying the evils of the world." Although in the novel to be 'undead' means to be immortal, it also means to be driven by the unappeasable urge to kill the living. And this also implies that vampires think that there is nothing wrong with doing so. Vampires are *psychopaths*. Of course, their intelligence sets them apart from the other members of the undead family. But this only means that they're *highly intelligent* psychopaths. They're not aware of any wrongdoing. In other words, they lack *moral* knowledge.

Perhaps, then, what makes the immortality of vampires a curse is what they are compelled to *do* with their endless lives—to kill innocent people in order to satisfy their thirst for blood. I'm pretty sure that Van Helsing wouldn't view vampires as cursed if he believed that they led peaceful, helpful, immortal lives. Furthermore, since vampires do not see anything morally wrong with killing innocent people for blood, this would also explain why they don't see their immortal lives as cursed and why they resist being killed.

Mercy Killing

Either immortality is inevitably tedious, or the life of psychopathy is a cursed life, or both. It seems that the only chance that vampires like Dracula have of avoiding being cursed is to change their ways and stop killing innocent people for their blood. And that is something they can't do.

The best thing that we can do with vampires, therefore, is to kill them, for their own sakes. All killing of vampires is actually involuntary euthanasia. All killing of vampires is mercy killing. As Van Helsing says about killing Lucy, "when this now undead be made to rest as true dead, then the soul of the poor lady whom we love shall again be free."

If you love Dracula, set him free. Kill him.[1]

---

[1] Thanks to my former student, Lauren Michnick, for making the point that having immortal friends would make immortality less tedious.

2
Why Fighting Dracula Is Absurd

Nicole R. Pramik

A vampire, a lawyer, and a doctor walk into a Transylvanian bar.

No. That's not right. They walk into a tavern. No. Maybe it was a blood bank. This joke definitely has something to do with a blood bank. And a taxi. I think.

In any case, wouldn't that set-up be a little absurd? Or do you believe that the seemingly impossible really can happen? Like, do you have faith that I can remember that joke?

Well, Bram Stoker's motley crew of Count Dracula, Jonathan Harker, and Dr. Abraham Van Helsing don't walk into a bar, but what is funny is they actually show us how to live a moral, faith-driven life. In fact, when you really examine the three of them, they prove that a life full of selfish pleasures isn't exactly wise. But living a life like a walking etiquette manual isn't advisable either.

So is there a third, better way? There is, but all jokes aside, you'll have to trust me and valk this vay . . .

Life in Three Acts

Before we head too deeply into *Dracula*'s stomping grounds, we need to trek to Søren Kierkegaard's neighborhood in Denmark. Kierkegaard (1813–1855) was a Danish philosopher who taught there were three stages of life in his works *Either/Or, Part II* and *Stages on Life's Way*. He dubbed these stages the "aesthetic," the "ethical," and the "religious."

In the aesthetic stage, we live only for pleasure without any regard for other people. If it feels good, you do it, and if it doesn't, feel good you don't. Kind of like Count Dracula. He does what he wants, when he wants. But as fun as that all seems, it leads to a rather hollow existence because pleasures are limited in time, such as when you've sucked all the blood out of someone. Pleasure-seeking doesn't present long-term solutions, let alone answers (that's why vampires have to look for new victims every night!). So if you're looking for a framework for your life that has more merit, better try morality and religion.

The second stage is the ethical stage, which is where we, very much like Jonathan Harker, establish a moral compass. But maybe to a fault. This stage can be filled with guilt and worry over whether or not you're doing the right thing, making the right choices, and pleasing the right people, so you perpetually live in a state of fret.

Which brings us to the third stage, the religious one. Like Van Helsing, we realize life isn't all fun and games but it can't just be about following rules for no good reason. Kierkegaard argued that we also need to ponder the reality of God and that a life without acknowledging God is empty. The key to personal emptiness is the realization that we are not happy with selfish pleasures alone but we also aren't happy just following rules. There's something more to life.

So the three male leads in *Dracula* depict Kierkegaard's stages with Count Dracula playing out the pleasure-driven aesthetic stage, Jonathan Harker fulfilling the morally-grounded stage, and Van Helsing representing the faith-filled religious stage. In the end, the religious stage, as Kierkegaard would argue, is the best stage because the kind of fulfillment that comes from true religious participation starts within you, not from external doctrine or by just going to church.

Granted, you could take all of this on faith from me. But I'll allow these gents to prove it to you instead.

Count Dracula—Bat Boy of Transylvania

I don't know about you, but I think I'd pass on any invite from Count Dracula—not to be confused with a friendly cereal mascot or a green-feathered duck who likes broccoli sandwiches. Seriously, that last one was a kid's show. Look it up.[1] At first, you might think, "Gee, Dracula is a nice guy." He tends to Jonathan Harker's needs, is helpful in providing information, and seems like the all-around perfect host. Pale and pompous, to be sure, but polite. Or so it seems.

Dracula lives, drinks blood, sleeps, and breathes (in his own undead way) the aesthetic stage. He keeps an immaculate physical appearance so he looks good on the outside. But on the inside, he's driven by pleasure-centered desires where he only cares about what he wants and how to get it. He behaves highly immorally (you kind of have to when you suck blood from the living), experiences emotional extremes (he gets enraged instead of just angry), abhors religious objects, and is prideful when it comes to his family line. With this laundry list of sins, he's in no way interested in behaving rightly or developing any show of faith in God.

But Dracula's desires and drives go far beyond just thirsting for blood. He also craves absolute power and control. For starters, Dracula is an independent bloke: he'll go where he pleases, do as he pleases, and don't try to stop him or tell him otherwise. Take his actions towards poor, unsuspecting Jonathan Harker. He tells Harker where to go and what to do, keeps him prisoner in the castle, makes offers Harker is told he can't refuse, and even steals Harker's belongings. Talk about being flat-out batty.

One key scene in *Dracula* occurs when three vampy vampire chicks come to call on Harker in the middle of the night. Dracula gatecrashes their would-be bloodletting orgy and blows up at them, insisting Harker belongs to him. These women might be Dracula's puppets, but they aren't afraid to shed light on their master's obsession with pleasure and they call him out for being unable to love. In other words, he's unwilling or unable to place another person's interests above his own. Even so, Dracula insists he can love. Just in a more selfish, possessive, psychopathic sense of the word.

In the same way, by depriving Harker of freedom, Dracula is relishing the fact he has total control. He can dictate Harker's

---

[1] Editor's note: Seriously it was an awesome show.

every move and even his words in his letters, which gives Dracula the satisfaction of putting another person under his authority, however unwilling that person might be. Possessive power is related to a pleasure-driven nature since possessiveness is all about focusing on oneself, about what other people can do for *you*, just as seeking pleasure is self-focused because the only person who gains anything from it is you.

Sadly, Dracula never seems to grow up and out of this selfish stage and possesses what Van Helsing calls a "child-brain," meaning his understanding of the world is basic and tinted by his self-centered, self-serving nature. Dracula, in fact, admits he relishes "the shade and the shadow," which has to do with much more than just avoiding a nasty, ash-inducing sunburn. He has no desire to change and loves being in the dark when it comes to ethical living or religious faith. Dracula also can't cast a reflection, both literally and figuratively. If we live only for pleasure, we can't reflect on ourselves, our actions, or even other people because we're too focused on meeting our needs and wants. Much like our not-so-dear Count.

So Dracula is the original vampire bad boy who thinks only about himself, lives for himself, and satisfies his own passions. You might write him off as a lost cause. But what about Jonathan Harker? Can he possibly show us a better way?

Jonathan Harker—Think Like a (Moral) Man

You have to feel for Harker, who doesn't have the easiest job in the world and also doesn't represent the easiest of the three stages. Harker lives out the second stage, the ethical stage, as he recognizes wrong from right and considers how his actions impact others. He might not be brawny but he does have brains. He finds a way to escape from the clutches of Castle Dracula using a bit of pluck and a lot of good sense. He's also fairly in tune with things. For example, he picks up something from Dracula that doesn't sit well with him, and Dracula's presence even makes him physically ill. If Harker was in the aesthetic stage, he would either ignore these internal red flags or not heed them at all. So being cautious as opposed to careless is a sign of moral concern for himself as well as a way of looking out for others so his actions (or even inaction) don't start a bad chain reaction of events.

Even when Harker is faced with the possibility that he might not be walking out of Dracula's castle alive (at least not in the un-undead sense), he keeps his wits and shows wisdom. In the end, Harker strives to see Dracula destroyed, not out of a sense of revenge, but out of a desire to see justice done on others' behalf, namely Lucy and Mina. He's guided by a moral compass that seeks to amend wrongs. What's more, Harker puts other people first, so it isn't all about Harker wanting to see Dracula get put six feet under for his own appeasement.

Even so, as good as he is, Harker's ethical strengths have their limitations. He gets stressed out trying to make the best choices, even to the point of being a tad neurotic. If he even thinks about doing something immoral (like make out with Dracula's babes), he feels guilty. Harker's knowledge is confined to his own self-reliance as opposed to having faith in God to clear a path for him in a seemingly impossible situation. Kierkegaard would agree that being an ethical person is better than living selfishly, but he claimed that living by ethics alone deprives a person of any sense of true self-exploration, which is a necessary element for attaining a religious faith.

In the same way, Harker lives according to a good ethical rule book but doesn't even grasp what religious devices have to do with keeping Dracula at bay. He just thinks they're merely handy trinkets vampires have an aversion to, but as far as any faith-related connection goes, Harker doesn't quite get it. Kierkegaard would say this is a mistake since having a religious life enables you to get a clearer glimpse of yourself as well as the world at large. But Harker isn't entirely lost since he does team up with everybody's favorite vampire slayer in the end (Sorry, Buffy!).

Van Helsing: Decoding the Divine

Van Helsing re-enacts the religious stage since it's his faith in God, and neither passing pleasures nor a strict adherence to an ethical code, that governs his life. Granted, you could label Van Helsing's attempts to protect Lucy with garlic and a crucifix, and even dismembering her after death, as superstitious. Seward, Van Helsing's friend, acts as the devil's advocate here, posing faith-challenging questions. Why does the doctor do what he does? What good will such frivolous or even gruesome tactics be in defeating Dracula? And, most importantly, will these methods actually work? Van Helsing's employment of such absurd tactics to ward off and eventually destroy Dracula require a seemingly absurd level of faith in God.

Van Helsing is patient with Seward and assures him that he must simply trust in God. Van Helsing knows it's crazy to believe God will intervene yet it's this assumption of God doing the possible with impossible odds that maintains his faith. He tells Seward that he wants his friend to "believe in things that you cannot," meaning have faith in God by virtue of the absurd to do the impossible. Kierkegaard said no one can actually believe in God because believing requires seeing some sort of proof; instead, you have faith in the things you don't fully understand. And it's this lack of hardcore logic that enables Van Helsing to have faith.

While Count Dracula is the antithesis of faith (because his only god is himself), and Harker and Seward are religious doubters, Van Helsing is a true believer from Kierkegaard's point of view. Van Helsing accepts things on faith because he's willing to suspend his belief in what makes sense from a logical standpoint. And since his faith is tested and proven right, which Kierkegaard asserts is necessary in continuing the cycle of faith, he continues along his path: Van Helsing's reliance upon God to do the impossible turns out to be justified again and again, which is why he holds on to it. After all, Van Helsing could choose not to deter Dracula, not to put Lucy to rest, or not to go after the Count. Yet he proceeds, assuming the impossible will become possible through faith, by virtue of the absurd. His choices reflect a constant renewing of faith, as he has faith God will fight for him and work on his behalf against Dracula.

"We want no proofs; we ask none to believe us," Van Helsing remarks in closing, meaning he recognizes that faith doesn't come by believing (which comes from seeing). True faith, as Kierkegaard and Van Helsing would explain it, comes only if we exercise the virtue of the absurd: that's when we suspend our disbelief in the seemingly impossible being revealed as possible. In other words, we have to be willing to grant that the absurd, impossible, and illogical can actually happen. There's no logical or scientific explanation for why a crucifix protects you against Dracula. You just have to have faith in it (and, of course, carry it with you!).

Now this concept of faith isn't some kind of catch-all sentiment that everything we believe in is actually true. (That would mean that all those folks who believe in the Bermuda Triangle, cookie-making elves, and vampires for that matter are going to be really disappointed.) Van Helsing's faith isn't careless in that he believes in everything and everyone. Instead, his faith enables him to act out of faith rather than fear (unlike Harker) and believe that God can do the impossible and intervene where human efforts have failed. According to Kierkegaard, faith is liberating, as our lives are made easier by having faith in God and accepting the absurd.

The *Dracula* Way of Life

Dracula, Harker, and Van Helsing take readers through Kierkegaard's three life stages with telling results. Van Helsing, as the religious man, recognizes the need for faith in God to do the impossible, no matter how absurd it seems to the logic-driven human mind. Jonathan Harker isn't too far behind with a strong ethical code but can't quite accept faith in God by virtue of the absurd. He's still just a touch too logical and reliant on physical evidence for that. Lastly, Count Dracula is just a lost cause, plain and simple. Give him blood and some dames and he's set for the rest of his quasi-afterlife.

In the end, Van Helsing is painted as the real hero since his character combines living rightly with faith in God, even if it seems absurd. Having a religious faith causes him to be a self-realized person who knows what's right, what's wrong, what his human limitations are, and where God can step in. In fact, faith in God is the only thing that makes life worthwhile since it frees us from the strain of our mundane, predictable human existence. That's Kierkegaard's take on it and we could suspect that was Stoker's position, too. Especially after seeing how Van Helsing turned out.

Now I remember that joke! And it has nothing to do with a bar. Did you have faith by virtue of the absurd that I would find it? Well, you might be too polite to tell the truth, so, here it goes:

What do you call Count Dracula when he's out of blood and ten miles away from the blood bank?
    Ready for it . . .

A cab!

But let's make it a cab operated by an ethical cab driver who has faith in God to do the impossible. That would be helpful. Otherwise, Dracula's just left behind in the dust (or make that ashes), proving that living for passion alone, without morals or faith in God, can kill you—even if you're already dead.

3
They Shall Become One Flesh

JAMES E. WILLIS, III AND
VIKTORIA A. STRUNK

Blood is why, over one hundred years since its writing, *Dracula* is still considered one of the scariest novels ever written. The tale is terrifying in a hauntingly beautiful way. In the darkest scenes of the book, Willhelmina—Mina—Murray is in pure white and held tightly by the darkly clad Dracula. The count reveals his chest, opens a vein on his breast, presses her lips to it, and makes her suckle, much like a mother offering milk to her baby. This deadly drink of blood curses Mina to become a vampire when she dies. It is at that very moment that her soul is damned to Hell.

It seems that all hope is lost for Mina when she both willingly and unwillingly drinks the blood from Dracula's chest. But strangely enough, the blood, and the curse, actually help Mina contribute to Dracula's defeat. When Dracula begins to turn Mina into a vampire, he also provides his enemies with a means to destroy him. It is this dark marriage, bound in blood, that reveals the deepest secrets found in *Dracula*. You see, when we think of vampires, we think of them drinking our blood . . . but we forget that Dracula wants *us* to drink his. There's a very dark reason for this . . . there's something more than blood that Dracula wants to steal.

A Dark Covenant

It's the connection between Mina and Dracula that shows us the importance of *connectedness*. Why is it that Mina's connection to Dracula is also dangerous to Dracula? Is it because each connection must be two ways?

The Greek philosopher Plotinus (204–269 C.E.) believed that everything is brought together in *unicity*, or the uniting of all beings. In a series of six books called the *Enneads,* Plotinus explores what it means to say that everything is 'one'. Plotinus's thinking helps us unravel the mystery behind the very strange connection between predator and prey, dead and undead, that is Mina and Dracula. *Unicity*, the uniting of all beings, is central to the scene of Dracula forcing Mina to drink his blood. It's true that the connectedness between Dracula and Mina is a good example of unicity, but, it is also a dark perversion of the beautiful idea that all things are connected . . . as we will see.

Lusting for 'the One'

At the beginning of the story, Jonathan Harker meets Dracula. Dracula's a charming host, albeit a tiny bit conceited. He says, "The common people know me, and I am master" (Free eBooks edition, p. 30). So despite his caring, hospitable side, there are signs that there's more to Dracula than meets the eye. Dracula remains a shadowy character, the victimizer of others, the thief of life and the broker of death.

When Dracula forces Mina to drink his blood, he victimizes her, but did he mean to victimize her by forcing her transformation into a vampire, or to connect them spiritually and physically through the blood transfer, or did he intend to induce his own demise? The scene of Dracula consuming human, living blood, and Mina consuming deathly, vampire blood is the idea of Plotinus's unicity in a nutshell. By mutually drinking each other's blood, Dracula and Mina become united; they become "one." Death and life become connected in a way we cannot understand today.

But what would it mean for a creature of death to become "one" with the living? Dracula's taking of Mina's blood not only means feeding upon what he, as a vampire, needs to survive. It is also an injection of lifeblood into his cold veins. Mina ingests death, and, as a result, is becoming death. In a parasitic relationship, the parasite must feed upon the host. In this way, Dracula's relationship with all other victims is a conventional parasitic one, yet his relationship with Mina doesn't follow the usual parameters. Dracula's lust for life is clearly parasitic, but unlike her host, Mina will benefit from this parasitic relationship by herself attaining everlasting life. Death, in modern times for those who believe in an after-life, can bring people closer to The One, but Dracula must continue to sojourn from place to place for eternity.

For Plotinus, oneness is a positive and beneficial state of being because it is the root of all meaning—we come to know the truth through oneness. The blood transfer between Dracula and Mina casts Plotinus's idea of oneness in a new light. In *Dracula*, oneness is no longer a good thing because it signals death for both characters. But what's more, it also creates a new meaning of what it means to live and to die.

The One Who Becomes Divine

In many ways, Dracula seems human. He looks human (well, most of the time). He speaks and moves like a human. He even seems to think like a human. But there's also a highly inhuman side to Dracula. Dracula's incredible strength and, of course, his immortality are inhuman.

Despite his ability to escape the chains of time, Dracula was equally confined by having to steal life from others. Dracula converges on the living and the dead because he is neither; he possesses awareness and an ability to master all situations like a living person, but he also pulls the life out of his victims. So there's one downside to Dracula's existence. Despite possessing super-human strength and immortality, Dracula lacks one key thing: *agency*—the ability to act the way he desires. We, as humans, can choose what to do and even what to consume. Dracula is damned to live through death, like a savage animal that must hunt its prey to survive—only to repeat this cycle. Dracula is a killer who follows his necessary instinct with super-human awareness and reasoning; he is neither mere animal nor mere human.

Plotinus taught that people ought to be self-sufficient, that they should know themselves as persons. This is how they gain *meaning* in their lives. Dracula is not able to do this because he's dependent on human blood to live. But he isn't gaining human blood when Mina suckles from him. What is Dracula gaining . . . could it be that he is seeking to draw on her agency by connecting to her? In this way, he might be trying to create unicity for himself!

When Dracula preys on Mina and takes in her blood, he is ripping out her agency, her ability to make choices for herself. With each feeding Mina loses more and more of her ability to make her own choices. Does this mean that in some way Dracula is gaining the agency Mina is losing? Dracula is ingesting blood, but he is also taking her essence—what makes her fully alive, what makes her human. Their minds become interconnected in the transfer, enough that he can know her thoughts and so much that she floats in and out of a harrowing trance.

There was something in Mina's spirit that Dracula wanted, craved, desired—he seems especially drawn and determined to be with her. Perhaps it was her spirit, her strength, and self-sufficiency—her ability to give her own life meaning—that drew Dracula to her. He sought Mina's agency, perhaps because in their unicity, he could know true freedom to choose his own meaning.

To Be One with the Damned

When Dracula takes in Mina's essence, and forces her to gorge herself on his death, she becomes one with the damned. This is where Plotinus's view that a person should be united with The One comes in. 'The One' to Plotinus is totally transcendent and indivisible, beyond all human ability to categorize or understand. Dracula, though, in his imperfection, demonstrates how this unification can go awry. The ever-increasing trance that nearly overtakes Mina's mind and body ultimately leads to Dracula's true death at the hands of Van Helsing. When this happens, Mina is freed from being cursed.

But when Mina is finally free, she takes back her agency and her own meaning. She must wonder, though, "Is he finally dead. Is he really gone?" You see, unicity now becomes a problem . . . Much like a human understanding of death as "going" somewhere, what happens to the macabre essence of Dracula? Perhaps the final terror of Dracula's death is not that he is permanently "removed" from life, but that he continues on, both in Mina's essence as well as in the deepest fears of all who encounter this character because of their *connectedness*.

In life—and in death—Dracula *becomes* more than he was. The true power of Dracula is not the ability to overcome death with the blood of life, but rather that he might well live on within Mina in some other gruesome way. Dracula's power, not just over life and death, but also of redefining what "life" and "death" mean in his own terms, is best described as becoming hideously divine. Instead of Plotinus's view of Oneness as redefining what it means to exist as unified with everything else, Dracula's redefining life and death is a twisted vision of that unification. This perversion between living and dying means that *Dracula* truly exposes a great human fear: that maybe the veil between life and death really isn't that far apart.

Death Is Near

We live in a world that evades death for as long as possible, and it does so quite well. Advanced health-care, graveyards, nursing homes, the nice men who cart corpses away all set our living spaces and our death rituals apart. Unless you work in the healthcare sector or at a funeral parlor, you likely have very little contact with human corpses, dying people, and the scent of the grave.

Our unnatural separation between life and death would've been unimaginable in the time period in which *Dracula* was written: rather than calling an undertaker, family members tended their own dead. They washed and dressed the bodies of their dead relatives, and kept them for days at a time in the family parlor to be visited by relatives. In the late spring and summer, the putrefying corpses' death smell would linger in the family home and intermingle with the plethora of flowers brought in to mask the indelicate odor. Food was prepared and eaten, many times in the same room as the deceased, and family photographs were taken posing with the bodies as they had been in life ("Smile, Grandpa!").

People behaved as if the deceased were still, well, sort of alive. Death was everywhere around us. Only our modern time has seen fit to *preserve* the corpse in such a way that metaphorically, and often literally, removes the life force of blood. Because of this, on the rare occasion we do deal with death, it seems very permanent. The distinction between life and death is so clear that we know the dearly departed won't ever rise again.

Death is not only something foreign to our daily lives; it's also misunderstood. Death becomes something that happens to someone else. The "problem" with death, then, is that it is constantly outside of our ability to know. We remove most reminders of it from our daily lives, and we cannot experience what it means to *be* dead (and in case you do, you usually don't have much time to tell others what it's like). Things are different when it comes to Count Dracula. We imagine him as *un*dead—unlike us, he lives with the constant reminder of the nature of death. To live requires death, but does death somehow include life? Plotinus believed that everything was connected, that seems to include life and death.

Dracula and Mina's dark sharing of blood represents a lust, an irrepressible and insatiable desire, which flows between them. In his connection to Mina, Dracula achieves a kind of unicity, oneness with all things. Dracula's path to truth lies in unicity, but if he is to reach true oneness, according to Plotinus he must achieve it through reflection and contemplation . . . not through blood!

Brainy Yearning

Count Dracula's ability to reflect and contemplate, his intellect, is first noted by his choice of residence. His castle is in "one of the wildest and least known portions of Europe" (p. 2). Not only would he be able to escape quickly into any of the bordering territories, but the mountains would make it difficult for anyone who was trying to hunt him down. Dracula was known by all the villagers; a mere mention of his name caused grown men to cross themselves. Jonathan Harker comes to know Dracula not only as a thoughtful host but, also, as a fascinating person to talk to. When Harker converses with Count Dracula, he discovers, "In his speaking of things and people, and especially of battles, he spoke as if he had been present at them all" (p. 42). Dracula has first-hand knowledge of all these events because he had, indeed, been there. Think of how much Dracula must know after several lifetimes!

We understand life, in all its strange complexities, difficulties, and joys, through experience. Our lengthy list of experiences shape and form our sense of reality. What makes death so scary is the fact that no one knows what it's like. Dracula is a terrifying character because his experience is formed by life *and* death; his understanding of the world and what life means is based upon living for many decades, as well as "being" dead. Dracula's intellect is fundamentally different for this reason.

We can only imagine that Mina's mind is completely transformed by her experience of what it is like to be both alive and dead as she begins to see through Dracula's eyes. Mina's intellect becomes one with Dracula's, and ultimately leads to her helping Van Helsing hunt down the vampire. Why would Dracula, who surely knew the problem with taking over Mina's mind and body do something that would ultimately lead to his own final death by giving her insight into his knowledge and power?

Plotinus thought the intellect has a relationship with desire. If an individual, in this case Dracula, is keenly aware of his own identity as a vampire and is able to locate his bodily desire for Mina's blood, then he would be able to separate himself in what Plotinus calls the "Intellect." If Dracula is free from his own desire, he could possess Plotinus's "Intellect," but he doesn't. Instead, Dracula is a victim of his own desires.

Mina's intellect possessed a connection with Dracula's prior to their shared blood exchange. Something in her mind also entranced Dracula, much the same way his vampire mind nearly overcame her human mind. While it may not be possible to say exactly what that was, perhaps she possessed a certain knowledge of life that highlighted how deficient Dracula's was. Dracula ultimately becomes the hunted, due to Mina's intellect. The oneness of their intellects reaches its pinnacle in Dracula's death: the superhuman vampire becomes a victim to his vulnerabilities while the human becomes the victor.

People desire to believe that they are connected to something bigger than themselves. In this way, Dracula's self-exposure by connecting with Mina's mind, as well as Mina's vulnerability to Dracula's forcefulness, completes their very flawed and deadly tango. What Mina could not provide with her body, for her blood was the same life-force as any other victim, was met with Mina's unusual intellectualism. This contrasts with what Plotinus called "the Intellect," however, because they were not moving away from uncontrollable desire, but instead moving directly toward it.

Soul: Theft in Desire

Alongside the One and the Intellect, Plotinus also discusses the soul. According to Plotinus, there's first a thing called the 'world soul'. This 'world soul' contains numerous single souls, that is, the souls of all other people. That's why Plotinus believed all people are sympathetic to each other—we're all interconnected by partaking in the one world soul! So basically, the Soul's a sort of bridge: first, it partakes in 'The One' because it's always a unity. And second, it shares into all the different single souls and thus relates to diversity, which is the opposite of 'The One'.

Dracula needed Mina's human mind, and her agency, but he also needed the completeness of her soul: in his act of revenge for the plot against him, Dracula seeks out Mina's soul in its totality; by transforming her into the same monster, he would not only get his revenge, but he would also strip Mina of the very same soul that connects her to the world soul and thus, to every other living thing. In other words, his revenge carried out in near rapturous desire would not only demean her humanity, but it would also give him a "proxy" soul.

Dracula has no hope for redemption or salvation, in this life or the next. He's neither alive nor fully dead. He's aware but soulless, a thinking being yet not free of his animalistic and uncontrollable need for blood. Dracula is caught between worlds. Mina represents the ultimate desire for Dracula: in the Intellect, in her Soul, she is the object of his bloodlust, as well as the object of his revenge. This is why his forcing her to drink his dead blood and his ingestion of her living blood is the ultimate unicity: they become One together. He gains something of her humanity, and she dies slowly as she becomes a victim of his curse. By taking in part of her Soul, there's a part of Dracula that lives on beyond his death at the hands of Van Helsing.

A Beautiful Death

As we journey through the nightmarish scene between Dracula and Mina and use Plotinus's understanding of the One, we discover that Dracula is a twisted reflection of what Plotinus taught. The blood exchange between Dracula and Mina is particularly scary when we apply Plotinus's ideas because we see that death is a continuum of life, and even more strangely, life is a continuum of death—a moving toward death, no matter how hard we try to ignore it.

Plotinus teaches us that unicity is from the One, Intellect, and Soul, but what we realize through *Dracula* is that life and death are bound together. This inversion and perversion of Plotinus's thought reminds us that even though we try to pretend death doesn't concern us, it will sooner or later find us anyway.

4

Dracula's Rules

DOUGLAS JORDAN

Only at certain times can he have limited freedom. If he be not at the place whither he is bound, he can only change himself at noon or at exact sunrise or sunset . . . It is said, too, that he can only pass running water at the slack or the flood of the tide. Then there are things which so afflict him that he has no power, as the garlic that we know of, and as for things sacred, as this symbol, my crucifix, that was amongst us even now when we resolve, to them he is nothing, but in their presence he take his place far off and silent with respect.

—VAN HELSING

Dracula stood at the door, confused. He was unable to enter, even though he wanted to. There he was, King of Vampires, thwarted by the wishes of a mere mortal woman that he not enter her home. Her sweet blood was just over the threshold of the wooden frame. Soon, he would make her one of his, a vampire in her own right. If only he could overcome the barrier formed by this wooden door frame and Lucy's lack of consent, then he could make her his. It was not until several days, and much charisma later, that he could finally make it into Lucy Westenra's home to turn her into a vampire.

There might be no rules in Hell, but there are definitely some rules for vampires: They can't enter your home unless you invite them in, they need to drink blood, and they need to sleep in their native soil to regain strength, which is why poor Dracula always has to carry all those boxes with him. But what is the source of these rules? Are they something essential to Dracula, like the biological need to drink blood? And besides, what even makes a law a law? After all, you would think that if anyone could break a law, natural or unnatural, it would be Dracula!

Vampiric and Natural Law

Perhaps Dracula is following natural laws, the laws that govern the natural world. Aristotle (384–322 B.C.E.) taught that nature was the same everywhere, which means that the laws of nature are also the same everywhere. If Dracula needs to feed on blood to survive in Transylvania, then he will also need to drink blood to survive in England. That Dracula needs blood is a biological fact which isn't trumped by change of location.

The way we look at natural law today is that it explains how the world works, from the laws of gravity to evolution. Put more simply, natural law is about physics and science. This view is much the same today as it was in ancient times. Natural laws explain how the body works. Even in our fantasy worlds, like the world in which Dracula lives, the characters and the author try to give explanation for why things are the way they are. Van Helsing gives explanations for Dracula's nature in ways that make sense to him, often using God as an explanation. Dracula, for example, is repulsed by holy artifacts because Dracula is rejected by God. We could say, then, that in the world of Dracula natural law is defined by God. You would think that if Dracula existed he must follow these laws. Perhaps, though, as he is undead, he simply has to follow a different set of them.

Natural laws are interchangeable with properties, rules, laws, and biological facts. These five factors work together to produce an understanding of how the world works, and why it works. In Dracula's world, those laws are set by God, so there need not be as much uniformity in a world where the laws are produced by some universal process. In other words, God, being all-powerful, could create a set of laws that govern the living and a different set of laws that govern the dead. But whether natural law is produced by God or by the natural processes of the universe, those laws would be unchangeable by us and would be universal for all those to whom they apply. For example, a vampire's inability to enter a home without consent is a rule or property of vampires in general. So whether created by

God or by the laws of physics, *all* vampires have no choice but to follow that rule.

Don't Tell Me What I Kant Do!

There are, of course, other ways to look at laws, specifically morally. Natural law would only tell us what actually is or is not possible given our biology and the laws of physics. Moral law, though, deals with what we *should* and *should not* do. There is an excellent question, for example, whether Dracula's inability to cross a threshold without being invited in is the result of a natural law—*he physically can't*—or perhaps it's a moral law—*he's obligated not to.*

The philosopher Immanuel Kant identified three act-types of action: obligation, wrong, and permissible.

An act-type refers to the moral status of the action. Simply, if it is something we *should do* it is an "obligation," if it is something we *should not do* it is "wrong," and if it is not wrong, but we are not obligated to do it, it is "permissible." Permissible means the absence of an obligation or the absence of a wrong. The majority of actions taken in any given day are permissible actions. Dracula going to visit England, Jonathan Harker choosing to talk to the sisters in Dracula's castle, and Dracula choosing when to go to his coffin to sleep at night are all permissible actions.

Obligation entails a requirement to act. It seems that Dracula might have certain obligations. As in our classic example, he is required to get permission before entering a household. We do have to ask ourselves, though, whether this is an obligation or a matter of natural law. The answer is probably pretty simple. Dracula isn't the kind of guy who follows rules. Obligations, though, are rules. And, unlike the laws of nature, those rules can be broken. For example, we probably think that Van Helsing and Harker had an obligation to kill Dracula. We probably think this because Dracula was so evil and if he continues to (un)live he will kill more people. Just because they have this *moral* obligation to stop him doesn't mean that they will succeed, only that they *can* and *should* try to succeed.

Kant famously pointed out that we can't make it an obligation for someone to do the impossible. In other words, moral laws don't make sense if they ask us to violate natural laws. To say that Van Helsing should close his eyes really tight and wish Dracula dead is just silly, and it is unreasonable to blame van Helsing if he failed to kill Dracula in such an impossible way. Rather, we can only say that people *ought* to do what they *can* do! So, given the fact that Dracula doesn't care much about rules and *really* likes killing people, it probably isn't his obligation that keeps him from crossing the threshold of Mina's door; it is probably natural law that keeps him out. In fact, Van Helsing states,

> He can do all these things, yet he is not free. Nay, he is even more prisoner than the slave of the galley, than the madman in his cell. He cannot go where he lists, he who is not of nature has yet to obey some of nature's laws, why we know not. He may not enter anywhere at the first, unless there be some one of the household who bid him to come, though afterwards he can come as he please. His power ceases, as does that of all evil things, at the coming of the day. (*Dracula*, Chapter 18)

Dracula is physically unable to enter Lucy's home without her consent. The properties of Dracula and all other vampires forbid him from doing so.

(Un)Natural Law

There's more to Dracula, though, then just what natural law demands of him. Although evil, he does make decisions. Perhaps we're assuming too quickly that his actions are just the product of natural law. He does have relationships with others, though perhaps a bit dysfunctional, and those relationships are governed by things that Dracula can and cannot do. Wesley Hohfeld explains that any legal or rule-based relationship can be explained by a series of elements. This bunch of elements includes *duty, claim, liberty, power, liability, immunity,* and *disability*.

A Hohfeldian relationship is between two individuals. Some of the most important relationships here are the Dracula-Lucy relationship, Dracula-wives relationship, and the Dracula-Harker relationship. Some of the relationships Dracula has are with many different partners, like the relationship between Dracula and every vampire he creates. There is a relationship between Dracula and the first vampire he created, and the same sort of relationship exists with the second vampire he created and so on.

A *duty* exists when one person owes an obligation to another. The person who has a duty must perform a given action. In this relationship, the person in the weaker position will have a duty. The other person in the relationship has a claim. Dracula's brides have a duty not to harm (or seduce) Jonathan Harker. This is a restriction Dracula has imposed upon them. As the stronger partner in this relationship, he has a claim against the wives that they follow this restriction. This duty exists simply because Dracula has established the rule that they shall not harm his guests. His precise reasons for making that rule don't matter. Even though he intends on letting them have him later, this doesn't affect the binding nature of Dracula's rule.

A *claim* is the ability to enforce a duty. Dracula has a claim against his brides living in the castle, as well as all the people that he has turned into vampires and many of the people in Transylvania who serve his will. Due to this claim, he is able to enforce action from the less powerful people he commands. They owe him a duty, whether it is cleaning the castle, carrying his coffin, or getting him coffee while in London. Liberty is the absence of a duty or a right not to act. To have liberty means to have freedom of action. For example, Dracula has a liberty to travel to England as there is no duty owed to anyone to not travel.

Some people in relationships have more power than others. *Power* is when one party is able to negate a claim or duty. The dominant person in the partnership has a power. The other person in the relationship has a liability. Dracula has power in his relationship with each of the vampire brides in his castle. This is because he can remove their duty to not harm Harker. In fact, he does just that, telling them that they can have him when he leaves for London. In other words, Dracula has the power to keep the rules the same, or he can change them to suit his preferences.

Immunity exists when one individual is immune from having a duty created for them by others. The person in charge of the relationship has an immunity. For example, Dracula's servants cannot create a duty for him, so he has immunity and no liability. Those people for whom Dracula can create a duty have a *liability*—someone else can create a duty for them that they have an obligation to fulfill. It seems like Dracula gains immunity over the people he turns into vampires. This is because once these people become vampires, they're unable to change or eliminate the relationship between themselves and Dracula. Only Dracula is able to modify their relationship. This is why Dracula has such power over the people he turns into vampires.

Disability is when the person is unable to modify a relationship due to her minor position—the person has "no power." Poor Lucy has such a disability in her relationship with Dracula. Since she's Dracula's minion, she cannot make or change the rules in their relationship. Lucy is forced to accept Dracula's duties. Likewise, also all those people Dracula has turned into vampires have such a disability relationship with him. It might be said that we have the power to deny Dracula entrance into our homes. We're "immune" from any desire of his to create a duty that we let him in. *But* once we let him in we lose that immunity, and, certainly, from Dracula's perspective we now have a liability—we "owe" him the duty of letting him in.

Rule Enforcement for Beginners

So what we have so far are three options for why Dracula follows any rules at all: 1. Dracula holds himself to the rules, or at least some of them. 2. A family of ruling vampires enforces the rules, like in the *Blade* Trilogy. 3. The third option is that these rules are laws of nature, and as such are indistinguishable from the properties of vampires and Dracula. In other words, some rules are rules we have to follow because they are natural law (Aristotle), some rules are moral rules that we choose to follow (Kant), and some are forced on us by those in power (Hohfeld). So which of these theories, Aristotle, Kant, or Hohfeld help us understand Dracula's actions when it comes to issues like having to get permission to enter a home?

I'm pretty sure that many of the rules for vampires are not self-enforced. Questions like when they can change shape and their aversion to garlic are likely rules of their biology—rules of nature. The rules governing Dracula are anything but self-enforced. If vampires are following self-enforced rules this would mean that each individual vampire makes the decision to follow those rules. It's like asking fourth graders to make sure that they do their homework. They'll say "sure" and spend the afternoon playing football. What I mean to say is that vampires, as well as humans, are very motivated by self-interest. Most humans would violate the rules if they could get away with it, what are the chances if Dracula would turn down a tasty morsel just because "He's supposed to get permission to enter the house"!? So let's say if Kant is right, and there are moral rules that should be followed like "Don't enter a house without permission." Most vampires, and Dracula in particular, wouldn't care.

So what about Hohfeld's understanding of rules? We have duties and obligations that are placed on us by our social relationships. Maybe there is a vampire clan that maintains the morality of Vampire's. But the same problem that exists for an individual making rules exists for a group making rules. Both self-enforced and cabal enforced rules fail when it comes to vampires for the same reason: the self-interest of the party involved is just too strong. Violating those rules is much more beneficial (or fun) than following them. Why on earth should Dracula tell himself *not* to feast on Lucy? Maybe vampires of lesser power can be forced to follow rules, but surely not the mighty Dracula!

As the enforcement capacity is not on an individual basis or group basis, and vampires are unlikely to feel much moral responsibility to anyone, then there seems to be only one option left—the laws of nature restrain Dracula.

Our Debt to Dracula

Dracula has many different abilities. He can defy gravity, transform himself into different shapes, mesmerize his victims, and summon beasts and other animals. He has extraordinary charisma and the strength of twenty men. Despite all the powers and abilities that Dracula and other vampires have, they still encounter severe limitations. He has many weaknesses and restrictions, like the thirst for blood, the inability to enter a home uninvited, being disabled by religious relics, and the requirement to sleep in native soil to regain his strength. These properties can be explained best by natural law, as there is little reason to believe Dracula would make limitations for himself or follow the rules set on him by a vampire cabal.

But what about Dracula's ability to defy gravity? Gravity has a liability in its relationship with Dracula. This is because Dracula is able to modify his relationship of strict adherence to the laws of gravity when he negates the gravitational force on himself. He can bend the rules of gravity. Isn't that a violation of natural law?

Dracula possesses incredible charisma and hypnotic abilities. He uses these on the people of Transylvania in order to have them assist in moving his coffin and other personal items to London. This charisma allows him to create relationships with other people. But in so doing he seems to again violate natural law by invading the minds of others.

Dracula can transform himself into mist, shadows, and various animals like wolves, dogs, and small rodents, and even control the weather. In addition, he's able to summon beasts of the night to come to his aid. Dracula has a claim over those animals and beasts he commands surrounding his castle. All of this seems again to violate the laws of nature. It's as if nature itself has a duty to obey Dracula! In fact, we can start explaining those violations in Hohfeld's terms!

For example, unless a vampire sleeps in the native soil of his homeland, he does not regain strength. There is a mystic connection to the homeland of Dracula which restores his strength during the day. This relationship cuts two ways. There is a claim by Dracula against the soil, in that the soil replenishes the strength of Dracula. Does this mean there is a duty on behalf of the soil to restore the strength of Dracula despite the laws of nature?

In fact, the most interesting relationships that Dracula and other vampires can enter into is when they turn a mortal into a vampire. When this process starts, there's no relationship between the vampire and the person who will become a vampire. This relationship is established first and foremost when the mortal is being bitten. The new vampire owes a duty to Dracula, and he has a claim over them. Dracula has power over the relationship!

So perhaps it's actually Hohfeld who best describes the world's relationship with Dracula as a kind of duty owed to the Count. On the other hand, the requirement to consume blood is one of the most notable features of vampirism. There is an unquenchable desire to drink human blood in order to sustain the vampire. As Dracula possesses superior abilities to that of other vampires, he is able to hold off longer between feedings. He is able to resist the urge to constantly drink the blood of the humans he views as beneath him. Nevertheless, the thirst has a claim over Dracula. Dracula, as well as all other vampires, has a disability in relation to the thirst. This is because all vampires are unable to change the relationship between the thirst and their biological make up, so again natural law comes to life! On one hand it seems that Dracula can force others to have a duty to him in violation of natural law, and on the other hand he seems bound by physical laws!

Even worse, what we can't get past is Dracula's inability to enter a victim's home unless invited. We have no reason that Dracula would follow this rule, even if it is "wrong." It *must* be a rule that it is imposed on him, either by virtue of some natural biological fact or by God—natural law. In the story, God plays an important, though unseen role. So perhaps the best way to understand the rules Dracula must follow is through a combination of natural law and Hohfeld. God, in the story, decides what the rules are and creates liabilities for Dracula. We see this when Dracula is unable to enter Lucy's home until she unknowingly lets him in. Dracula owes a duty to Lucy to not enter her home.

Lucy has a claim against Dracula to not enter. When she gives consent to enter, Dracula gains power over the relationship and Lucy enters into a liability, as she is no longer able to revoke the consent given to Dracula. So Dracula's not as powerful as he might seem. Even he must obey the laws of nature—even to the whim of a mere mortal woman—when those rules are enforced by nature or by God. So maybe, the best question to ask, when thinking about the seemingly arbitrary rules Dracula follows is why would God enforce some of the rules of natural law, but not others? As pressing as that question may be, I do not suggest inviting Dracula in to discuss the issue . . .

5
Dracula's Dilemma

ROBERT ARP

The vampire live on, and cannot die by mere passing of the time, he can flourish when that he can fatten on the blood of the living. . . . But he cannot flourish without this diet, he eat not as others. . . . When they become such, there comes with the change the curse of immortality.

—ABRAHAM VAN HELSING

First, a little refreshment to reward my exertions. You may as well be quiet. It is not the first time, or the second, that your veins have appeased my thirst!

—COUNT DRACULA

The fair girl, with a laugh of ribald coquetry, turned to answer him. "You yourself never loved. You never love!" On this, the other women joined, and such a mirthless, hard, soulless laughter rang through the room that it almost made me faint to hear. It seemed like the pleasure of fiends. . . . This was the being I was helping to transfer to London, where, perhaps, for centuries to come he might, amongst its teeming millions, satiate his lust for blood, and create a new and ever-widening circle of semi-demons to batten on the helpless.

—JONATHAN HARKER

Sucks to Be Him

After reading these quotations from the *Dracula* text—and if you're familiar with the whole plot line—there are a few things that we know and can infer about the Count:

41

- He has a thirst for blood, also referred to as a lust for blood;

- Drinking blood doesn't really satiate him completely, since he always seems to want more blood;

- He doesn't have the capacity for love, probably because he's undead and you need to be alive in order to feel that kind of deep emotion;

- He's immortal, but it's a curse of sorts.

Imagine being Count Dracula and having the capacity to live for several lifetimes driven by a thirst for blood, while not really being able to feel satiated or satisfied. At best, there seems to be some sort of momentary relief when you've had your fill of blood, but that quickly goes away. The hollowed-out life of a junkie might be the closest thing to Dracula's un-life we could imagine, with the desire for the next "fix" consuming all of his existence. Think of Jason Patric's vampire character, Michael, in the movie *The Lost Boys* (1987) or Louis in *Interview with the Vampire* (1976), when they start to thirst for blood. Try as they do to resist their urges, they can't, becoming wild-eyed (or red-eyed like Dracula and Lucy do in the story), frantic, and driven to "feed the need."

Add to this picture the fact that Dracula and typical vampires are *aware* that they can't feel satiated, and then you can kind of see how the vampire's un-life kind of, well, sucks (pun intended)! Talk to *ex*-junkies, and they'll often tell you that they knew their lives were hollowed out, devoid of anything other than the desire for the next fix. Dracula knows he can't experience joy, love, or contentment, as many scholars of (and commentators on) *Dracula* will note, despite the fact that the Count responds to the "fair girl" vampire: "Yes, I too can love. You yourselves can tell it from the past. Is it not so?" And Dracula knows that he'll never experience the things that mortals do, even though he lives for such a long, long time. What an unfair un-life!

Doomed, Damned Dilemma . . .
and Draculology

Such is the plight of Dracula's un-life, in a nutshell. Not all vampires have such an un-life, however, as some seem to be content with who and what they are, as appears to be the case with the vampire community in the *Underworld* (2003–2012) series. But, there are a great number of vampires in a great number of stories modeled after Count Dracula whose un-lives really *do* suck.

Dracula's un-life can teach us valuable lessons about our own real lives, believe it or not. After all, as Draculologists (yeah, I just made that word up) like Nina Auerbach (*Our Vampires, Ourselves*, 1995), Bob Madison (*Dracula: The First Hundred Years*, 1997), Andrew MacKenzie (*Dracula Country: Travels and Folk Beliefs in Romania*, 1977), and J. Gordon Melton (*The Vampire Book: The Encyclopedia of the Undead*, 1999) tell us, vampire lore emerges from our innermost desires. These desires include not only the longings to live forever, indulge in our basest passions, and be subversive, but also the desires to embrace our mortality, control the animal within, and blot out evil wherever it may lurk. Bram Stoker was aware of a lot of this lore when he penned *Dracula* in 1897.

Besides the Count himself, there are many different kinds of vampires who've been written about before and after the *Dracula* story. As you might expect, the personalities of vampires, and the stories told about them, are as varied as the authors who tell us the tales.

Dualism, then More Draculology

What's the fundamental nature of a vampire like Dracula? How and in what form exactly does a vampire exist? These questions are metaphysical in their tone, and *metaphysics* is the area of philosophy that investigates the nature and principles of things that exist. Metaphysicians want to know what really exists in reality, what kinds of things make up reality, what they're made of (what constitutes their nature), and how things are related to one another.

We all know vampires don't really exist, but if they did we would see that, as members of the undead community who make their way around the world, vampires seem to be a composite of 1. a dead material body and 2. an immaterial mind/spirit/soul (for us here these are all the same thing). This view is akin to a version of *metaphysical dualism* in the philosophical sub-discipline of metaphysics known as *philosophy of mind*. According to dualism in philosophy of mind, a person like you or me is made up of a material body and an immaterial mind; again, Dracula and other vampires, being undead, have a *dead* material body (that apparently doesn't decay) and an immaterial mind.

Two popular versions of dualism are *substance dualism* and *property dualism*. According to substance dualism, a person is made up of two wholly distinct *substances*, a mental substance (a mind as well as mental states and capacities) and a material/physical substance (a body as well as physiological parts and processes), which can exist apart from one another. Those who believe in the immortality of the soul are substance dualists because they think that the death and decay of the body doesn't mean that the soul ceases to exist; the soul lives on after the death of the body.

Your standard Christian is a substance dualist since, according to this religion, someone's soul ultimately goes to Heaven or Hell for all of eternity, while anyone who believes in reincarnation—like your standard Hindu, Buddhist, Jain, and Sikh—is also a substance dualist since the soul lives on in some other body. Plato (around 428–347 B.C.E.), the student of Socrates and teacher of Aristotle, was a substance dualist. He believed that, since people seem to be born with knowledge of certain things already, their soul must have existed prior to uniting with their bodies at birth, and that learning is the process of recollecting or remembering all of what you knew when you were in that pre-existent state but forgot in the first several years of your life.

According to property dualism, a person is one whole substance that is made up of two wholly distinct *properties*, an immaterial mental property (which is the mind and mental states and capacities) and a material property (which is the body and physiological parts and processes). According to this way of thinking, the mind and brain are distinct properties of some one person similar to the way "whiteness" and "sharpness" are distinct properties found in Dracula's canine teeth. Just as we can distinguish the property of whiteness from the property of sharpness in the Count's left canine, so too, we can distinguish an immaterial mental property (your mind and its mental attributes, qualities, features) from a material bodily property (your brain and all of the physical bodily processes connected to it) in some one person.

However—and this is one of the main things that separates property dualism from substance dualism—just as the whiteness (as a property) and sharpness (as another property) of that particular tooth (one whole substance) can exist only while that particular *tooth* exists, so too, according to property dualists the mental and bodily properties of a person can exist only while that person exists. So when we destroy Dracula's left canine, presumably by turning the Count himself to ashes, the properties of whiteness and sharpness in that particular canine cease to exist along with the canine. Likewise, when a person dies, decays, and ceases to exist, both that person's body *and* mind cease to exist.

Thus, unlike the substance dualist, the property dualist thinks that the mind is ultimately wholly dependent on the brain and body for its existence: no brain, no mind. Such a view of mind in relation to body seems to be consistent with scientific data, and is appealing to those who do not believe in the immortality of the soul. After all: as the brain starts to deteriorate, so does the mind, as with older people who have dementia; when damage is done to the brain in an accident, certain mental capacities go away completely; and when someone is born with a part of the brain missing or malfunctioning, they lack the mental capacities associated with the missing or malfunctioning part. Plus, a snarky property dualist might ask the substance dualist in a rhetorical way, "Have you ever seen a *disembodied* mind, soul, or spirit floating around somewhere or somehow?" following that up with, "Uh, yeah, I didn't think so . . ."

Preying on Bodies and Souls

According to some vampire stories, the vampire's cursed soul will continue to live on in Hell or some other non-worldly realm after its dead body has been destroyed, indicating a substance form of dualism. Bram Stoker undoubtedly was a substance dualist who also wrote about characters in *Dracula* as if they were substance dualists since on several occasions he has them speaking about their belief in Christianity and the fact that Count Dracula has always been and will always be "preying on the bodies and the souls of those we love best." Stoker also has a conception of Hell in *Dracula*, and in several places it may seem that Count Dracula's soul may go to Hell when released from its body.

Consider Harker's comment about the Count, which isn't disputed by anyone, including the original Draculologist, Van Helsing:

> May God give him into my hand just for long enough to destroy that earthly life of him which we are aiming at. If beyond it I could send his soul forever and ever to burning Hell, I would do it!

Also, there's obviously a conception of Heaven in *Dracula*, and it looks as if poor Lucy's soul will be "set free" and go there once her vampire head is cut off and her mouth stuffed with garlic. Once they do the deed, "instead of working wickedness by night and growing more debased in the assimilating of it by day," Van Helsing tells his vampire hunters, "she shall take her place with the other Angels."

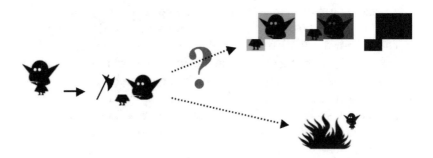

In other vampire stories, the bloodsucker's mind ceases to exist when its undead body is destroyed by sunlight, a stake through the heart, or beheading, indicating a property form of dualism. This seems to be the case in Marv Wolfman's *Blade the Vampire Slayer* (since 1973) comic book series as well as with Carol Jones Daly's vampire novel from the middle of the last century entitled, *The Legion of the Living Dead* (1947). It may be the case that *destruction of the mind* is what actually happens to the Count's mind in *Dracula*, since we are told that once Harker slashes his throat and Morris plunges his bowie knife into his heart, the Count's whole body "crumbled into dust." But we aren't given any indication if the Count's mind or soul went to Hell or some other place, or possibly jumped into someone else's body. Draculologists still debate and speculate about what happened to Dracula's soul, actually.

In either form of dualism, the dead body—or some physical/material medium like a bat, wolf, wind, mist, or something else—is necessary for a vampire, including Count Dracula, to exist in this Earthly world. At the same time, in both substance dualism and property dualism a distinction can be made between characteristics or properties of your mental life, and characteristics or properties of your bodily life. In other words, both substance dualists and property dualists think that there is something about the mental realm that makes it *distinct* from the bodily realm; again, either in *substance* or in *property*.

You Yourself Never Loved

Many vampires are portrayed as unable to experience the pleasures and pains associated with loftier things like love, or with even baser things like food and drink. Recall in *Dracula* the Count's seeming inability to love or even partake in meals with Harker in his castle. Consider this anonymous quotation from the Internet I found on one of those Dracula fan sites that does a good job of capturing the bittersweet-ness of being a vampire:

> How long have I shunned the caress of soft light upon my cheek, how long have I yearned to feel the gentle wind in my hair, love in my heart, and hate? Yet, my soul is dead; I cannot feel, cannot see the light of day. Still, my curse is the greatest of gifts. The taste of blood is sweet as the sweetest honey to me. I embrace each passing night of my unlife, and the call of blood is my blessing.

Not only do Lestat and Louis have this problem in the Anne Rice stories, but the vampires in Jeff Rice's *The Night Stalker* (1974), Jacques Cazotte's *The Devil in Love* (1991), and James Gunn's *The Immortals* (1958) have a similar problem as well. The vampire Strahd bemoans his lack of feeling in *I Strahd: The Memoirs of a Vampire* (1993) and even Dracula himself in Francis Ford Coppola's movie, *Bram Stoker's Dracula* (1992), can't seem to get any satisfaction.

These portrayals should strike us as strange because the vampires usually appear to be in some state of anger, pain, or anguish when describing their state, indicating that they can, in fact, feel something . . . pain! Consider the movie version of *Van Helsing* (2004) when, during a conversation with his two female vampire minions, Dracula screams in anguish that he feels nothing, but longs to feel nonetheless. Or consider what George Hamilton's vampire character says to Renfield in *Love at First Bite* (1979) when Renfield asks the vampire if he's happy:

> Happy? How would you like to dine on nothing but a warm liquid protein diet while all around you, people are eating lamb chops, potato chips, Mallomars . . . Chivas Regal on the rocks with a twist?!?

Maybe it's just that, because they are cursed in some way or damned by a god, vampires can only experience pain and never will be able to experience pleasure as part of their continual cursedness or punishment. If the idea of vampires experiencing some form of *pain* seems unconvincing, there are plenty of instances where vampires seem to be experiencing *pleasure* while sucking blood, deceiving, wooing women (or men), or engaging in sexual intercourse.

The most straightforward reason usually given as to why vampires cannot feel pleasure or pain is that their bodies are dead, or no longer functioning. Since pleasure and pain are feelings requiring a functioning body to experience them, it makes sense that vampires can't have these feelings. Yet, Dracula's frustration in *Van Helsing* is a common theme among vampire personalities and their stories. Again, recall Dracula's exchange with his three henchwomen in the original *Dracula* story where the Count seems to have to convince himself that he's capable of love. So, it seems that vampires both *do* and *do not* have experiences of pleasure and pain. What accounts for this contradiction?

What a Pleasure It Would Be . . .

A way to clear up this problem might be to distinguish between two different senses of pleasure and pain, the way that the famous moral philosopher John Stuart Mill does in his book *Utilitarianism* (1863). There are those lower pleasures or pains that are most appropriately understood as *feelings associated with a body*. Examples of these pleasures and pains would be aches, pains, and "butterflies in the stomach" as well as euphoric surges and adrenaline rushes. Normally when we think of pleasure and pain, we think of them in this bodily way, associated with the neurophysiological processes of a living animal with an intact nervous system. The vampire in the Internet quotation above simply wants "to feel the gentle wind in my hair." When Harker first meets the Count's three vampire henchwomen in Dracula's castle, he articulates the base pleasure of bodily, sexual desire: "I felt in my heart a wicked, burning desire that they would kiss me with those red lips. It is not good to note this down, lest someday it should meet Mina's eyes and cause her pain, but it is the truth."

Then there are higher pleasures and pains understood as *qualitative experiences associated with a mind*. Examples of these would include the pleasure of discovering the solution to a complex math problem, the pain of having made an immoral decision that cannot be undone, or the pleasure of knowing one is loved by a friend. Here, the pleasures and pains are less bodily and more mental, and have names like *joy*, *contentment*, *satisfaction*, *regret*, and *sorrow*.

Besides having the bodily sensation of feeling the wind in her/his/its hair, the vampire in the Internet quotation above wants to feel love and hate, which are more than simply a bodily sensation. There are sixteen instances of the word *pleasure* found in *Dracula*, and almost every one of them has to do with one of the characters finding contentment or joy of some kind—in conversation, in joking, in sarcasm, or for other reasons. Even the Count speaks of the books about London in his own library giving him "many, many hours of pleasure" during one of his chats early on with Harker. This is pleasure that isn't merely bodily in nature.

My Bountiful Wine-Press for a While

Armed with this distinction between lower and higher pleasures and pains, we might be able to clear up some of the confusion concerning what a vampire experiences. For example, we can make sense of the above Internet quotation from the vampire by noting that the cursed soul/spirit/mind of such a being—its immaterial, mental part—is expressing regret or sorrow (qualitative experiences associated with the mind) at being unable to be pleased by wind in its hair or the taste of fine wine (feelings associated with the body). The vampire is expressing a higher, mental pain about a lack of a lower, bodily pleasure. On the other hand, a vampire like the Count can derive great bodily pleasure when sucking blood, but "can't get no satisfaction" in the forms of contentment or love, though he seems to experience mental anguish because he *realizes* he "can't get no satisfaction."

Even though we hear vampires lament the fact that they cannot experience pleasures and pains, we have to question their sincerity. They seem to be in some kind of pain while lamenting and seem greatly to enjoy sucking blood from their victims. In *Dracula*, the Count expresses a *longing* to go through the streets of London, a *desire* for Harker to stay, an *excitement* about conversations with Harker early on, and other emotions, too. The distinction between higher and lower pleasures may help us out here. Vampires may be cursed with a higher, mental pain while lamenting their lack of feelings in their bodies. Similarly, they may gain a higher, mental pleasure from satisfying their need for blood. (By the way, it is a curious thing that vampires should need blood in the first place. What do they need it for? On most vampire accounts, their bodies are dead, so the blood does not act like a food product.)

From several accounts, it appears that the vampire is deriving a kind of base, physical, bodily pleasure from its evil pursuits of blood-sucking, deception, and "turning." Dracula seems really to enjoy himself when he sucks Mina's blood, much like "sweet honey" and a "blessing" as claimed by the vampire in that quotation from the Internet I noted earlier. And consider what Louis says about Lestat in *Interview with the Vampire*: "Lestat killed two, sometimes three a night. A fresh young girl, that was his favorite for the first of the evening. For seconds, he preferred a gilded beautiful youth. But the snob in him loved to hunt in society, and the blood of the aristocrat thrilled him best of all."

Dracula's Dilemma Dissected

If we put aside the obvious problem that a vampire's body is dead, and we imagine that there is some connection between its bodily desires and its own cursed mental satisfaction, then there is another way in which we can make sense of the vampire's plight. It may be that the vampire "can't get no satisfaction" because of its inappropriate focus on the pursuit of "bodily" pleasure. One of the reasons why the vampire Lestat is so fascinating in the Anne Rice stories is that he's somewhat of a pleasure-seeker who continually searches, but never really finds, satisfaction or contentment in his cursed life. His cursed, fictitious life reminds us of our own real lives.

Both vampires and mortals must confront what is known as the *hedonistic paradox*, a term that was first introduced by Henry Sidgwick (1838–1900) in *The Methods of Ethics* (1874). The basic idea behind the hedonistic paradox is that whenever pleasure itself is the object sought, either it is not found or it is found. If pleasure is not found, the result is the pain associated with not finding the pleasure one seeks. In an episode of *Buffy the Vampire Slayer* (1997–2003) that I watched recently, one of the vampire characters says to another vampire that he "hates not getting what he wants," in reference to having to suck the blood from a less-than-desirable woman.

On the other hand, if pleasure is found, especially on a consistent basis, the result is still pain. The pain results from either finding pains that are *mistaken for* pleasures in the long or short term, or from the boredom of always getting the pleasures you want. Think of the way that Louis fools Lestat into sucking the blood from the already dead twin girls in *Interview with the Vampire*, and how Lestat mistakes this painful experience for a great pleasure; albeit it was a mistake, in part, prompted by Louis's deception. Or, think of the vampires who are destroyed by Blade (presumably, a great pain) at the rave in the beginning of the movie *Blade* (1998) and how they mistakenly think that they have come to a bloodfest featuring fresh young human meat (presumably, a great pleasure). Or, think of the Don Juan lecherous character from the Spanish and Italian stories of the seventeenth century who never finds the contentment he's after with the opposite sex because he's so focused on the pleasure of sex, hopping from one female, to the next, to the next, to the next.

Concerning the issue of boredom, consider Lestat's complaint of virtually "seeing it all" and being bored in *The Vampire Lestat* (1985), or a deluded man who thinks he's a vampire in the book by Katherine Ramsland, *Piercing the Darkness: Undercover with Vampires in America Today* (1999), claiming that "it's somewhat boring, living forever." Why do you think Count Dracula wants to leave Transylvania and go to London? Because he wants to keep pursuing the pleasure associated with "turning" and sucking, sucking and turning, turning and sucking, on and on and on. If he could, he would turn the whole world into vampires. Presumably, since he can live forever, he would get bored with this. Once there's no one left to turn or suck on, what's he going to do?

The hedonistic paradox is "hedonistic" because of the focus on the pleasure being sought (*hedon* is Greek for pleasure). Either way, whether pleasure is not found or it is found, the result is still pain. Rather than a paradox (which is really two seemingly contradictory things that are both true), I prefer to call this predicament one finds oneself in a *dilemma*. (It's really more of a no-win situation—you're damned (pun intended) either way—but the word *dilemma* completes the alliteration.) Dracula's dilemma is that he consistently finds the exact opposite (pain) of what he set out to find in the beginning (pleasure) no matter if he finds pleasure or doesn't find pleasure.

Defeating the Dilemma?

Is there any way out of the no-win, Dracula dilemma for a vampire who wants to continue pursuing pleasure for the sake of pleasure itself? Actually, vampires might be able to win in the end, for a couple of reasons.

One of the problems with pursuing pleasure is the boredom associated with always getting what you want. A central question that needs to be answered is whether there could be innumerable pleasures to be had at your disposal. Put another way, given the number of possible activities imaginable, and the pleasures associated with those activities, is it possible to exhaust all of those activities, gain the pleasures, and become bored with the pleasures attained? If there could be innumerable pleasures out there to be had, then, even for a vampire with many lifetimes at its disposal, it seems like it would not be possible to achieve all of those pleasures. In which case, boredom would never ensue.

Now a vampire, who has the capacity to live several lifetimes, surely would become bored after a certain amount of time. But this would depend upon whether that vampire had experienced each and every possible pleasure to be experienced. If you're inclined to think that the amount and range of possible pleasurable experiences are limited or finite, then it's more likely that boredom would result for a vampire who lives several lifetimes. On the other hand, if you're inclined to think that the amount and range of possible pleasurable experiences are unlimited or infinite, then it's more likely that boredom won't result for a vampire. Again, the primary question that needs to be answered is whether there could be innumerable pleasures to be had at your disposal? If the answer to this question is *yes*, then you never get bored, never experience pain, and it seems that one of the losses in this no-win dilemma can be avoided. If the answer is *no*, then you do get bored, do experience pain, and you lose like you're supposed to in this no-win dilemma.

The distinction between lower bodily pleasures and higher mental pleasures may help us out once again. Within the bodily realm, there seem to be a variety of different pleasures associated with a variety of different bodily activities. In fact, any pleasure or pain is only a pleasure or pain as it is associated with some form of bodily or mental activity for a human. There are no lower or higher pleasures or pains without bodily or mental activities. This being the case, pleasures are aligned with activities that run the gamut from hurting us in the short-term and hurting us in the long-term, to helping us in the short-term and helping us in the long-term. For example, there's a difference between the pleasures had from smoking crack and the pleasures had from pursuing a variety of extreme sports. All things considered, the likelihood of the crack harming you regardless of the precautions you take is much higher than consciously and cautiously pursuing an extreme sport.

Dodging the Dilemma?

Is it possible to pursue pleasure and avoid the no-win situation altogether? It's easy to see how a life of pursuing lower, bodily pleasures leads you into the pains of either not finding what you seek, mistaking pain for pleasure, or even boredom. This becomes all the more obvious in the case of a vampire that can live several lifetimes. But could you actually "win" in the pursuit of higher, mental pleasures? Let's think about the difference between pleasures that result from *on-going activities* and pleasures that result from *the knowledge of being in certain completed states*.

Recall the earlier examples, solving a math problem and being loved by a friend. These aren't on-going activities, but completed states of being, where you have knowledge of these states. The knowledge of these states brings with it a sustaining, almost satiating, form of mental pleasure. Aristotle had something like this in mind when he investigated various forms of pleasure in his famous work in moral philosophy entitled, *Nicomachean Ethics*, specifically Book X. It may be that bodily pleasures are more the result of on-going activities, while mental pleasures are more the result of being in a certain state.

With this distinction in mind, we may be able better to understand how hard-core mathematicians or true friends achieve satisfaction, contentment, or joy associated with these states. If math equations don't do it for you, think of some tough project, assignment, or task that you completed and are happy about having completed. Or, think of the runner who trained all of her life for, and actually finished, the big marathon, the father of three who finally got his Master's in Business Administration through night school, or the hero who saved a child from drowning. Now think of these folks reflecting upon their accomplishments with joy. Such joys are of the kind which, when reflected upon, last a lifetime. A stronger case might be made for you falling victim to the dilemma and "losing" in the *pursuit* of either the solution to a math equation, a lasting friendship, a marathon race, or an MBA *prior to* achieving a completed state, in that one may never find what one seeks. However, once in a certain completed state it would seem that the pleasure is continuous with the knowledge of the completed state.

Virtuous Vampires?

If a vampire engages in physical pleasure-seeking for the sake of that pleasure-seeking, then we can see how such a lifestyle would lead to a kind of hollowed-out existence, not unlike that of a junkie. A junkie gets to the point where they physically must have the drug in order to survive, at least in the short-term. Most junkies, at least at first, *choose* to use drugs and can change their ways. Maybe vampires should be pitied for their blood-sucking ways. After all, it seems that they are unlike junkies in that they are just built to suck blood. For most vampires, human blood is a necessary food source. As Angie says to Joel, the serial killer who is becoming a vampire in the movie *Addicted to Murder* (1995): "You can't change your nature. You can't contain it, you can't shift it. You can only be what you are meant to be."

Consider, too, the way Van Helsing and others portray the Count and other vampires in *Dracula*: vampires are seen as being enslaved by their nature and in need of being set free. It's as if vampires can't help their evil ways—they still need to have their heads cut off, no doubt, but there's a sense in which the vampire is more akin to an animal, stricken with killer instinct that is beyond their control.

Yet even those members of our community who cannot control themselves, like pedophiles, must regulate their desires or have their desires and actions regulated for them. Vampires could ask members of the human community to donate enough blood to their cause so that they need not take it forcibly, and I am sure that there would be kind-hearted souls willing to oblige. In Barbara Hambly's book *Those Who Hunt the Night* (1990), we're told that vampires "can—and do, at need—live upon the blood of animals, or blood taken from the living without need of their death."

Starting in the 1960s with vampires like Barnabas Collins in the series *Dark Shadows* (1966–1971) and Forrest J. Ackerman's comic book character Vampirella (1969), and continuing through the 1980s and 1990s with Chelsea Quinn Yarbro's vampire hero, St. Germain (1994), and Nick Knight in the series *Forever Knight* (1992–1996), there've been "virtuous vampires." These vampires actually recognize that, although they must feed upon blood to survive, they can do so without either giving in to their most basic needs or harming people in the process. Further, they've been able to generate moral codes, establish vampire cultures, create strong bonds with mortals, pursue "loftier" activities such as are found in academia and the arts, and find contentment in using their "dark" powers for the good of their own kind as well as humankind. In other words, these vampires have been able to dodge or even defeat the Dracula dilemma altogether either by pursuing higher mental pleasures or by engaging in activities for the sake of the activities themselves, rather than for the pleasure to be gained from the activities.

Blessed and Cursed

Vampires, like the humans who invented them, have varying degrees of desires for different kinds of things. Dracula wants to go to London, Lestat wants to be a rock star, numerous vampires on the TV series *True Blood* (2008–2014) want the same rights and privileges as humans have. If your focus is consistently the pursuit of bodily pleasure itself, then we can see how pain will result, especially if you're a vampire with the capacity to live several lifetimes. More banal vampires could live lives that are both blessed and cursed. They could be blessed in that they have the potential to live forever, indulge in their every physical desire, and do what they want irrespective of any moral code. Yet, these are the very things that ultimately become cursed for them. Living several lifetimes gets boring because they have "seen and done it all." Indulging their physical desires becomes either painful or boring, and doing what they want makes them targets of evil and corruption to be hunted down and destroyed.

You need not be a vampire, nor live several lifetimes, to see that the pursuit of pleasure *solely*—especially bodily pleasure—offers little blessings in the long run. Base pleasures don't seem to equate to happiness. This is probably at least part of the reason why Van Helsing notes that "there comes with the change the curse of immortality." The cursed part is that you're like some junkie or an animal going around constantly looking out to feed the need, Feed The Need, FEED THE NEED! **FEED THE NEED!!!**

There's wisdom in John Stuart Mill's claim that happiness in life is attained by not making pleasure one's focus:

> Those only are happy who have their minds fixed on some object other than their own pleasure. . . . Aiming thus at something else, they find happiness along the way. . . . Ask yourself if you are happy, and you cease to be so.

II

A Vampire's Values

6
What's Wrong with Being a Vampire?

GREG LITTMANN

> It seemed as if the whole awful creature were simply gorged with blood. He lay like a filthy leech, exhausted with his repletion.
>
> —JONATHAN HARKER

There's something appealing about the idea of "living" like Count Dracula. Nobody tells Dracula what to do. He takes whatever he wants, and eats whatever he pleases. Up until Jonathan Harker and Quincy Morris finally decapitate and stab him, he has a clear run of about four hundred years getting his own way on everything. Best of all, he has all the time in the world to enjoy his freedom. If Dracula feels like brushing up on the complete works of Shakespeare, penning the proud history of his native Szekely clan, or just roaming the Transylvanian forest enjoying the hunt, he has forever to do it. Sure, he has limitations: he must avoid crucifixes, has to take it easy on the garlic sauce, and can't walk into a building without a direct invitation (the social awkwardness should he ever need a public toilet after a night's hard drinking would be awful—"Pardon me sir, but if I gave you a shilling, would you invite me into the lavatory?") All the same, the (un)life of Dracula has a lot going for it.

But despite Dracula's freedom, security, and wealth, the reader is not expected to look up to him as a model of successful ambition. Rather, we are to condemn him as a fiendish villain. But what's so bad about being a vampire? We ourselves prey on other animals whenever we eat meat.

Jonathan is horrified by the idea that Dracula feasts on humans, writing "A terrible desire came upon me to rid the world of such a monster." But when Jonathan is staying at the Hotel Royale in Transylvania, and is presented with the spiced corpse of a chicken for dinner, he eats it with delight and makes a note to himself to get the recipe. Why the double standard? Unlike Dracula, few of us even need to make a choice between eating meat and extinction. Instead, like the mental patient Renfield, who eats blowflies and spiders in his cell at the asylum, we consume animal life without need. So perhaps the way Dracula behaves isn't really so bad. Perhaps we should regard him not as a monster, but simply as a predator like ourselves, one that simply perches one link higher than us on the food chain.

Mem., Get Recipe for Mina
— Jonathan Harker

Of course, *Dracula* is a novel and none of this really happened. No real chickens died or memos got written. So can't we just ignore the whole situation as fantasy? Asking whether vampires are any less justified in feasting on us than we are in feasting on animals is not just an intellectual game. Vampires aren't real, but hypothetical situations make useful "thought experiments" with which we can test our theories by seeing whether our theories seem to give the right answer in all possible circumstances. For instance, let's say that you have a moral theory that it's always wrong to break a promise. This theory doesn't stand up in the face of a hypothetical situation in which you had promised to help a violently dangerous asylum inmate like Renfield to escape.

Of course you should break a promise like that! The fact that the case is fictional and that you would never make such a promise is beside the point—the mere fact that the theory doesn't give the right answer in this imaginary situation shows that the theory is flawed. In the same way, thinking about what the moral duties of vampires would be if they existed can help to cast light on our own moral duties. More specifically, considering vampires can help us to work out whether it is morally alright to eat animals. If we want to insist that it wouldn't be morally alright for a vampire to prey on us, then we either have to find a justification for preying on animals that wouldn't also justify vampires preying on us, or we have to give up preying on animals and become vegetarians.

> **. . . strike in God's name, that so all may be well with the dead that we love and that the Un-Dead pass away.**
>
> —PROFESSOR VAN HELSING

In the novel *Dracula*, the moral lines are marked out by God. Dracula must recoil before the power of a crucifix or the host, but Jonathan Harker can eat as many chickens as he likes without being ejected from churches by gusts of wind or bursting into flames whenever he sneezes and someone says, "Bless you." Our own universe, on the other hand, is either Godless, or contains God(s) who don't reliably intervene to identify wrongdoers—you can wave a crucifix at a Nazi all you like, but it won't make them recoil like Dracula. If we want to know our moral duties, we'll have to try to reason them through for ourselves.

In *Dracula*, God does more than just provide clear moral signposts. He also (according to the heroes) assigns humans to an afterlife. When Jonathan Harker considers climbing down the high walls outside Castle Dracula to get to the count's room, he comforts himself about the perilous drop by thinking "At the worst it can only be death; and a man's death is not a calf's, and the dreaded Hereafter may still be open to me." In other words, because Jonathan can live again in paradise, his death is not as bad as the death of an animal. In fact, he'd be getting a significant lift in "living" standards! If you agree with Jonathan and think that humans go to Heaven after death but other animals do not, this would be reason to treat the death of a "calf" as more tragic than the death of a human. After all, a human death would just be a move from one place to a better one, the death of other animals, though, would mean utter oblivion for them.

To be fair, Heaven is not the only place where humans can wind up in the universe of *Dracula*. Perhaps the greatest threat posed by the vampire is damnation to Hell. When Lord Arthur Goldaming objects to Van Helsing's plan to open Lucy Westenra's tomb to impale and behead her, the professor reminds him, "This night our feet must tread in thorny paths; or later, and forever, the feet you love must walk in paths of flame!" So we might say that what makes being a vampire so much worse than eating animals is that vampirism endangers the victim's immortal soul. But if the moral superiority of eating animals over vampirism comes down to nothing more than the fact that damnation is not involved, then this gives us not just the right to eat and exploit animals, but to eat and exploit humans in exactly the same way: Unlike Dracula, our predations don't endanger the victim's soul. If we want a standard that permits eating animals, but doesn't allow us to be treated in the same way, we'll have to find morally relevant differences between humans and animals other than the theoretical existence of a human soul.

I rushed up and down the stairs, trying every door . . . but after a little the conviction of my helplessness overpowered all other feelings.

—JONATHAN HARKER

One common justification offered for humans using animals however we like is simply that we have the power to do it. Someone who takes this approach will often point out that in nature, the strong eat the weak. They say that we humans may have settled on some rules for mutual protection, but between species, right is whatever you can get away with.

But this view doesn't stand up when applied to a case in which we humans are the ones who are out-powered. Dracula's supernatural gifts make hunting us down so easy that it isn't even sporting. He can come after you as a bat, a wolf, a mist, and who knows what else? He can hypnotize you with a stare, snap your spine with his superhuman strength, suck out your blood, or just send his packs of rats, wolves, and lesser vampires to do the killing for him. Professor Van Helsing even assures us that "he can grow and become small," indicating that, though he never does it in the novel, Dracula can transform into Giant Dracula, at which point even a Jonathan Harker is going to declare "Mina, my darling, you are on your own" and run.

It's true that the novel *Dracula* ends with the count's defeat, so there are limits to his power, but Dracula had shockingly bad luck. If he hadn't happened to prey on the beloved of a friend of vampire specialist Van Helsing, or if a series of "thirsty" workmen hadn't been readily bribable by the heroes for information and help, or if the gypsies transporting Dracula from Galatz to Castle Dracula hadn't been so overawed by Jonathan's "impetuosity, and the manifest singleness of his purpose" that they let him walk by to cut off their master's head, then the novel would have ended not with Van Helsing bouncing Jonathan and Mina's child on his knee, but with Dracula grabbing Queen Victoria by the hair and forcing her face onto a wound on his chest to drink his blood.

What's more, Van Helsing acknowledges that if the count had had just a little more time to acclimatize himself to nineteenth-century Britain, all the bad luck in the world wouldn't have stopped him. The professor notes, "In some faculties of mind he has been, and is, only a child. But he is growing, and some things that were childish at the first are now of man's stature. He is experimenting, and doing it well." He adds, "Well for us, it is, as yet, a child-brain; for had he dared, at the first, to attempt certain things he would long ago have been beyond our power."

So, if might makes right, then Dracula has a perfect right to drink your blood, or even to turn you into his slave. Let's abandon the view that might makes right, then, unless you feel like offering up your throat to the vampire's hungry kiss. Let's allow that there is no reason, in principle, why one type of creature can't have moral duties to another type of creature. Can we come up with a reason why it would be immoral for Dracula to feast on us, but not immoral for us to eat animals?

He is of cunning more than mortal, for his cunning be the growth of ages.

—PROFESSOR VAN HELSING

One common justification offered for eating animals but not humans is that our human intelligence sets us apart. On this view, it's immoral to eat humans because humans are so clever, but okay to eat non-human creatures because of their limited intellect. Again, though, Count Dracula foils us at every turn. If we humans are free to eat animals because of their limited intelligence, then Dracula should be allowed to gorge on us because of *our* limited intelligence. After all, compared to him, we have the minds of chimps.

Van Helsing explains, "He was in life a most wonderful

man. Soldier, statesman, and alchemist. Which latter was the highest development of the science knowledge of his time. He had a mighty brain, a learning beyond compare . . ." and "for centuries after, he was spoken of as the cleverest and the most cunning, as well as the bravest of the sons of the 'land beyond the forest'." But Dracula was just getting started. In death, "He study new tongues. He learn new social life, new environment of old ways, the politics, the law, the finance, the science, the habit of a new land and a new people who have come to be since he was . . . He have done this alone, all alone! From a ruin tomb in a forgotten land. What more may he not do when the greater world of thought is open to him." The man (monster) learns fast!

Dracula's understanding is matched by his practical genius. Jonathan writes, "He certainly left me under the impression that he would have made a wonderful solicitor, for there was nothing that he did not think of or foresee. For a man who was never in the country, and who did not evidently do much in the way of business, his knowledge and acumen were wonderful." Dracula is affronted at the very thought of being opposed by inferiors in intellect and experience like Van Helsing and company: "Whilst they played wits against me—against me who commanded nations, and intrigued for them, and fought for them, hundreds of years before they were born—I was countermining them." He has hundreds of years of learning on even the wisest of their little band!

Dracula was just getting his brain into gear when he was unlucky enough to be assassinated by rampaging heroes better supplied with guts than good plans. If he'd been given a mere ten years to brush up his skills in London, the blink of an eye to him, he'd be running Parliament and the Church of England, while shipping boxes of earth to North America in preparation for visiting President Roosevelt at the White House.

We generally take it for granted that beings of superior intelligence would not treat creatures of our intelligence the way that we treat animals. We don't see Mr. Spock chowing down on Captain Kirk, or Doctor Who frying up his companion with his sonic screwdriver, or Gandalf whipping up a stew of Sam Gamgee and 'taters. Dracula, on the other hand, explicitly sees humans as animalistic in comparison to him, and so ripe for exploitation. He sneers at the heroes: "You think to baffle me, you with your pale faces all in a row, like sheep in a butcher's . . . you and others shall yet be mine, my creatures, to do my bidding and to be my jackals when I want to feed. Bah!"

The little bird, the little fish, the little animal learn not by principle.

—Professor Van Helsing

We could insist that the morally significant difference between animals and humans is not that we have greater *relative* intelligence, but that our intelligence reaches a certain minimum level required for the right not to be eaten. On this view, a creature with an intelligence below a certain level is fair game, while any creature of human intelligence (or above) has the sort of rights that rule out Dracula using us for some "light refreshment", as he puts it.

The biggest problem with this approach is that it seems arbitrary (or at least overly convenient) to insist that the level of intelligence that confers the right not to be eaten just happens to be the level of intelligence that we possess. What reason can we give as to why it is at our level of intelligence that consumption becomes a monstrous act, while at lower levels, consumption isn't wrong at all? What objection could we give to someone who insisted that the magic level is the intelligence of a pig, or the intelligence of Dracula, or simply that there is a sliding scale of wrongness, so that the more intelligent a creature is, the more wicked it is to consume it? It all looks like a case of tailoring the moral rules in whatever way benefits us, rather than trying to do what is right.

Besides, there are many humans who function at an intellectual level below that of many animals. We regard the idea of eating a seriously senile elder as horrific, even if they are functioning below the level of a chimpanzee or even a pig! But if it is reaching the minimum level of intelligence that makes the moral difference, then we are being hypocritical if we give a human any more rights than an animal of the same intellect.

What's more, the need to respect the rights of humans of limited mental capacity rules out any justification for eating animals that relies on animal's lack of any *particular* intellectual ability. For instance, some folk say that it is morally all right to eat animals because animals do not understand morality—they don't know right from wrong and so can't be wronged. But if we make an ability to understand morality a requirement for having the right not to be eaten, this would not merely justify eating animals, but also toddlers and the severely mentally ill, among other humans. If we accept that there would have been something morally awful about Van Helsing suddenly taking a bite out of the Harker's young son as he dandles him on his knee, then the right not to be eaten cannot come with moral understanding. Little Quincy may be too immature to know right from wrong, but gentlemen with "the kindliest and truest heart that beats" do not eat children.

> . . . poor dear, dear Jonathan, what he must have suffered, what must he be suffering now.
>
> —MINA HARKER

So what do people with "the kindliest and truest heart" do when faced with a creature or lesser power and intellect? I think that eighteenth-century English philosopher Jeremy Bentham hit the nail on the head in his *An Introduction to the Principles of Morals and Legislation* (1789) when he concluded that when determining our moral duty toward animals, "The question is not, 'Can they reason?' nor, 'Can they talk?' but, 'Can they suffer?'"

Bentham was an advocate for a moral theory called "utilitarianism". Utilitarianism, in its most common form, is the view that an action is right if it best promotes happiness over suffering and wrong if it promotes suffering over happiness. Utilitarians of Bentham's day concerned themselves with the abolition of slavery, better conditions for workers, women's rights, and improvements to the prison system, and launched the animal rights movement to boot. Bentham was not a vegetarian and did not think vegetarianism was a moral duty for humans. However, he recognized that there was no justification for the callous way that food and work animals were being treated in his society.

Bentham died sixty years before Dracula's fictional visit to England. However, given that Bentham was trained as a lawyer and that a hundred years' difference is nothing to Dracula, it is easy to imagine the count executing his plans a century early, and a young Jeremy Bentham being sent off to

Castle Dracula instead of Jonathan Harker, to assist the count's transition to London. Let's allow that the brilliant Bentham has twigged to Dracula's nature and plans. What might the philosopher say to try to convince the count to give up drinking human blood?

To be honest, I doubt anything he could say would move the diabolical vampire—Bentham is sure to end up either as Dracula's dinner or mangled at the base of the castle walls after he hurls himself out of the window. But in his final moments of futile pleading as the Count advances toward him, Bentham would beg Dracula to consider the suffering he is bringing into the world. No doubt, Dracula's way of life also produces pleasure, if only his own. Dracula loves a good drink of blood and laughs with joy as he closes in on his victims, and flying around as a bat must be fun as hell.

All of these pleasures matter on Bentham's model and are to be weighed in favor of the vampire's lifestyle. But for a vampire to maintain its "life," it must end many other lives, like the captive child in a sack Dracula feeds to his three female accomplices, and the vengeful mother of that child that Dracula has torn apart by wolves. More lives yet are shattered by the loss of loved ones, as Arthur's life is shattered by the death of his beloved Lucy. The more that vampires spread their kind, the worse the killing will be, and the more terrible the human suffering. The thing that's wrong about being a vampire, Bentham would explain, just before leaping from the window and plunging screaming to his death, is that it can't be done without inflicting so much pain that it outweighs any of the benefits the vampire gets.

If Bentham's desperate objections to Dracula are correct, and Dracula's actions are immoral because they bring more suffering than happiness, then we must apply the same standard to our treatment of animals. If we do, it becomes obvious that the way we treat animals must be drastically changed. Like Bentham, we may stop short of insisting on vegetarianism. After all, some animals, like clams, cannot suffer at all, while others could be given satisfying lives and humane deaths. But we should not tolerate common practices like exposing farm animals to extreme weather conditions, castration and detailing without anesthesia, and killing animals by letting them bleed to death, or the pervasive practice of factory farming animals by packing them into tiny living spaces.

The chicken that Jonathan tucks into with such relish at the Hotel Royale had probably had a pretty good life for a chicken, strutting around, scratching in the dirt, and doing other things that chickens like to do. The chicken you dig into at home most likely spent its life in a small cage packed with other birds, without enough space to ever stretch its wings, and with its beak seared off to prevent it from pecking the other chickens to death out of sheer stress. It's difficult and expensive to make sure that the animals we eat were humanely treated. If humane carnivorism is too hard, vegetarianism is a fine option!

Jonathan Harker's Journal

5 May. —The Count himself left my luggage inside and withdrew, saying, before he closed the door: "When you are ready, come into the other room, where you will find your supper prepared." I discovered that I was half famished with hunger; so making a hasty toilet, I went into the other room. My host, who stood on one side of the great fireplace, leaning against the stonework, made a graceful wave of his hand to the table, and said: "I pray you, be seated and sup how you please." The Count himself came forward and took off the cover of a dish, to reveal a steaming pile of unappetizing vegetables. Spinach, leaks and asparagus lay limp and soggy on the plate. I could not repress a shudder. A horrible feeling of nausea came over me, which, do what I would, I could not conceal. The Count, evidently noticing it, gave a grim sort of smile, which showed more than he had yet done his protuberant teeth, and sat himself down on his own side of the table. He picked out a wilting piece of greenery from his plate and lifted it to his lips, grimacing in disgust as he began to chew. We were both silent for a while; until I could contain myself no longer and cried, "Surely you have not fallen sway to vegetarianism, that foolish doctrine that flies in the face of the natural superiority of man to the beasts?" Count Dracula gazed upon me with a look so strange, it quite unnerved me; his dark and piercing eyes filled with some infinite longing and terrible sadness. "Shut up and eat your leeks," he sighed.

7

Expert Testimony in the Trial of Count Dracula

JOHN ALTMANN

Let the trial begin . . .

The history of Dracula's evil begins well before our time, and we can't know all of the evil he has committed during his long life. But we do know that Jonathan Harker was tortured at his hand. With malicious glee, Dracula trapped him, tormented him, and left Harker a broken man, his mind never able to recover. Then there was Lucy, a young woman who was engaged to be married and had a life full of love and happiness. When Dracula sank his teeth into her throat all of Lucy's hopes and dreams died alongside her humanity. What rose from the ashes was a monster who brought nothing but suffering to strangers and loved ones alike.

Next Renfield, a mental patient with a severe mental illness, was taken advantage of by Dracula—forcing Renfield to harm both innocent non-human animals and human beings. When Renfield was no longer of any use, Dracula savagely broke his back and bloodied his face before putting an end to his life. Ladies and gentlemen, what sits before you in this courtroom is not a man but a monster.

Dracula is a monster that, thanks to the bravery of Dr. Van Helsing and his friends, will be put on trial today. This will not be a trial of law; it will be a trial of morality. Three men have come forward to bring evidence against Dracula. The aim of this trial is not to prove that Dracula did wrong— we know that he is guilty. Rather, we seek to establish that he is *blameworthy*. Dracula's actions were not accidents and he cannot claim good intentions; he is unforgivable. The judgment you arrive at as a jury will ultimately serve to determine the fate of Count Dracula.

Biting Necks Is Not an Imperative

Ladies and gentlemen of the jury, I call to the stand first philosopher Immanuel Kant (1724–1804). Professor Kant is a man who believes that there are moral rules that must be followed. That there are acts that we commit that are by themselves considered right or wrong and are separated from the consequences they produce in most cases. Professor Kant is of the idea that there is a universal rule of morality that under no circumstances should be broken. Professor Kant thinks the defendant, Count Dracula, broke this very rule. This universal rule, this *Categorical Imperative*, proves Dracula's culpability.

Professor Kant's Categorical Imperative tells us that moral laws are universal and apply to everyone. The Categorical Imperative also tells us that people should always be treated with respect and are never to be taken advantage of. Finally, the moral laws we make for ourselves must also be agreed upon by the community we live in. What this means, ladies and gentlemen, is that the Categorical Imperative demands that we be fair. We cannot make exceptions for ourselves. If we believe it is okay for ourselves to do a thing, we must concede that it is okay for everyone to do that same thing! Mr. Kant has carefully reviewed the facts of this case and believes that the defendant Count Dracula's actions are in direct violation of the Categorical Imperative. Professor Kant, you may now proceed with your testimony.

> *I begin my testimony by directing the attention of the jury to evidence that shows the defendant violated the first aspect of the Categorical Imperative. I would like to share with the jury an entry from Jonathan Harker's journal from Chapter 4 of the collected interviews. Jonathan writes in this entry an account of a mother being murdered by a pack of wolves under Dracula's command after she confronted him over his abducting her child. The defendant killed this woman in a savage and remorseless fashion. So, reason tells us he must believe that it is*

morally acceptable to kill. So, logic tells us that he must be willing to universalize killing, yet he will not permit others to commit similar actions when he finds himself in the role of the victim. The defendant clearly contradicts himself. Dracula believes in killing when it is others, but makes a special exception for himself! Kant points dramatically at the startled Dracula.

The defendant proves me correct when he finds himself in a violent confrontation with Jonathan Harker, Dr. Van Helsing, Dr. Seward, Quincey Morris, and Arthur Holmwood. The incident was recalled in Dr. Seward's diary as seen in Chapter 23 of the collected interviews. Seward writes that while Jonathan Harker made two violent stabs at Dracula with his Kukri knife, Dracula avoided each blow and escaped to safety. Clearly, Dracula does not want to be killed and yet, he is willing to kill others. We can see that he cannot universally apply his rule— had the defendant been willing to fairly and justly universalize his own actions, he would have allowed himself to be murdered seeing as he has murdered others. By making the act of murder a law solely for his benefit over the benefit of man in general, Dracula has broken the Categorical Imperative.

The most compassionate and loving beings among us will remember that people should always treat each other with respect and never take advantage of someone else. The defendant Count Dracula, however, proves to have an absence of both compassion and love. The best example of this was the incarceration of Jonathan Harker within the walls of Dracula's castle. Dracula lured Jonathan Harker to his castle under the belief that Harker would be conducting real estate business with the defendant as he wished to relocate to London. The defendant told Mr. Harker that he wanted to move to London out of a deep appreciation for European culture. The truth is that the defendant wanted to spread his influence there and claim a countless amount of fresh victims.

Once Harker finalized the paperwork, he was no longer useful to Dracula . . . except as food. Jonathan Harker was now meant to be a means to the end of not only Dracula's hunger, but also of the hunger of his wives.

Jonathan Harker was no longer considered a human within the confines of Count Dracula's castle walls and suffered abuse that made him less than an animal. Jonathan's job, his wife, and everything else that made Jonathan Harker a human being were given no consideration by the defendant. Instead, Jonathan Harker had been reduced to a mere meal. This reduction makes the defendant a violator of my second rule.

Besides, no man lives in isolation. This makes it all the more important that any moral laws a person chooses to live by must be acceptable within the community they live in. Dracula's deceptive and murderous nature is something that has never been accepted by any community he has resided in. Jonathan Harker recalls in the very first entry of his journal when a woman who ran a hotel he was staying at in Bistritz gave him her crucifix when she learned he was doing business with Dracula. Mr. Harker also made note of how citizens would always cross themselves whenever they felt the defendant's presence nearby or even heard his name in conversation. When the defendant would then later relocate to London, he would find that the attitude towards his presence there was far more violent and hostile.

Ladies and gentlemen of the jury, such intense and fearful reactions to the acts that Dracula has deemed to be morally permissible demonstrate that the laws Dracula lives by are quite clearly not accepted within the community. With these facts before you it is my expert opinion that Dracula knowingly broke every single rule in my Categorical Imperative. He is therefore a threat to human society. I have no hope for the defendant to make any kind of recovery whatsoever. Should he be found innocent, he will most certainly repeat his offenses with the same lack of remorse. It is my recommendation that Dracula should be promptly executed. Given that Dracula believed it to be morally permissible to violently deprive others of their lives, he must, as a consequence, accept that standard as it relates to his life in the hands of this court.

Thank you Professor Kant, you may step down.

Weighing the Scales of Misery and Happiness

I will now call to the stand philosopher John Stuart Mill (1806–1873). Mr. Mill is of the belief that the consequences of acts should be the only thing considered when determining right and wrong. Mr. Mill believes that the greatest good always lies with the greatest happiness for the greatest number of people. If the consequences of an act produce greater happiness for the majority then it is right, and if the consequences of an act produce greater misery for the majority, then that act should be considered wrong. Mr. Mill has studied this case intensely and believes that Dracula's actions have caused the majority more misery than happiness. Mr. Mill, you may now share your results with the court.

Ladies and gentlemen of the jury, the defendant Count Dracula is someone who cares solely for his own satisfaction and happiness even if at the misery of good and innocent people. I want to direct the court to evidence dealing with Lucy Westenra's interactions with Dracula. When we look into Mina Harker's journal, we can see that the first time the defendant interacted with Miss Westenra was eleven o'clock P.M. on the tenth of August.

Mrs. Harker had gone looking for Miss Westenra at this time after Miss Westenra had another incident of sleepwalking. Mrs. Harker would soon find Miss Westenra in the arms of Dracula. When she approached Miss Westenra, she discovered her pale and barely breathing with two small holes on her neck that indicate that the defendant forcefully drank from her.

After Dracula drank from Miss Westenra, he began stalking her in his bat form to monitor the progress of her transformation and to potentially feed on her even more. One of the defendant's instances of stalking was particularly aggressive as Miss Westenra's bedroom window was shattered by a wolf moments after the defendant was watching her in his bat form. The presence of the wolf terrified Miss Westenra's mother to the point of a heart attack that she would instantly die from. Not long after the death of Miss Westenra's mother, Miss Westenra would lose her humanity and become a vampire. As a vampire the newspapers labeled Miss Westenra as "The Bloofer Lady," a woman who took children away from their parents.

As the Bloofer Lady Miss Westenra would lure children away from their homes and, after kidnapping them, bite into their necks and drink their blood. These events only further prove the threat Dracula poses even when he is not directly involved. Luckily, Miss Westenra didn't get to continue feasting on children for an extended period of time. Thanks to the efforts of her doctor and friend Dr. Van Helsing, Dr. Seward, and Quincey Morris, who were her former suitors, and Arthur Holmwood, her husband, Miss Westenra was stopped before even more people could be harmed. Miss Westenra feasted from all these children and because of that they, the men who deeply cared for Lucy Westenra, and several others all experienced great suffering in the name of the defendant's own happiness and desires.

It is in my expert opinion to the jury that the defendant Count Dracula should be found guilty and imprisoned for the sake of medical and scientific research. When we consider the consequences of sentencing Dracula to death as my peer Professor Kant suggests, we see that the consequences would be most harmful to the public. The court would be depriving the people of a chance to use Count Dracula as an instrument for good and prosperity. By discovering how a creature such as Dracula possesses the powers that he does and ultimately what makes him tick, we can promote the strengthening of the already fragile and brief human life, as well as ensure that the birthing of a monstrosity such as Dracula never occurs again upon this Earth. Such benefits far exceed those that would be gained from simply executing Dracula.

Thank you Mr. Mill. You may now step down.

Virtues, Violence, and Vampires—Oh, My!

I call to the stand our final expert witness Aristotle (384–322 B.C.E.). Mr. Aristotle believes that the purpose of morality is the promotion and strengthening of character. Mr. Aristotle believes that living with strong character means living in accordance with reason. Mr. Aristotle believes that when one lives by reason, then that person guarantees themselves a prosperous and happy life. Aristotle called this system of living Eudaimonism.

After examining every aspect of this case, especially the nature of the defendant, Count Dracula, Mr. Aristotle believes that based on the evidence the defendant is incapable of living the life of eudaimonia as defined for human beings and should not be punished for his actions. Please proceed, Mr. Aristotle.

The first argument I wish to present before the court is that the defendant Count Dracula is not a human being like you or me. Because of that, he cannot be morally judged by the same standard as any human being. The defendant is a vampire and his view of what personal happiness and flourishing is will be quite different from our own. I direct the jury's attention to Jonathan Harker's journal. In it we will see an entry from the twenty-fifth of June which details the first time that Mr. Harker saw the defendant sleeping in his coffin. What Jonathan Harker saw was the defendant with graying hair and mustache and pale cheeks.

When we skip to an entry from the thirtieth of June, Mr. Harker again sees the defendant sleeping in his coffin but looking significantly different in appearance. Mr. Harker writes in detail saying:

There lay the Count, but looking as if his youth had been half restored. For the white hair and moustache were changed to dark iron grey. The cheeks were fuller, and the white skin seemed ruby-red underneath. The mouth was redder than ever, for on the lips were gouts of fresh blood, which trickled from the corners of the mouth and ran down over the chin and neck.

These different descriptions seen first on the twenty-fifth of June and then again on the thirtieth are very important.

They show that the defendant does not drink blood out of a sense of being evil. Dracula drinks blood because doing so is necessary to continue flourishing. Mr. Harker wrote of how, when the defendant had not drunk any blood that he became gray, pale, and that Mr. Harker could not sense any breathing from Dracula. Had Dracula continued to be in this state, death was right around the corner. Blood is a natural means of survival to the defendant, in the same way as meat from cows or pigs is natural for us humans to eat.

When Dracula was drinking the blood of Mina Harker, this was an act of retaliation towards those who wished to do him harm. Dracula knew the likes of Jonathan Harker, Dr. Van Helsing, and the others all desired nothing more than to see his life reduced to a pile of ashes. This made Count Dracula panic because he knew his well-being was now in danger. Dracula had to defend himself any way he could and he even says to Mrs. Harker that he was drinking from her because her husband and his companions tried to end his life and were a threat to him. The defendant is on the record as saying cruelly to a terrified Mina Harker "And so you, like the others, would play your brains against mine . . . Whilst they played wits against me, against me who commanded nations, and intrigued for them, and fought for them, hundreds of years before they were born, I was counter-mining them." Dracula planned on using Mrs. Harker to kill his enemies and to continue flourishing in his environment. Van Helsing himself even noted how Dracula is like a child when he says "He, too, have child brain, and it is of the child to do what he have done." Thus, even the good Doctor acknowledges that Dracula is not fully competent mentally.

Because of this childlike brain that Dracula possesses, he only reasons so far as to know whether or not he is capable of a certain action. He pays very little mind to the consequences of the action once committed. Having this kind of mind does not grant Dracula the power of self-control and as a result, he cannot moderate himself and his behaviors. This is completely the opposite of our human nature because we can moderate ourselves due to our reason. Because Dracula is like a child, we must think about how we would treat our children in such a case. The punishments spoken of in this court would be far too harsh for a child and so I believe far too harsh for Dracula as well.

Ladies and gentlemen of the jury, it is in my expert opinion that the defendant Count Dracula should be found guilty of his crimes and that his punishment should be imprisonment. While I strongly believe that Count Dracula must be restrained so as to not cause any more unnecessary death and harm, I cannot agree with Professor Kant on the death penalty. As I said, even Dr. Van Helsing himself, an expert on vampire biology, believed that Dracula had the mind of a child. Children are incapable of moderating themselves because their ability to reason is still weak. If we permitted Dracula to die here today, it would set a precedent that it is permissible in a just society to murder children when they do wrong. If such a thing were to occur, we would be no less beastly than Dracula himself. Because of these conclusions, I find imprisonment to be the only suitable punishment.

Thank you Mr. Aristotle: You may step down.

Has the Jury Reached a Verdict?

Ladies and gentlemen of the jury, you have now heard evidence from three different expert witnesses. Immanuel Kant is of the opinion that the defendant should be found guilty and that he should be sentenced to death because since Dracula has killed multiple people, his actions indicate that he finds killing to be morally permissible. Because of this moral rule that Dracula himself established, it is the duty of the court to hold him up to his self-imposed standard. Dr. Kant believes that by applying Dracula's standard of murder also to himself, we keep our sense of morality strong and the dignity of the Categorical Imperative intact.

Our second expert, John Stuart Mill, believes Count Dracula to be guilty but disagrees with Kant on the punishment. Mr. Mill has stated that he believes the defendant should be sentenced to undergo experimentation. The benefits of unlocking the secrets of Dracula's biology from a medical standpoint far outweigh those gained from simply executing Dracula from both a moral and legal standpoint.

Mr. Mill believes that understanding Dracula's powers and the nature of his immortality could promote and strengthen the human race in ways we could have never hoped for. Our final expert witness, Mr. Aristotle, believes that Dracula should be found guilty but only face imprisonment. Aristotle made the argument that the defendant was of a childlike mind and because of that, could not sufficiently moderate his actions and simply acted as a child would in these circumstances.

I ask the jury to please consider all of the evidence presented and testimonies given in full. I will not be giving any sort of opinion or handing down any sort of verdict concerning the fate of the defendant. That responsibility rests entirely on your shoulders. So when you have made a decision, please email DraculaVerdict@Gmail.com with your verdict and why you came to it. I thank you all for your time, keep your necks covered, and court is now dismissed.

8
Why Count Dracula Can Never Be Evil

COLE BOWMAN

When his name is uttered, those who know it quake with fear of his evil. He has the strength of twenty men and likes to use it on unsuspecting victims. He makes diabolical plans and wants to slowly devour the population of London. He kidnaps, kills and stalks in the night. His eyes flame red when he's angry and he uses sorcery to drive men mad with a cannibalistic psychosis. He owns a big, creepy castle. He drinks blood and probably fed a baby to his three hungry, seductive, vampire brides. He is the last of a legacy of Székely warriors and he intends on regaining the former glory of his family.

He's Count Dracula and he's the world's most infamous vampire. He started and has continued to inspire a genre that has shaped the way that we look at the undead for nearly a century and a half. While reimaginings of him have ranged from stars on the silver screen to puppets, Dracula has remained the cornerstone of vampirism. And, the spreading of his image has helped to define what it means to be a vampire, highlighting the struggle between humankind and the outsider as he has become more and more well known.

Because of this, Count Dracula has become one of the most influential examples of evil in literature and art. But what makes Dracula evil? The problem with Dracula is that he is *not* inherently evil. Like many others who might be labeled "evil," he doesn't have an innate quality that makes him evil. Instead, he acts out of ignorance for human value and in his own self-interest: he's thoughtless and selfish. This is where his particular kind of "evil" comes from, not from some underlying force that causes him to commit crimes against humanity. To prove this, we must look closely at Dracula's motivations and his methods. As we do so, it becomes obvious that Dracula is much more mundane, more ordinary, than he appears at first glance.

What's Evil, Anyway?

Twentieth-century political theorist Hannah Arendt (1906–1975) provides a standpoint from which we can easily understand the very mundane nature of Dracula's evil actions. Arendt had a lot to say about evil, but said nothing explicitly about vampires. All the same, through Arendt's ponderings on the subject of evil, the centuries-old vampire can be resurrected once again, though this time, he might look quite a bit different than the malicious creature he has been depicted as in the past.

Born to a Jewish German family in 1906, Arendt was something of an expert on evil. She lived through the rise of Nazism in Germany, and worked closely with fellow Jewish refugees in France during World War II. Arendt witnessed first-hand one of the most horrific periods in the history of humankind and it helped her to get a keen perspective upon the nature of evil.

To begin, let's throw out the idea of an absolute, divine evil. This is the kind of evil that can be found in ideologies or religions. It's that kind of evil that, by its very nature, cannot be examined critically. In her *Origins of Totalitarianism* (1951), Arendt established the concept of absolute evil as "it can no longer be deduced from humanly comprehensible motives." If the motives are not comprehensible to humans, we have no way to form a meaningful discussion of them. While some form of an absolute evil may exist, it has very little basis in real life. Absolute evil is intangible and its effects on individuals (like Dracula) can't be measured.

So, if you think about it, absolute evil is boring. It is something we can't really make sense of, don't really know why it happens, and doesn't change. It wouldn't be something someone *becomes* but rather it would just be some abstract idea out there. On the other hand, what *is* interesting is the kind of good versus evil struggle that rests in our everyday decisions. It is the evil that can change throughout time, and it can be either supported or undermined by actions that a person takes.

Arendt is most famous for coining the phrase "the banality of evil," which was the primary conclusion of her book *Eichmann in Jerusalem*. While the word "banality" implies that there is a commonplace or trivial nature about evil itself, it's not *quite* what she intended for the phrase to mean. Arendt's aim for *Eichmann in Jerusalem* was to illustrate the ordinariness of the people who were responsible for perpetrating evil. She did this by addressing the crimes of notorious Nazi official Adolf Eichmann. This book detailed her thoughts on Eichmann's 1961 trial, which showed to the world that he was responsible for following through on the Nazi Final Solution plan in Eastern Europe. He saw to the deportation of *hundreds of thousands* of Jews to ghettos and camps.

Eichmann, Arendt argues, was not driven by evil, but committed crimes against humanity by simply living out his life as a Nazi official. Like so many others of his time, Adolf Eichmann was a part of a massive system of people who were culpable in the murders of millions. However, he didn't do this because he felt an irresistible craving to inflict pain, but because it was his day job. Likewise, the people who raided ghettos and exterminated entire family lines were just ordinary folks doing their *jobs*. By calling this "banal", Arendt is not trying to undermine the impact of evilness itself, but instead show that the people involved are not doing so for the sake of evil. They are committing evil actions for banal reasons like, "it's my job" or "because I was ordered to do it." In other words, they don't do it for evil's sake; they do it because they want a paycheck or to stay out of trouble—for *themselves*.

Paths of Good Intentions

So, what does this mean for Dracula? Well, everything really. The unfolding of *Dracula* is the unraveling of his character. While he seems to have at least some capacity of goodness in him during the beginning of his tale, this capability decreases more and more as the story advances. By the end, there isn't a scrap left of that possibility of redemption. He's just a bad guy. What Arendt's theories illustrate, in spite of this clear path of evil actions, is that the very nature of Dracula's evil should not be taken for granted. It is not something to be taken lightly because it is not a *part* of the vampire. Evil does not drive

Dracula; it is a *result* of what he has already done. Dracula is not perpetrating evil acts for their own sake, simply to cause harm and chaos. Dracula is selfish and is attempting to reclaim the former glory of his family.

Dracula and Eichmann are very similar in their treatment of others because of this. They are careless and both objectify the people in their way. Their thoughtlessness causes them to treat people simply as a means to an end. Like Eichmann, Dracula does not value the people that come through his afterlife as people. Like Eichmann, he sees them as a cog in a much larger machine. So, when he wrongs a person, his actions are exercised not in the spirit of malice, but of thoughtlessness. While he appears to be evil from the perspective of those involved, his actions are just careless rather than intentionally cruel.

What Arendt argued was that evil is not a state of being, but a choice that is made by the person actually committing evil acts. The person *chooses* to wrong others. What makes it worse, though, is that the person in question is often not actively making the choice for the sake of its impact on others, but as a means of simply benefiting herself. That is, a person who commits evil actions does so because she does not consider the human dimension of the consequences of her action. She does not see a person before her, but simply the means to an end— her end. Arendt's ultimate statement about Eichmann is that his nature is not evil *per se*, but that his actions were driven by thoughtlessness. She stresses that thoughtlessness leads to evil. It is the mechanism that allows for evil actions to be taken. A person, therefore, can do evil but not *be* evil. So, what exactly is the difference? To *be* evil, one must choose malice for its own sake and others suffer for it. To *do* evil, malice is not a factor, but suffering is still the result.

Let's look at an example: There are two men, Louis and Edward and each are making their way down identical streets, each with a delightful ice cream shop along his route. An identically gleeful set of eight-year-old girls with a double scoop of bubblegum ice cream exit their respective shops in front of the men along their route. Louis bumps past the child, making her drop her ice cream on the ground and continues obliviously on his way. Edward, however, spots the child happily about to take her first bite of the cone and slaps it out of her hands and onto the dirty pavement. Edward then proceeds to mock the girl for the loss of her ice cream as she cries. While Louis is a jerk for his carelessness, Edward is evil. In both scenarios, the children are deprived of the joy of bubblegum ice cream, and suffer because of it. But, the second scenario is the only one in which deliberate action is taken to cause this suffering.

Similarly, the good doctor John Seward gives us a perfect example of how this would look in the case of an individual. Seward has a strange man, Renfield, in his asylum undergoing treatment for a peculiar psychosis that drives him to consume various life forms. Beginning with flies, Renfield is driven to feed small creatures to larger and larger ones. It rather resembles a macabre set of matryoshka nesting dolls, with him taking the place as the largest doll after having fed animals to one another. While it becomes clear later on in the novel that he acts this way because he is under the control of the Count, his actions are inexplicable at first to the young doctor. To better understand his patient's condition, Seward denies Renfield access to cats, the next step in his carnivorous psychosis. Renfield snaps and lashes out at the man. It is obvious that the disruption in his scheme has caused him great grief. But this doesn't mean that Dr. Seward is evil. He is just attempting to *help* Renfield, but the necessary actions to do so cause Renfield great distress.

While he suffers because of Seward's treatment, Seward is ultimately acting in his patient's best interests. In this way, Dr. Seward is like Louis. He causes Renfield to suffer, but only because he does not fully understand the distress it will cause the other man. If he had done this out of a specific intent to hurt Renfield, he would be like Edward. His intention is decisive. While the outcome is the same whether or not he intends to harm Renfield, his own character is determined by the motivations which make him act the way he does. And, so, Dr. Seward is not evil.

Blood and Violence

To really understand Dracula, we must understand his methods. Dracula will never be mistaken for a pacifist, no matter how much he tries to convince those around him that he is harmless. He is prone to lashing out, doing so on many occasions throughout the course of the story. The Count's violent actions are used by the good guys as another nail in the coffin of his morality. But Dracula's violence doesn't provide a simple distinction of good and evil. It is not nearly so simple as that. The Count's fondness for violence is understood easily enough, though, if we allow for a little perspective on the matter.

Firstly, it must be noted that he is often *intentionally* violent toward the people who populate the rest of the book. From the perspective of those at his hand, Dracula's actions are appalling, but from his own standpoint, the Count's violence is quite constructive. Simply put, acting out of violence helps him to get his way. It is a mechanism for getting what he wants and so long as it does, the object of his violent outbursts doesn't matter.

Arendt addresses this specific issue in her appropriately named work *On Violence* (1970). There, she discusses the creative potential of violence itself. She suggests that violence can act as a catalyst for change. And in *Dracula*, violence is definitely a catalyst of change. It is the primary tool for change in Dracula's repertoire. For example, Dracula reacts violently when Harker leaves his rooms to wander about the castle. Although unharmed by the count, the solicitor is scared enough to comply more carefully with Dracula's wishes. This, in turn, confirms Dracula's belief that violence is effective in accomplishing his will. But does any of this make him evil? No, not really. Yes, Harker does suffer because of his treatment, but that is simply incidental to the Count's primary goal.

The second thing that has to be understood before we condemn Dracula for his violence is his very nature. Dracula is a vampire. Vampires consume human blood in order to survive. So, Dracula must consume human blood in order to survive. The fact that getting access to blood is often a horrific, violent event is not something that he likely considered, well, bad. That is just *how you get blood*. Especially in a time that hypodermic needles are at the height of medical technology and the idea of a synthetic blood substitute is literally inconceivable. So, when Dracula gorges himself on the blood of a child in Transylvania, he does so to survive, not because he delights in the horror of his own doings.

But that brings up yet another question: is it morally reprehensible to choose a child victim? Well, from a human perspective, it absolutely is. Dracula, however, is rather out of touch with human morality. This question wouldn't even occur to him. While the murder of a child is generally considered one of the greatest crimes amongst humankind, it is likely that a vampire would judge the situation very differently. Dracula has never had children, though he does have an almost parental bond with the new vampirelings that he creates, and he does not have a healthy understanding of what it means to be in a human parent-child relationship. He's disconnected from the experience entirely, so he's unable to fully understand the moral implications of his actions. He simply does not know the importance of what he does. Humans are his *prey* and it just so happens that children are easy prey. In his mind, so long as his victim is human, it's fair game.

This brings us to our final point about violence in Stoker's *Dracula*: Violence is not just confined to Dracula himself. Other than the vampire, the most violent person in the novel is Van Helsing, the savior of the humans who have become ensnared in Dracula's plot. Van Helsing is on a crusade to rid the world of supernatural creatures, and will stop at nothing to make sure that it happens. He is ready to kill any vampire he comes across, no matter who they once were or what they are up to because that is the only way he knows to stop their bloodlust. He sees violence as a catalyst, just as both Count Dracula and Hannah Arendt do. When viewing the body of the freshly dead Lucy, Van Helsing tells Seward: "I want to cut off her head and take out her heart." The image his statement brings to mind is horrifying. Seward is shocked by it, but Van Helsing sees it as a way to ensure that Lucy will not rise from the dead again.

The most poignant example of Van Helsing's own approach to violence comes from the very reason he's in London in the first place: He's there to hunt and kill Dracula. He is ready to kill him on sight, offering no other option than the vampire's immediate extermination. After all, it's his *job* to hunt down and destroy supernatural beings. Sound familiar? Van Helsing never states just how many other supernatural creatures he has hunted, but it would be fair to assume that there have been at least a few. Given his knowledge of vampirism, it may be that he has had many such encounters. Violence is just as much a tool for Van Helsing as it is for Dracula, and he's the leader of the *good guys*, the Crew of Light. So violence doesn't necessarily tell us whether or not someone is evil.

The Thoughtless Immortal

The root of Dracula's evil may well come down to his careless-ness. While he is manipulative and cunning, he has only his own goal in mind, and disregards the needs of everyone else in his pursuit of that goal. This thoughtlessness has become something of a shroud around him, affecting all that he does and how he interacts with the world. This, according to Arendt was also the root of Eichmann's own evil. Arendt states:

> The longer one listened to him, the more obvious it became that his inability to speak was closely connected with an inability to think, namely to think from the standpoint of somebody else. (*Eichmann in Jerusalem*, p. 49)

Eichmann and Dracula are both alike in this and in a few other ways. They are both unable to understand someone else from that person's own perspective. They simply refuse to put them-selves into someone else's shoes. Should they do so, they would inevitably have different feelings for the other people that their actions impact. So, is it this *lack* of feeling that's at the core of our vampire's evil?

Dracula's conversations show us that he acts in much the same way as Eichmann does with respect to those "safeguards" Arendt mentions. He protects himself from even acknowledg-ing his own cruelty by establishing *rhetorical* safeguards against his own actions. More plainly, Dracula traps his victims with a verbal waiver of sorts, allowing him to excuse his own actions throughout the novel. When he holds Harker captive in his castle, he does so by beginning his stay with the conversa-tion: "Welcome to my house! Enter freely. Go safely, and leave something of the happiness you bring!" (Barnes and Noble Classics edition, p. 7). While it's plain to see that Harker is cap-tive in the building, Dracula has provided him with an explicit permission to leave at any time. By asserting (even just in his own mind) that Harker was welcome to come and go as he pleases, Dracula safeguards himself from having to think too deeply about the position that he has put the solicitor into.

Even if he had a fragment of humanity in his conscience, Dracula's safeguards protect him from feeling guilt for this. He mustn't be concerned about his role as a captor if he has given Jonathan a chance to back out of their arrangement upon his arrival, even if he does lock him in his chambers during daytime. To Dracula, these measures are necessary and he will use any excuse he can muster to give himself permission to get away with it. It's possible that the vampire may choose to protect himself from humanizing too much on purpose, but this looks unlikely. The ability to forge an emotional bond with others is an important human characteristic, but the vampire would have very little need of it. What good can come of a predator thinking too fondly on his prey? Not much.

At one point, when Harker wakes up, he observes that he had been placed abed undressed. He then observes that his diary is still intact in his pocket, noting that Dracula would likely have taken or disposed of it if he had found it there when he undressed him. While it is reasonable to argue that the Count simply did not notice the journal there, it is more likely that he simply did not care about what Harker was writing in it. And what reason does he have to worry about it? He knows that whatever thoughts the man puts in it are trapped with him in Transylvania. There is no way that it can avert his design to infiltrate London, so it is useless to him. This serves to further highlight Dracula's complete disregard of Harker's, or any other person's, perspective. If it is not even valuable enough to threaten him in its most candid form, it's not valuable to him at all.

The Crew of Light

While Dracula is careless with other people, the members of the Crew of Light are decidedly considerate of the needs and desires of the others. Dracula's thoughtlessness stands in stark contrast to the thought*ful*ness these other characters display. In fact, the entirety of the novel is based from their perspectives, with each of them providing us with a slightly different view of Dracula during their ruminations. It is by their comparison to each other that Dracula is painted as evil in the first place. This merry band of do-gooders is the means by which the Count's evil is truly measured, so their presence must also be examined to fully comprehend Dracula.

Throughout his journal, Jonathan Harker repeatedly mentions Mina's feelings in the eventuality that she might come across his writings. He reflects on how she might feel to read his seduction by the three vampiresses within Dracula's keep, noting her potential shame for learning the lurid details. On top of this, Harker thinks frequently on her well-being while he's away. He even makes memos to himself about recipes and other keepsakes he wishes to bring back to her. Jonathan consistently has Mina's interests in mind during his travels. It is in this very same journal that Dracula is first introduced, and where his character is being established in a way that literally contrasts him with all of the love and caring that Harker holds for Mina.

Harker's consideration of Mina is not isolated, though. This sort of thoughtfulness resonates through the entire group, creating an effective foil for Dracula's thoughtlessness. Lucy's suitors all remain gentlemanly friends, despite their competition for her heart. Mina cares for Lucy, protecting her when she starts to sleepwalk. Van Helsing takes it upon himself to protect Mina once she, in turn, falls to the Count's influence. These behaviors by the protagonists serve to further highlight Dracula's disregard, giving it a basis by which it can be contrasted. Dracula's outright selfishness is even more apparent when compared to these others, especially to them in their dealings with him. They perceive him as malicious more so in contrast to their own kindness than for his transgressions against them. And it is only these perceptions that we have to consider when looking at Dracula himself. Certainly, there are no journal pages of his to defend him.

Thoughtfulness is something of a key to goodness amongst people. This is implied through the relationships between the characters consistently. In fact, as though to underpin his overarching point about goodness, there's an exact comparison between goodness and thoughtfulness in Chapter 17: "How good and thoughtful he is; the world seems full of good men— even if there are monsters in it." This, written in Mina's journal, is in reference to Dr. Seward's gentle kindness to her. Mina herself cares for others deeply and that is reflected through her actions and thoughts on them. Because of this, she's able to recognize the same kinds of traits within others. The monster she mentions is Dracula, of course, and she is unable to recognize any sort of thoughtfulness in him. Thoughtfulness and goodness go hand in hand.

As Mina is something of a beacon for goodness amongst the characters, her commentary is made even more compelling.

She is the embodiment of the traits Arendt considers necessary for choosing right action. Mina is pointing out the importance of empathy to the formation of valuable relationships, which extends from the same place as does Arendt's previous argument about being able to think from the perspective of another. If you can imagine yourself in another person's position, you feel empathy for that person. Empathy makes it possible to ease another's suffering, to ensure that a loved one's life is affected by as little evil as possible. That's the foundation for caring.

By contrast, the Count's actions are more disturbing for his initial guise as a caring, thoughtful person within the narrative. Indeed, one reason for Dracula's perceived evil may just be his attempts at propriety in the first place. He spends a great deal of time and effort trying to make Harker feel comfortable while he is in Transylvania. The denouement that occurs upon Harker's coming to understand Dracula's manipulations is intensified by the shattered image of care that the Count had presented in the first place. The consideration that he put into Harker's initial time there was a pretense of sorts, inauthentic and hollow. Once Harker realized this, the betrayal was complete.

The Banality of Evil

Dracula is, indeed, devoid of empathy for the people that suffer at his hand in the novel. When he is holding Jonathan Harker prisoner, he doesn't take a moment to consider the young lawyer's opinion on the matter. He simply sees Harker as a means to an end, a way to begin his revenge anew in his "beloved" England. He does not reflect on Mina's wishes before beginning the process to make her into his bride. He does not care about Arthur's love for Lucy as he kills her. This detachment from empathy is far from the gnawing, desperate desire that evil has shown itself to be. It is mundane. If anything, it is lazy evil. *Evil Lite*, if you will.

Like Eichmann, Dracula has committed terrible crimes. He has murdered, manipulated, kidnapped and mutilated. But the reason for this was no malicious desire to cause suffering. It's Dracula's thoughtlessness that makes him commit greater evils than he likely would have committed were he acting out of malice. As Arendt famously said, "The sad truth of the matter is that most evil is done by people who never made up their minds to be or do either evil or good" (*Thinking*, p. 180). Arendt does not use this discourse to excuse Eichmann's actions, and neither should we excuse Dracula. But by thoughtlessly calling him "evil" without fully understanding him we become no better than the Count himself.

For Dracula, his very nature betrays him in the end. He cannot be considered by human measure because he isn't human. While Dracula's interactions with the cast of characters (especially Harker) implies that he has a deeper contract with humankind, the most important function that humanity plays in the "life" of the vampire is that of food. To a vampire, humans are food first and foremost. While lively conversations that help the Count to perfect his English inflections are a delightful bonus in the deal, every human that crosses through Dracula's plane are mostly just potential snacks. Dracula's objectification of others is somewhat more understandable then, as humans are more akin to livestock than to kin or peers. He culls from humanity what he deems to be the greatest specimens to turn into other vampires (like Mina), while he converts other, inferior, specimens into servants (like Renfield).

Unlike Eichmann, however, Dracula is not one with humanity. He therefore shouldn't be held to the standard of good and evil that we expect of others. Dracula will also never be a beacon of good like Mina for the same reason. No human can bite a vampire and make him understand the profundity of his actions. While the crimes that Dracula has committed are egregious, they are committed out of ignorance. That's why Arendt's argument about Eichmann falls short of fully comprehending the vampire. Eichmann, at least, understood what it meant to be human before he helped in the murders of thousands.

That's why Eichmann, though banal, is truly evil, whereas Dracula, though careless, can never be evil.

9
Baring Fangs, Bearing Responsibility

JOHN ALTMANN

Imagine that you're standing outside the walls of Castle Dracula, and out of the corner of your eye you see a distant beckoning shape. Cautiously, you step closer and see Jonathan Harker mouthing to you from the window. You can just make out that he's a prisoner and that he's not safe where he is. His face is wearing an expression of fear and dread, and you can sense that Harker is in grave danger. If you take action and attempt to help him, you may expose yourself to the many dangers of Castle Dracula but you may also be able to save his life. If you ignore Harker and walk away, you remain alive but you have Harker's fate on your conscience.

What do you do? That's a problem of moral agency. Moral agency is our ability to make moral decisions on the basis of right and wrong and being completely responsible for those actions. When Dracula has his fangs full of Lucy Westenra's flesh, is he really making a free choice? When Dracula forces himself on Mina Harker and steals her blood, or when he coldly and brutally murders Renfield, is he truly responsible for these acts? I realize it sounds crazy, but he really may not be responsible. Dracula may not have enough free will to be blameworthy for his actions!

Freedom and Slavery

When we hear 'free will', we often take it to mean possessing the ability to do whatever we want, but this definition can't be correct, because we can never do whatever we want. If we

91

could, there would be no reason why Jonathan Harker couldn't walk through the walls of Dracula's castle and escape to safety or why Dracula couldn't drink blood and satisfy his thirst in broad daylight. The fact that we're restrained by our biology and the laws of physics means that free will has to be something else. It is more likely the ability to act freely within a given set of possibilities. Dracula, throughout the novel, commits murder, theft, abuse, and other actions that seem evil. He does these things constantly, without any regret or remorse. So it seems Dracula does not possess the free will to be good and if that's the case, can he still be held responsible?

Contemporary philosopher John Martin Fischer would answer my question with a resounding "Yes!" Fischer believes that whether we have free will or not, there are actions that come entirely from us. So even if all Dracula is capable of is evil, even for reasons outside of his control, as long as Dracula makes the active choice to be evil then he can still be held morally responsible. Making the choice to walk down a path even if it's the only path available would be exercising what Fischer called guidance control. Dracula still has guidance control. He makes decisions. Even if he has no other options, those decisions are ones that have their origin in his wants and desires. So even if he has no freedom and no choice, the fact that his actions come from him and are not forced on him means he's responsible. In other words, his actions come from his *reason* not because something or someone forces him to do it. He thinks about what he wants, then does it.

The Selfish and Selfless: Dracula and Rationality

Dracula has demonstrated time and time again that he's a creature of great intelligence. Dracula uses his extraordinary intellect in the pursuit of his own interests. Dracula poses as a carriage driver to lure Jonathan Harker away from safety. Once in Castle Dracula, the Count used his powers of reason to make sure Harker has no available exits. Even when he kidnaps a helpless child to feed his wives, Dracula still committed the act with his interests in mind, so that they would not devour Harker whom Dracula claimed was his! In other words, Dracula figured that if he didn't want his wives feeding from

Harker, he would have to give them other flesh. So he used his reason to do something heinous!

Immanuel Kant (1724–1804) would have found Dracula highly immoral for using reason to manipulate others to his will. Kant believed the use of reason is at the very center of morality and moral judgments. So, Dracula acts immorally if he uses his reason to further his own interests at the expense of others, as when he attacks Mina Harker so that she won't be able to help Dr. Van Helsing and the others against him. But when we use our reason to help others and to uphold dignity and respect, we're acting morally, as when Dr. Van Helsing convinced Arthur Holmwood to let him cut off Lucy's head and kill her in her vampire form so that her soul could be at peace.

Dracula's life and actions after he became a vampire show a clear and consistent pattern of him always pursuing his own interests and never showing one shred of caring or concern for the well-being of others. He has demonstrated through his actions that he is capable of reason more than most, yet him using it for his own ends makes him amount to an immoral monster and a blameworthy one at that.

Yes, But How Does That Make You Feel?

When we think about how the people of Transylvania or anybody that has come in contact with Dracula react to him, to say that he would never be invited to any Thanksgiving feast or Christmas party is putting it mildly. When Jonathan Harker told the old woman who ran the hotel he was staying at that he was meeting Dracula on business, she wept and pleaded with him not to go, and when he refused she gave him her cross to take with him to make sure he had a fighting chance. When Jonathan Harker witnessed Dracula transform and scale his castle walls to take flight, his face went pale with horror. When Mina Harker remembered how Dracula forced himself on her and drank from her neck, she wept in utter despair and agony. If there is anybody out there who has any love for Dracula, I'm pretty sure it would just be Dracula himself.

These reactions our heroes and the average person have to Dracula's monstrousness are at the core of David Hume's moral philosophy. David Hume (1711–1776) believed that our emotions and how they presented themselves to certain people or events, express a feeling of either "approval" or "disapproval." Basically, we experience a feeling of "yay" or "boo" when we see what other people do, and that feeling determines if the other person is moral or immoral in our eyes. These feelings take the form of reward or punishment towards the person in question, and that is how responsibility is determined. Take for example when Dr. Van Helsing, Jonathan Harker, and the others all rush into Mina's room and discover that Dracula had forced himself on Mina and taken a significant amount of blood from her. She would later weep and be utterly disgusted with herself as she recalled how Dracula cruelly drank from her.

Everyone around Mina as they heard her tell them of her horrifying experience with Dracula is in a state of pure anguish. This is especially true of her husband Jonathan, who curses Dracula to the darkest depths of Hell and who lets out tormented cries of suffering to God for what has happened to his family at Dracula's hands. Such violent emotional reactions towards Mina's state of well-being as well as how she got there show that not only is there disapproval from these men towards the act of violence on an innocent woman, these reactions also show disapproval for Dracula himself. To put it lightly, when they hear about Dracula's actions they all think and feel "boo!" These men then place responsibility on Dracula and commit to the plan of punishing him for his crimes by way of death.

Biting Back: Dracula and the Existence of Luck

So Dracula deserves to die a hideous death, but, then again . . . When Dr. Van Helsing spoke to everyone in the later chapters about when Dracula used to be human and an excellent military general who fought for the freedom of his country, did any of you think to yourselves "Man, what rotten luck that he became a vampire!"? I sure did and from the sound of it, much like Lucy Westenra, the transformation was anything but consensual. All of the murders and theft of blood that Dracula has committed over his long, long life can all be traced back to that fateful night he was transformed. It's as if everything since then has just been out of Dracula's control. So while we all think "boo" about Dracula's free and rational choices to do evil, his evil begins with a force outside of him!

The living philosopher Thomas Nagel believes that assigning responsibility to a moral agent is an impossible task because of the existence of luck which he defines as circumstances that lie outside our control. If everyone was completely to blame or to praise for their actions, then Jonathan Harker would be immoral entirely for helping Dracula acquire property in London because he helped him even when he discovered that Dracula was a monster! Yet, Jonathan Harker, through everything, actually emerges from the story as the hero because the evil that he helps with is accidental—it's luck.

Dracula's entire existence and everything that ever resulted from it is a product of luck. Dracula himself showed us that the supernatural powers a vampire possesses include inhuman strength and an ability to command wolves to do his bidding. Jonathan Harker's imprisonment is proof that such powers are hard to overcome through resistance. So, Dracula, before his transformation could have struggled mightily to resist the vampire that ultimately made him into the monster that we would come to know and loathe. If a vampire with ridiculous strength and a wolf army ready to serve isn't an extraordinary circumstance outside anyone's control, then I don't know what is.

Powerlessness Means Innocence

Jonathan Harker had a moment early on in the novel where he was shaving and, as many shavers have done before and since, accidentally cut himself. Dracula walks in as Harker is bleeding (apparently having never heard of knocking) and upon seeing the blood, goes into a crazed state and lunges for Harker's throat. The only reason Harker doesn't die in that moment is because Dracula's hand touched the beads of the crucifix Jonathan was wearing which allowed (or perhaps compelled) Dracula to regain his composure. At the end of the day, he amounts to a being who is absolutely powerless over his own life.

The belief that we're powerless to do anything other than what we end up doing is known as fatalism. Theological fatalism is the belief that God controls all the events of the universe and we're unable to change them. When it comes to God and his relationship with Dracula, the least you can say is that they're not the best of friends. Jonathan Harker is probably grateful for it: After all, if it wasn't for the crucifix he was wearing around his neck in Dracula's castle, he would be dead.

The crucifix is an object in the novel that represents purity, goodness, devotion to God, and the power that God possesses. When we see the crucifix save Jonathan Harker's life, we know also that it means that God rejects Dracula and judges him to be beyond salvation. Thanks to this rejection, Dracula is fixed on his path of tainted character with no hope of being anything more than that. If you need any more proof of the power of God's rejection and the inability of the rejected to change, look no further than Mina Harker who, after being bitten by Dracula multiple times, was considered tainted in the eyes of God when the holy wafer held by Dr. Helsing during a group prayer burned her forehead.

Now Mina Harker was a person of exceptional character throughout the novel. She was a devoted wife to Jonathan Harker and took care of him when he returned from Transylvania terribly ill. She also helped Dr. Van Helsing and Dr. Seward keep records of events involving Dracula to have a better understanding of him. She was a person of exceptional moral fiber and yet, despite all of these past deeds, God still rejects her and judges her to be tainted. If someone as good as Mina can be rejected by God simply because Dracula bit her, it logically follows that the possibility of redemption for Dracula is something that will always be out of his grasp even if he made a conscious effort to change. This seems a bit unfair doesn't it? Almost like where we started at the beginning. Despite Dracula's bad luck, his forced transformation into a vampire, he is damned, just as Mina would have been had she not been saved by her friends.

Because It Is My Nature

Yet, Dracula is a monster of a very cruel and malicious nature. Dr. Van Helsing describes this nature late in the novel when he's addressing his companions before they head out to kill Dracula. Dr. Van Helsing says that Dracula is a being void of heart and conscience. This is a nature that is inherent in Dracula and cannot be overcome. So because of that fact, all the arguments that lay claim to Dracula being morally responsible are on shaky ground.

Beginning with John Martin Fischer and guidance control, he would have argued that even if being evil was the only possible choice Dracula had available, that he would still be responsible for that choice if he actively chose it. The problem with active choice is that it requires both recognition of the choice you're making, and recognition of the choices you didn't make. By Dracula lacking a conscience, he is unable to recognize not only the wrongness of his actions, but he even doesn't know what right and wrong are in general. It's not merely that Dracula doesn't wish to change; it's that he lacks the ability, to begin with, to see any reason to change. To say that Dracula is making an active choice in harming others when he can't even register in his own mind what is right or wrong seems really unfair.

Dracula's lacking a conscience also challenges Kant's claim that morality is derived from reason. Though Dracula is incredibly intelligent, his lacking a conscience means that he is incapable of weighing his self-interest against the interests of others. When Arthur Holmwood at first angrily tells Dr. Van Helsing that he would not permit him to decapitate the corpse of his wife Lucy Westenra, we can see that he is acting out of love but also out of self-interest in not wanting to see harm come to *his* wife. But, when he sees his wife in her monstrous state harming innocent children, he gives Dr. Van Helsing permission to do the dreadful deed. We see here that Arthur recognizes in that moment the dignity and well-being of others, something that Dracula is completely incapable of because his nature knows no other way of being.

The problem with David Hume's idea that morality can be based on "yays" and "boos" and so can moral responsibility is that the reactions people have towards Dracula are absolutely useless in changing who he is: Dracula simply doesn't perceive these reactions. Consider when Lucy Westenra and Mina Harker are attending the funeral of the sea captain whose ship was attacked by Dracula during the violent storm: At the funeral, there is a man with his dog who keeps barking nonstop and to correct the behavior, the man yells at and hits the dog and because of that it stops barking. Because the dog took note of his owner's violent disapproval, he changed his behavior to be more acceptable and to gain approval. People have reacted to Dracula with fear, anger, disgust and many other emotions but because he lacks a heart, these reactions are meaningless to him and do not cause him to reflect on his behavior for even a millisecond.

The Murderer Misclassified

So, let's return to our original question of whether Dracula can be morally responsible for his actions. I don't think so. Recall the words of Dr. Van Helsing regarding Dracula's nature. We've seen how Dracula lacking a heart or conscience is a problem for the ideas about morality of Fischer, Kant, and Hume. We rely on our conscience to deliberate on our actions and how they relate to the concepts of right and wrong. We rely on our hearts to empathize with one another, and to recognize pain, suffering, joy, happiness, and every other emotion that exists under the umbrella of the human condition.

Dracula didn't choose to no longer have a conscience when he became a vampire. That's just how vampires are naturally and is just one of many things outside of Dracula's control, as Nagel would point out. It's not that we can't say that Dracula is evil. He is. But when we blame him, we can't just dump it all on him and wash our hands of his blood. Morality is complicated, and we have to be careful of holding others one hundred percent guilty for things beyond their control. In the end Dracula, like all of us at one point or another, is a victim of circumstance and certainly deserves no blame for that.[1]

---

[1] Thanks to my family and friends. You made this chapter possible.

10
The Denial of Dracula

NICOLAS MICHAUD

"Weak."

I can think of no better word to describe humanity than very, *very weak*. And what's the solution we've chosen to address that weakness: Dedicating the world's resources to the cure for cancer? Turning the military might of all the world's super powers to the colonization of space? Dedicating spare time to working out, meditation, and intellectual development?

No.

Humanity, rather than solving the problem of its weakness, instead escapes from it. In one year, the entertainment sector will generate over 564 billion US dollars. Approximately 100 billion dollars is spent on alcohol in the US each year. And, chillingly, some 15 percent of all Internet traffic is cat-related. If one were to consider not just entertainment, but drugs, pornography, and even art, one would likely find that the majority of our efforts are spent distracting ourselves from our very greatest weakness . . .

Death.

Of course, humanity does spend *some* money and *some* effort on life-extending technologies and research into the causes of the ailments that come with old age, but, obviously, not nearly enough. Every human living now will die. And how does humanity deal with this fact? . . . With distractions from death.

Humans tell stories about those who lack humanity's many weaknesses . . . makes monsters of them, and then executes them. I can think of no more pathetic recourse than—rather than lifting oneself up—to seek to drag one's betters down. What is *Dracula*, if not one more human expression of delusion? What a marvelous distraction! . . . Telling oneself that a small cadre of "righteous" humans could hunt and kill an immortal lion—Count Dracula?

With Giant's Power

Friedrich Nietzsche (1844–1900) once wrote, "God is dead." His statement is both overused and misunderstood. He did not mean that God was literally dead or even necessarily that there was no God. What his statement really means is that God is unnecessary for explaining the universe. There was a point when understanding the complexity and majesty of the universe seemed to require nothing less than the belief that an all-powerful and perfect God created it. Nietzsche thought that by the time of his writing, God was no longer necessary to humanity. Now that science provided an even simpler explanation, God was an additional complication in understanding the world. Humans no longer needed God, Nietzsche thought.

He was wrong.

In over a century since the authoring of Bram Stoker's *Dracula,* humanity has done very little to overcome its need for God. While Nietzsche was writing his philosophical works, Stoker was writing his story, his distraction—his tall tale that has generated movies, TV shows, more books, and even philosophical reflections. Both Nietzsche and Stoker wrote about God, death, and the afterlife. But whose work has proven to be far more popular, far more influential—the writing of a man who believed that humanity should seek to lift itself up to the highest possible levels, or a story about how very evil it is to be better than human? Stoker's narrative about the importance of godliness and the dangers of power is beloved, while, by many, Nietzsche's heretical work is reviled. Humans still very much rely on the idea of God, but not really to become better people so much as a way of consoling themselves that they will go somewhere nice when they die.

Nietzsche's work is heretical because he argued that humanity uses God as an excuse—as an excuse to be pathetic. Nietzsche wrote about the ability of humanity to "overcome."

This overcoming though, generally is not a matter of kindness and thoughtfulness. It's the overcoming that means the ability to become powerful. It's the kind of philosophy that seems to describe Count Dracula—a "will-to-power." This power is something that everyone wants, but not everyone can have. It's the power Dracula had and Van Helsing envied.

To Be My Jackals When I Want to Feed

Is Dracula's will-to-power, and his willingness to seek his own self-fulfillment *without* God really that bad? It seems a twisted question, but shouldn't we ask, "What did Dracula do so worthy of destruction?" The obvious answer is that he killed humans and converted others into demonic monsters like himself. So it isn't unreasonable for humanity to defend itself, right? On the other hand, why is Dracula treated as such a monster? Yes, he feeds on humans, and, yes, he seeks to make more of his kind, but how is that worse than a wolf hunting its prey? Or worse than a wolf who seeks to make more of its kind by hunting other animals to feed its young? Sure, if a wolf tries to kill you, you defend yourself. It might even be fun to tell terrifying tales of the "killer wolf." But it's pretty obvious that the wolf is not actually evil. It follows its instincts and seeks to survive, just like you. Blaming Dracula for hunting humans seems somewhat like blaming wolves for hunting sheep.

If anything, shouldn't we respect the power and strength of a mighty predator like a wolf, a lion, or even Dracula? After all, how many humans had to band together to destroy the Count? No one man had a chance. The sheep had to gather together to kill the lion. And why did they do it? Because Dracula hunted them. Fair enough, they were protecting themselves. But does that truly make Dracula hellish Satan spawn? Or do humans just think so highly of themselves that when *they* hunt it is heroic, but when someone hunts them it is *evil*? It sounds like humanity suffers from a serious case of *whiny*.

You with Your Pale Faces All in a Row, Like Sheep

To Nietzsche, no one has the right to whine when someone else is superior. Everyone experiences the desire for power, but only some will accomplish it. Because of this, the weaker will band together, like the so-called "Crew of Light" to destroy the "Overperson"—the person whom they resent for their power. These human "sheep" will even go out of their way to justify the destruction of the Overperson, arguing that they're evil and deserving of destruction *because of their power* (Nietzsche, *Thus Spake Zarathustra*). Dracula represented a danger to humans, and rather than respecting that danger and power, the Crew of Light decided that he had to be stopped not just because of his power, but because he must be evil, for doing the same things that humans do—hunting those less powerful than themselves and trying to reproduce.

The real problem is the realization that the Overperson is something that has less to do with physical strength or physical power, but more with your ability to free yourself from the constraints of morality—the morality created by the weak to protect the weak. This may seem crazy. Morality is a good thing, right? It helps keep everyone in line. It reminds us of the rules.

But think about so many of those rules; they're usually not about justice or truth. Instead, morality is often just reduced to "law." Counterintuitively, those laws are often immoral or irrational—think of how long slavery was legal, how the law protected segregation even after the end of slavery, how the law prevented women from voting and how it was legal to beat one's wife in courthouses on Sunday for centuries! The law is not necessarily moral. It is made by those who have shared interests, and often it is used to prevent others from rising up (Nietzsche, *Beyond Good and Evil*).

Even worse than often questionably moral laws are the rules of society. Think of the rules that tell us what to buy, who we have to be, what kinds of jobs we have to have, who we are supposed to marry, and what makes life worthwhile, in general. Society tells us we're supposed to work hard, to make money, and immediately spend that money on stuff that we will later sell at a garage sale for only twenty-five cents. We're supposed to do all of this to help the economy, and because having more money and stuff supposedly makes us worthwhile.

Are these social rules really good for us? What about the person who realizes that working overtime so their children can have cable and designer sneakers doesn't make much sense, if it means that they spend less time with their family? So he says, "Screw it," and stops working so hard, falls in social class, is considered lazy by his co-workers, and has less stuff. Society would have little respect for his rejection of its norms. In fact, if everyone did it, our economy would slow, and our GDP would decrease, and we would likely not be the wealthiest country in the world *monetarily*. But isn't that "lazy" man doing something excellent? In other words, shouldn't we admire people who realize what *really* matters to them and *pursue* it?

How do we treat people who realize those social rules are just stigmatizing nonsense and choose to be their own best person? True, Dracula is something of a jerk, but do we really have a right to classify him as evil because he chooses to seek his own self-fulfillment in ways that we don't like? Or are we just being sheep complaining that the wolf is playing unfairly? Funny thing is, if we actually think that beings who are more powerful should be more moral then why, when *we* are the killers, don't we seem to have any pity for our mutton?

I Fell to at Once on an Excellent Roast Chicken

Really, what Nietzsche's work tells us is that we should be the best possible version of ourselves. Instead of resenting other people who are excellent, we should strive to be excellent, ourselves. If we fail, well, so be it, but that's no reason to blame those who defeat us. In fact, if we were to realize that we're responsible for our own excellence and our own betterment, we likely would realize that the rules put on us by society that tell us who we're supposed to be are nonsense. We would develop rules for ourselves, and the Overperson wouldn't be some immoral monster. The Overperson would still loathe war and cruelty, but they would do so because they realized that they didn't want to be that kind of a person, not because society forced those rules on them for society's own sake.

True, Dracula may not be the best Overperson. He doesn't seem to be striving for excellence so much as striving for existence. Even worse, he doesn't seem to live a life without resentment. To Nietzsche, it was very important that the Overperson not resent others who succeed. Admittedly, Dracula does resent those who thwart his plans. Even so, humanity makes him a villain for the wrong reasons. He isn't cast as a villain because he is resentful or unwilling to be the best version of himself; he's cast as a villain because he's willing to do what's necessary to survive and reproduce. His superior strength, power, mind, and health are used as reason to fear and hate Dracula.

While humanity recognizes his power, that same power becomes a reason to envy and resent him. The Crew of Light do not cast down their fallen foe with admiration for the struggle and power of a mighty adversary, but with the revulsion of one casting out evil *because of the danger Dracula represented to all of weak humanity*. We sit down to our own meals of tortured flesh with glee, but when it is ourselves on the plate we squeal and cry out, "Morality! Morality!" Where was that morality when men beat their slaves, when women were legally raped by their husbands, and, still today, when children are forced to work in factories so we can have cheaper sneakers? Van Helsing is a hero for saving us, but any man who takes video inside of a factory farm where other animals are killed and tortured may be charged as a *terrorist* under the Animal Enterprise Terrorism Act. Morality seems awfully flexible to human self-interest . . .

Your Girls that You All Love Are Mine Already

So maybe tales like *Dracula* are told for the wrong reason. Ernest Becker (1924–1974), in *The Denial of Death*, argued that everything we have created in society is really just a massive distraction from the knowledge of our impending deaths. We build governments, wage wars, buy stuff, teach students, have children—even write books—all as ways to either 1. distract ourselves from the constant reminder that we will die (and soon) or 2. as a way to try to compensate in some "heroic" way for that death. Simply, we can immortalize ourselves by some heroic act—an act like Van Helsing's.

There's something to be said for Becker's idea. It does seem that humanity often distracts itself. One wonders why there is so much mindless entertainment in the world and some intoxicants that are *literally* mind-numbing? Perhaps we seek to numb ourselves because the realization that we will die is just too much. We need to distract ourselves. And when we aren't numbing our brains, we're doing something to pretend that we will be immortal, like write *Dracula:* "Maybe if I write a best-seller, I will live on in the minds of my readers."

We don't want to consider the fact that, regardless of our accomplishments, we will likely die alone and be forgotten immediately. The one thing that can be guaranteed is that the relatively few people who attend our funerals will likely cry a bit and then go out to lunch. And we know this is true, *because that's what we all do.* We go to the funeral, say goodbye, and then make it to dinner in time for happy hour. Others will do the same after our funeral. Heck—some will even go home for some life-affirming sex. Your funeral becomes an excellent way for some jackal to "pick up chicks."

And Time Is on My Side

Dracula takes on special meaning when we think about Becker's work. *Dracula* was written by a mortal man who, through his writing, was both distracting himself from the grains of sand draining out of his hourglass and simultaneously hoping to live on through his work. It is *also* used by Becker's readers as a way to distract themselves from the looming shadow of the grinning reaper. *Dracula*, though, is especially meaningful, as it is *a book about killing immortality.*

The immortal being whose immortality we resent must be killed. The heroism that Becker describes in his book becomes real in the Crew of Light whose members take extreme measures to ensure their immortalization as good men and women who will risk their lives to stop evil. They can rest easy, knowing that even their lost members are in heaven and, even if forgotten, are immortalized through the reverberations of their holy actions. Think about what this means, though: the Crew of Light, in order to save a bunch of humans *who will die inevitably anyway killed a man who would have lived forever!* It really makes no sense!

Why go through so much trouble to prevent Dracula from killing people who inevitably die anyway? Sure, it's nicer (seemingly) if we get to grow to a ripe ol' arthritic, bed-ridden, colostomy-bagged ninety-five-year-old, but it's not like the Crew of Light actually *saved* anyone. They just delayed the deaths of humans by destroying one of few people who suffered virtually none of humanity's frailties!

I'm beginning to think that *Dracula* is just an instance of humanity trying to justify two basic—and desperate—beliefs: 1. That immortality really isn't that great—It's better to be a "good" person and die than live forever, and 2. Humanity's so awesome that it can defeat super-powerful, near-immortal beings who can shapeshift, fly, and read minds. Reading and viewing the many incarnations of *Dracula*, we see a group of good and honest heroes defy impossible odds—reminding us that really, it would *suck* to be immortal. "Heaven forbid I should be so cursed!" we think to ourselves. To be immortal would mean to be "undead," "soulless," and "evil." So don't fret, all you tiny, frail, dying humans; immortality really isn't that great . . . you wouldn't want it anyway!

Bullshit.

It gets worse. Those who possess immortality . . . They *must* be evil. Let's try to kill them—both for having something we want and to remind ourselves that even the super-powerful have to die eventually. So rather than respecting how terrifyingly awesome it must be to be Dracula—recognizing that we are basically just cattle to him—and trying ourselves to be similarly awesome, we write book after book, script after script, movie after movie, that shows pandering little humans defeating the immortal lord of evil.

The arrogance of it all is astounding. What hubris! Oh, the extremes humans will take to make themselves the heroes of their stories before they die! It's kind of like beating your computer at chess, bragging about it, and omitting the fact that it was set on "easy." Or like all of the movies and stories we have of humans defeating killer robots. Robots wouldn't miss with their evil laser beams. You can't dodge lasers; *they travel at the speed of light.* We see film after film, though, of humans avoiding a hail spray of lasers fired by, apparently, very poorly constructed robots. It would take a killer robot *one* shot to kill you. It would, in a fraction of a second, analyze the vectors, your speed, the firing speed, and distance, and, without fail, every time, *kill you.*

What chance did Van Helsing *really* have against Dracula? The true story would have been much shorter. Dracula realizes Van Helsing is trying to destroy him, and then chooses to

1. turn into mist and slip under his door and kill Van Helsing; 2. break down the door and kill him; 3. Mind-control him to kill himself (in the movie version at least); 4. send one of his many immortal minions to do the dirty work; 5. send *lots* of his immortal minions to rip out his entrails and use them for jump rope; 6. turn into a wolf and rip out his throat; 7. make other wolves rip out his throat; 8. turn into a bat and annoy the crap out of him . . . and so on . . . The story is delusional. *Dracula* makes us feel better in the face of our mortality. It gives us both the *right* and the *ability* to destroy immortality. We get to feel good about our rejection of immortality, *as if we have a choice in it.*

In That Moment of Final Dissolution, There Was in the Face a Look of Peace

All these stories about immortal robots, villains, and vampires show us that real heroes destroy true physical immortality for a greater "spiritual" immortality. *Dracula*'s really a story about how we should be willing to give up hope for an "inferior" physical eternity for a far better holy and heroic spiritual one. We see, as Dracula dies in the book, a look of peace come over his face. He's so very glad to be dead, to be spiritually cleansed.

It's that "spiritual" component that's the real kicker, isn't it? We realize that it isn't just a metaphor to most of us when we say "spiritual." Van Helsing, by killing Dracula, isn't just going to create an immortal life for himself as a good guy through memory and the stories people tell of his heroic deed. Somewhere in the back of our heads, we know that isn't enough. Van Helsing is doing more than that . . . he's guaranteeing himself a place in *Heaven*. You see, Van Helsing is saving Dracula's victims not from death, because everyone dies a bodily death, but from an eternity in *Hell*.

And, so, we return to Nietzsche. Nietzsche didn't just think that we didn't need God anymore. He thought the belief in God was bad for us. Basically, we use God as a way to hold other people back from being excellent. We create religious rules that require that people be kind, charitable, and self-sacrificial so that those who excel have to hold themselves back and everyone else can catch up. Morality, to Nietzsche, was often just a manipulation by the sheep to cage the lion.

True, we also realize that being a real Overperson would likely mean realizing that kindness and compassion are often good traits. Not because they force the Overperson to hold themselves back, but because they are qualities that connect humans together and enable them to support each other in excellence. In his own work, Nietzsche notes that the Overperson would likely feel the need to share their realization that the rules about who we're supposed to be are nonsense forced on us by society. This sharing is a compassionate act; the act of a person who believes excellence is important and something for which everyone should strive.

Well, maybe we don't need to take Nietzsche's work to its furthest extreme. Maybe religion doesn't exist to hold the Dracula-like Overperson back—or maybe it does, who knows? What's far more important is the realization that many people use religion as an excuse not to hold others back *but to hold themselves back*. Think about it. How many people, right now, believe that they have an eternity to be excellent? In other words, even if they do not become excellent now, humans will achieve a "perfect" state upon death. Forget being like Dracula and having to kill and suck blood to survive (or being a human who has to kill plants or animals to eat and survive)! Life after bodily death will result in a kind of perfection of which even Dracula could only dream.

So, for the moment, many people are biding their time, satisfied in the idea that there is a better life just around the corner. True, not all religious people are just sitting around, assuming life after death is waiting for them; some are very dedicated to being as devoted and excellent as they can, working diligently to become the most loving, the most holy, the most faithful people they can. That dedication, though, is rare, and you wonder if those few are just built that way. In other words, you wonder if they would still be dedicated to self-improvement even if they were atheists? But many, if not most of us, are taking life for granted under the assumption that there is *more life* waiting for us—*better* life—and watching TV in the meantime.

Despair Has Its Own Claims

Most of us, devout or otherwise, don't put much effort into excellence. We put far more effort into distraction. What a truly terrible irony. On even the small chance that Nietzsche is right, and there is no God, are we—by the very way we're trying to gain immortality—ensuring that we will never have it? What if humanity doesn't feel the *pressure* to try to cure old age, stop cancer, and stop as much violence as possible because it thinks that by devoting a life to religion immortality is guaranteed? I wonder if human beings would suddenly get off their collective couches and *do* something awesome if they thought that death was even just *maybe* the end? Would they *really* put some time and effort into death-defying research, or at least try to become Overmen themselves . . . the best possible versions of themselves? Are we using our stories—religious stories and even entertainment like *Dracula*—as an excuse to avoid the effort of trying to defeat death or even to better ourselves?

Maybe.

There's one small consolation. . . . If all humanity is doing is distracting itself from death, and, sometimes, humanity creates art like *Dracula* to give itself hope and diversion, there will always be something good to read while we're waiting to die. It's an odd thought, though, to realize that someday, someone will be reading this and I will be long dead. To you I say, thanks for reading, but I'd rather be alive. . . .

Oh, and it'll be your turn soon enough. . . .

III

What's It Like to
Be Dracula?

11
Being Count Dracula

SHAWN MCKINNEY

. . . If there be aught that may be learned I shall learn it.

—ABRAHAM VAN HELSING

The famed vampire hunter, Professor Abraham Van Helsing, is a man of learning, knowledge, and discovery. He is a scientist, philosopher, and metaphysician. But he acts like a hot-headed maniac: He declares, "I am a student of the brain." But if he were truly a student and a man of reason, shouldn't he have studied Dracula instead of slaughtering him? Dracula could tell us so much about how the mind and consciousness works!

For example, there's a question of whether the mind is physical and material like everything else in the natural world, or is somehow non-material and outside the laws of nature. There's a good chance that our minds aren't some special non-material stuff, because if they were then supernatural mental powers like Dracula's wouldn't seem fantastic and impossible. Things would be different in Van Helsing's world, though, and Dracula's mind would hold the key to understanding human minds.

Let's Experiment, Renfield!

Dracula makes for a great "thought experiment." We can ask ourselves questions about him and the things he can do in our imaginations and then ask if those same answers could apply to our own world. Specifically, he gives us a chance to understand minds. If our idea of the mind allows for the possibility of the kind of magical shenanigans Dracula can do, maybe we're wrong about the mind and a bit, well, batty . . .

Here's the problem in a nutshell: the body is obviously physical and is subject to cause and effect (and the various laws of nature that govern the physical world), but the mind doesn't seem to be governed by these rules. This raises the question of what the mind actually is and how it interacts with the body. Humans seem to have thoughts and feelings and hopes and desires and all these non-physical parts that do not seem determined by preceding events. This seems to mean that my *non-physical* free will determines where my *physical* arm will move next, instead of some physical cause. If that's true, then the chain of cause and effect that makes up the natural world is broken by every person.

Most of the physical world follows laws, like a line of dominos falling over, but when humans are involved, those laws don't seem to hold—because of our free will. Supposedly, when something acts on us (like someone trying to push me over) I have a choice how to react—I don't have to just fall over like a domino! On the other hand, if the state of the physical world is what causes my arm to move, and not my free choice, then free will seems a misleading concept.

Free will is just one of many issues that arise from the mind-body problem. The more philosophers have studied the mind, the more they have found that it doesn't work the way most of us think it does. That's why, if Dracula was in our world, Van Helsing shouldn't have killed him: his brain is so amazing that any scientist worth his salt should be chomping at the neck to study it. Dracula's brain would answer so many of the questions in philosophy of mind. It might even give us some clues about the mind-body problem! The first step would be to finally understand what the mind actually is.

Brains in a Bat

Sometimes I say brain and sometimes I say mind, but we're really talking about the mind. Today we use the terms 'mind' and 'brain' almost interchangeably, but we shouldn't. When I talk about the mind, I mean the thinking, believing, knowing, feeling, conscious thing. This mind is probably the seat of our identity, the thing that (we think) makes us, us. But, is the mind really the exact same thing as the brain? The crux of the difference is that the brain is physical and bound by the laws of nature, whereas the mind doesn't seem to be (my imagination is not bound by gravity, for example). It's this difference between the mind and the brain that makes Dracula's mind the most amazing one ever, because whether or not his mind is connected to his brain, his mind seems to be completely free of any physical limitations. It isn't even limited to his body.

Every living human has a brain. They've all been pretty similar: connected to the spine, in the head (usually within a skull), lobes, cerebrospinal fluid, electro-chemical activity, lots of synapses, and tens of billions of neurons. They are all explicitly physical—even made of the same general human organic matter as the rest of our organs, and they don't change sizes (except for getting bigger as we grow up). Dracula's brain changes every time he transforms into a bat or a wolf or mist. Since he's undead, his brain might not even have electro-chemical activity. He can even control the minds (brains?) of other people and even other species. Yet, through all of these physical changes, the Count still has *his* consciousness.

This means that in Dracula's world the mind isn't restricted to one's brain or body. And it doesn't suffer from any physical restrictions. If our minds are likewise non-material, we should be able to put our consciousness into rats and mist and other people as well, maybe even into computers. But let's face it, we just can't. This is good evidence that the human mind is just as material and bound by the laws of physics as is the rest of the universe. Even if we know it's physical, we still don't know what exactly consciousness is or how the mind works.

I Am the Monster that Breathing Men Would Kill

The mind matters because of consciousness. By every measure, Count Dracula seems to be just as conscious as we are. One problem with studying consciousness is that it seems to be inherently subjective and that subjectivity is muddled, or even lost, when we try to describe it in objective ways.

About forty years ago, the philosopher Thomas Nagel pointed out that even though bats (non-vampiric, non-undead ones, presumably) may have a consciousness, we as humans could never ever know what's it like to be a bat. Think about it like this: you have woken up before, and you have seen another person before and you have probably felt another person before, so if I tell you that I woke up this morning next to my wife, you could have a fair understanding of what that was like. You probably can't do the same thing with a bat. I have never echo-located anything. I have no frame of reference to know what it is like to echo-locate my bat-friend after doing bat-things. Dracula, on the other hand, could echo-locate his bat-friend after doing bat-things.

Dracula could also rat-sense his rat-friend after doing rat-things, and wolf-sense (super-smell?) his wolf-friend after doing wolf-things. Then he could tell us about it. He could describe it using human words and relate it to human concepts and human sensory experiences. He has first-hand, experiential, subjective experience of these non-human subjective experiences. As such an expert on different experiences, Dracula could provide us with an objective understanding of consciousness.

Studying Dracula's mind also helps us avoid the problem of having to define consciousness in a clear, technical manner. Whatever intelligence we have, Dracula also has. Practically all of his adversaries say that Dracula is cleverer than they are. We know that the Count reads books like we do, used to lead armies of men, and even gets upset and is motivated by revenge. "What exactly is consciousness?" is a very important question, but it's one we can postpone answering when we consider what Dracula can tell us about the mind. Whatever consciousness is, we're probably most interested in what we have (human consciousness, perhaps), and the Count certainly seems to have that.

The Blood Is the Life

If the mind is the same sort of thing as everything else (that is, something physical), then there are quite some ways we can understand our minds. Supposing that the mind is physical doesn't end the investigation, it actually opens up new questions and theories. One physical theory of mind says that the mind and the brain are identical (philosophers, cleverly, call this the Identity Theory).

If this is true, then all of my thoughts have corresponding physical states in my brain (a certain neuron is in a certain synapse while a certain chemical is present, something along those lines). This has been a very popular theory in our world, but Van Helsing could have saved his world a lot of trouble if only he had *studied* Dracula instead of killing him. Even a passing survey of Dracula's brain would have made clear that identity theory offers no answers for how the mind actually works.

Dracula can transform himself into a wolf, a bat, even mist. The brains of humans aren't the same as the brains of wolves and bats. When Dracula is moving towards Mina as mist, he has intentions and desires just as he does when he's in a human form. The same thing goes for his bat and wolf form. Dracula maintains a mind, *his* mind, across all these different shapes.

If Dracula has the same thoughts as a bat that he does as a human, his mental states can't be identical to his brain states. If Dracula has the same thoughts as a human that he does as mist, then his mental states might not even be physical in any way like any brain we've ever seen. Mist lacks a spine or a head or neurons or synapses. And even though the Count has a human shape, he's undead. So he may not have electro-chemical activity in his brain like we do. Perhaps his blood doesn't even carry oxygen into his brain. Given all these peculiarities of Dracula's mind, it's pretty strange to hold that the mind is somehow identical to brain states.

Let's Get Physical

Another possibility is that all this stuff we think we're talking about when we say "mind," or "mental," or "consciousness," is just pseudoscientific baloney like alchemy or astrology. Maybe we should eliminate all this talk of consciousness and whatnot from our investigation of the mind. But still, even if we're wrong about what consciousness is, learning about how Dracula's mind works could still help us learn about the workings of *our* minds.

The most interesting possibility for a physical mind is, well, not all that physical. This interesting theory says that whatever functions like a mind is a mind, regardless of the thing doing the functioning (if a computer does what our mind does, then it has a mind). Philosophers call this theory Functionalism. Think about a song, let's say, Mozart's *Requiem*. You could hear a live performance of the *Requiem*, and then you could hear the same song on the radio, on a CD, on a record album, as an mp3, as a .wav file, and probably in other formats. Even though the physical component of the musical piece is different in each instance, radio waves, sound waves, digital bits, grooves on the album, the song is still Mozart's *Requiem*. No matter which physical form the song takes, it's still the *Requiem*. If this is how minds work, then minds are more like a bunch of functions, so whatever thing performs that function is a mind.

Think of calling whatever you sit on a seat. What's a seat? It's whatever somebody sits on. What is a mind? It's whatever somebody thinks with. What is Dracula's mind? Whatever thinks Dracula's thoughts. In the Dracula thought experiment case, sometimes his mind seems to come in different formats: in a rat brain, a human brain, a wolf brain, and sometimes in mist (and sometimes in a very, very flat human brain). Since the Count's mind seems to be the same in all these different physical shapes, his mind is never identical to his physical brain. If Dracula's mind is not identical to his physical brain, then it can't possibly be true that all minds are just brains. Furthermore, Dracula's mind seems a whole lot like our minds. He even used to have a human mind and brain and now that his brain changes all the time, he still seems to have the same mind. Dracula's mind seems to be like a song that can have many different physical formats, but is still the same song.

The importance of the Count's mind to understanding our own minds is pretty broad. Dracula can control human minds. He and Mina can share thoughts and sensations across vast geographic distances. This telepathic interaction means that Dracula's mind is either the same as our mind, or it's at least translatable and compatible with human minds. So, even if some magic weirdness changed the essence of his mind when he became a vampire, his mind is at some level the same sort of thing as our mind. This is just like saying that Romanian and English are the same sort of thing, they are languages, because Romanian sentences can be translated into English sentences and vice versa. But, the applicability of this theory to

Dracula seems to count against the theory in the real world: my mind doesn't work anywhere but in me. I can't put my thoughts in your head or transfer my consciousness to a computer. Human minds seem locked in our brains. And, if you twiddle with my brain, it does seem to change how I think and feel, as in the case of people who suffer from brain damaging diseases like Alzheimer's or from strokes.

We've all become God's madmen, all of us.

—VAN HELSING in the movie *Bram Stoker's Dracula*

Maybe there are two sorts of things, mental things and physical things, and they are essentially different. This view seems to be championed by Van Helsing. The traditional name for this view is Cartesian Dualism—named for René Descartes (1596–1650) who thought the body and mind are two separate substances. And that dualism seems to appeal to our common sense and our desire for the spiritual. For whatever reason, humans seem interested in the non-physical, whether in a religious soul, a psychiatric psyche, ethical notions like freedom or justice, immaterial things like love, happiness, respect, or even vague beliefs in the supernatural.

Cartesian Dualism appeals to us because it says that our bodies are physical and work just like science says, but we also have an immaterial aspect not bound by any natural laws. We have an aspect that can love and believe and imagine whatever it wants to and that aspect is in charge and moves the meat around. Dracula is an extreme manifestation of this belief that the immaterial controls the material. Dracula's body is as mutable as my imagination.

Unlike Dracula, I can't fly. I can't turn myself into a wolf, or a bat, or even a rat. I seem to be bound by the natural laws of the universe, by the laws of physics. On the other hand, I can imagine flying and shape shifting. I can choose to believe whatever I like. I can understand and think things that don't seem to have any cause and lead to unpredictable results. I can be completely delusional and see dancing clowns when you see oranges. I may even run from what appears to you to be tasty citrus fruit. In short, my mental activities seem ungoverned by any discernable natural laws, and certainly not by the laws of physics.

So, according to my common sense, it seems that my mind can't be physical. It has to be something different, something non-physical. That there's more to us than simply our physical bodies (that we're more than mere meat, so to speak) is a widely shared view (not necessarily by Dracula, though). Most of us would somehow connect this view to religion, but even the pre-Christian philosopher Plato (429–347 B.C.E.) thought that humans had an eternal soul that continues to exist after the body died.

Now, it might be quite appealing to see our bodies and minds as completely different entities. But this raises more questions than it answers! Most importantly, we're left without any explanation for how mind and body are supposed to interact. Does the mind control the body, or does the brain control the body? Why can't my mind control your body? Can my mind be transferred into a different body? If my mind is not bound by the laws of nature, but controls my body, does that mean that also my body isn't bound by the laws of nature? Dracula certainly seems capable of putting the saying, "Mind over matter," into practice, but do I need vampire powers to do that as well? If the mind controls the body, why can't I think myself into mist? If I can't, does that mean my mind is subject to the laws of physics? It might well be that my mind is a completely useless by-product of my brain with no effect on the physical world whatsoever. But if our imaginings of violating the laws of physics don't have any effect on our outside world, do we have good reason to believe our mind is actually non-physical?

Making Stuff Happen

Many traditional explanations of how the mind and body interact assume some sort of "divine intervention." The idea is that every time Van Helsing thinks about paling a vampire, God moves Van Helsing's arm exactly how Van Helsing thought about doing it. It has also been claimed that God constructed a pre-ordained universe. According to this view, Van Helsing's thoughts of moving his arm to pale a vampire would exactly coincide with the physical operations of the universe leading to his arm moving (Van Helsing's mind and the universe working in parallel, though never interacting). So the world's greatest vampire slayer would be neither Buffy nor Van Helsing, but

God. On the other hand, this idea also implies that it's God who puts Dracula's teeth into Lucy's throat, and it is God that kills Lucy, not the Count. God would also have been responsible for slaughtering the crew of the *Demeter* and for killing the babies we thought Vampire Lucy murdered. Frankly, I think you don't even have to be an atheist to regard this idea a bit far-fetched.

More recent philosophies imagine that mental stuff and minds emerge from physical stuff (generally brains), but can't be reduced back to physical stuff. Still, all explanations for mind-body interaction share the same basic problem that they can't provide any useful information about how the heck they interact. Dracula's mental abilities clear up some problems but leave others. His mind is not restricted to his own body: it travels to Mina's body and the bodies of rats, and possibly even to the body of Renfield. But, when the Count's body is killed, his mental influence also expires. If his mind can move between bodies and shapes, why doesn't it just move into a new body when his own body is killed? If the Count's mind can do all this stuff, why couldn't poor Jonathan Harker send out his own mind to get help when he was held captive by Dracula? Dualistic theories would generally answer this by claiming that "God did it this way" or "It's a mystery we haven't figured out yet," or "Mental stuff has no impact on the actual world." That's a bit unconvincing if you ask me.

The Knowledge of the Brain

From the point of view of our thought experiment, it's a pity that there hadn't been anyone checking on Van Helsing as Dracula did on his vampire brides. Instead of slaughtering Dracula, Van Helsing should have studied him. *That* would have been a valuable enterprise. But thanks to Van Helsing's craze, we've lost a whole century figuring out how the human mind actually works. What's more, the killing of Dracula wasn't even obligatory: Van Helsing knows how to contain vampires, as he demonstrated with Lucy in her crypt. Also Dracula could have been contained, so that we could study him.

From Dracula's mind we could have learned that the mind cannot possibly just be the brain. We would have learned that consciousness can travel between bodies, but dies with them. The mind is like a song, because that's the only way to account for the Count's mind. If scientists and philosophers had this knowledge, then we would know that all kinds of creatures could be just as conscious as we are. Space aliens and robots could have minds too. We might even figure out how to communicate with wolves, rats, and other animals. Our cell phones might be able to send psychic messages as well as text and audio. But sadly, Van Helsing didn't quite live up to his claim to be a student of the brain. Far from it.

But before we're too hard on him, we should remember that, despite our imaginings, Van Helsing isn't real, nor was Dracula. In the real world, our minds don't work without our brains. There's nothing else that's conscious like we are without having brains like ours. Psychic phone calls only exist in late night commercials, and intelligent aliens are just fiction. We don't have to make Van Helsing's mistake. We can read *Dracula* and see just how farfetched the idea of an immaterial mind is. If our minds were non-material it would imply that all the crazy stuff the Count can do, mentally, might be possible, but we have no evidence of any of that in our world; so maybe our minds are not made of the non-material "stuff" we imagine.

Stoker's novel may not tell us exactly how our minds work, but it gives a great picture of what our minds are not.

12

What Manner of Man, Monster, or Person?

Trip McCrossin

A week into his fateful stay at Dracula's Castle, Jonathan Harker is at last properly terrified. "I am in fear—in awful fear—and there is no escape for me," he admits in the final passage of his May 12th journal entry. "I am encompassed about with terrors that I dare not think of . . ." But had he not dared only moments before, in beginning the same passage, having just witnessed the Count descending "just as a lizard moves" the walls of the castle? "What manner of man is this," he'd asked, "or what manner of creature is it in the semblance of man?"

An answer doesn't come for another month and a half, but finally, in his June 29th entry, Harker tells us. The Count is a "monster." For one, there's the "lizard fashion" in which the Count leaves the castle. Then there's also Jonathan's imprisonment and presumed death sentence, at the hands of the "three terrible women," whom the Count commands, as he does the wolves. Finally, there's the nasty business of discovering the Count in the vaults of the castle's decrepit chapel, in a state Jonathan can only describe as *undead!* And so again in his June 30th entry, Dracula is a monster.

That the Count is a monster, "something so unhuman," is beyond doubt for Harker, and probably for most readers as well. Dracula is no human, yes, but is he also not a *person*?

Old Centuries and Their Powers

As Harker records in the last bit of his May 15th journal entry, the first since he dared question Dracula's personhood, he pon-

123

ders his immediate surroundings. He is sitting "at a little oak table," where an occupant "in old times" would have written out an "ill-spelt love-letter," but where he is now writing in shorthand. "It is nineteenth century up-to-date with a vengeance," he concludes, but "unless my senses deceive me, the old centuries had, and have, powers of their own which mere 'modernity' cannot kill."

We can easily imagine that among these is the powerful new theory of personal identity offered by John Locke (1632–1704) in *An Essay Concerning Human Understanding*. In this book, Locke develops a whole new way of looking at and understanding what it means to be a person. Locke was particularly worried about the question, "What makes me the same person over time?" When things change, they often become different things. So how is it that I am still the same person I was when I was a baby? What keeps the infant "me" the same person as the "old man" me?

To get at the problem Locke was worried about, let's first think about Mina's "Traveler's typewriter," a gift from Quincey, which she describes with gratitude in her evening diary entry on October 30th. Suppose in the days she's been using it, on the road from London to Castle Dracula, she finds it in need of repair. At first, it needs a new ribbon, and then several type bars and corresponding keys need to be replaced, and eventually the rest do, and then the carriage as well, and so on.

At some point, while she's typing out a new diary entry, she might come to realize that, one by one, *all* of the parts that made up Quincey's original gift have been replaced. Is *this* typewriter, she might then wonder, in fact *the same* typewriter that Quincey gave her? It has the same design, yes, but that design is the same design used for thousands of other similar typewriters, none of which are considered to be the same typewriter, because they are made of different material. This one, though, that she is now typing on is also made of all new material! So while it may have seemed to her the same all along, is it *really* now the same *identical* typewriter? You might think now that *this* isn't really such a serious worry. But just imagine what this means when applied to *us* instead of typewriters!

Mina might well wonder now, that is, about *herself*. Over a certain period of time, all the cells that make her body in the beginning are eventually replaced with new ones at the end, and, yet, it seems perfectly clear to her, and to others interacting with her, that she's *the same person* she was earlier on— even though her body, taken cell by cell, is in fact different material. Isn't she much like the typewriter, changing out old parts one-by-one for new parts? If her typewriter isn't the same typewriter, can she be said to be the same person?

This question, though, wouldn't bother Locke at all—who Mina *is*, as a *person*, is about more than her body. The crucial point is Mina's *mind*: Personal identity is not about our looks, but about our awareness of ourselves. Mina will remain the same person even after she becomes a white-haired, wrinkled old lady as long as she is conscious of herself.

Locke argued that you know you're the same person today as when you were at high school because of the way you relate to your past self. Our memories and reflections play a crucial role in shaping our personalities—once bitten, twice shy! (or as dead as poor Lucy). That's why Locke underlines that as "a thinking intelligent being, that has reason and reflection," and can consider herself "the same thinking thing in different times and places," personhood is a function of our "consciousness, which is inseparable from thinking," and "can extend to actions past or to come," and can do so, it seems, independently of what becomes of our body. That said, it should be clear why we're anything but typewriters. We can reflect on our past and imagine ourselves in the future!

Naming and Shaming

To get at the point Locke's making here, let's think now about a more fanciful example than Mina's typewriter. What would we say, for instance, if we found that Quincey and Dr. Seward had mysteriously exchanged bodies, each now remembering doing only those acts otherwise associated with what is now the other's body? And what if at least some of these acts were either laudable or blameworthy—acts associated with, in Seward's case, a certain taste for "chloral, the modern Morpheus," and in Quincey's, a certain expertise with a "great bowie knife"? Would we want to direct our praise or blame to the one who remembers committing the act (though with a different body), or would we direct that praise and blame at the one who doesn't remember the act but whose body was there for it? Locke urged us to choose the first of those alternatives: Pick on the guy who actually *remembers* what he's done! Locke thought that this should be done mainly for moral reasons.

In his view, the concept of personal identity is a *tool* we need in addressing the moral dimensions of our daily lives. "In personal identity," he tells us, "is founded all the right and justice of reward and punishment." This means that we judge Quincey and Seward each morally accountable *only* for behavior they can remember and are *conscious of*—regardless of what others may sincerely testify, as to the bodies otherwise associated with the same behavior. That no one may recognize either Quincey in Seward's body or Seward in Quincey's is simply irrelevant. Our job is to uncover the persons *truly* accountable for what we praise and blame.

You might wonder, "What does reward and punishment have to do with personal identity?" Well, Locke's idea is that in order to develop a meaningful sense of ourselves, we need to relate to some sort of jurisdiction which allows and bans certain acts. This helps us to connect each of our actions with a certain emotional state: fear of punishment, anticipation of reward. Such expectation enables us to identify with our actions.

Reflected in the pages of *Dracula* we find not only the problem of personal identity, but also a new and interesting response to it. Locke's perspective helps us to make sense of the idea that Dracula is both a monster *and* a person, while at the same time we see Mina and company disagreeing amongst themselves, at least for some time, and on occasion vehemently.

Who's the Saddest of Them All?

"Seven years ago we all went through the flames," Harker begins his concluding "Note," and "the happiness of some of us since then is, we think, well worth the pain we endured. It is an added joy to Mina and to me that our boy's birthday is the same day as that on which Quincey Morris died." As we read this, though, not as Harker's writing years later, but only moments after experiencing the sad moment in the last bits of Mina's final diary entry, with all that's happened in the preceding month still fresh in our minds, we may find it hard not to feel that something's missing. If this were *Mina* writing, that is, given the way she speaks to Harker and company after dinner on October 3rd, as Seward records in his diary later that night, would we not expect something more? Did someone else not die, and die memorably, on young Quincey's birthday seven years earlier?

As we learn from Seward's entry, Mina and company are discussing the unsuccessful London assault on the Count earlier in the day, and what lies ahead now, preparing for what will eventually be the month-long period leading up to the final confrontation at Dracula's castle. Mina makes a surprising plea, reflecting a dramatic change in her perspective. She had written differently of the Count's culpability, earlier in her September 30th diary entry, after learning of Lucy's death. But this was before she had herself been assaulted by the vampire. "I suppose one ought to pity any thing so hunted as is the Count," she'd said, before all of this, because "this Thing is not human—not even beast." She *supposed* this, but *now* her tone has changed, her point of view strengthened.

"I know that you must fight," she acknowledges to Harker and company, "that you must destroy," both for her sake, and for London's and humanity's more generally. But this should not be "an act of hate," she insists, any more than when they "destroyed the false Lucy so that the true Lucy might live hereafter." Speaking of the Count, she insists "that poor soul who has wrought all this misery is the saddest case of all," and she asks the others to "think what will be his joy when he, too, is destroyed in his worser part that his better part may have spiritual immortality." And so, she urges, "be pitiful to him, too, though it may not hold your hands from his destruction."

Why on earth does she implore Harker and the others like this? Because, as she goes on to say, "perhaps . . . some day . . . I, too, may need such pity." Mina is concerned about herself because she knows she might turn into a vampire in the near future. Her view of herself, of her own person, extends into the future.

If our consciousness were limited to the present, it wouldn't be a consciousness at all. We need a temporal perspective in order to build a meaningful sense of ourselves. It's this viewpoint which makes us save money and take care of our health.

Mina is worried because she knows she's been different, non-vampiric in the past and because she fears of what might become of her person in the future.

At first, Harker resists, insisting that he would not only destroy the Count, but "send his soul for ever and ever to burning hell," but ultimately, all were persuaded. All "wept openly," including Mina, "to see that her sweeter counsels had prevailed." And she is again, a little over a month later, witnessing the Count's final demise. "I shall be glad as long as I live that even in that moment of final dissolution," she says, "there was in the face a look of peace, such as I never could have imagined might have rested there." She is not just glad he is dead, but glad he is at peace.

Mina is relieved because she now knows that Harker and company have indeed been merciful to Dracula. In turn, this also means that they would have treated her—had she turned into a vampire—in the same way. And still more consoling is the fact that death is apparently some sort of redemption for vampires, as the "look of peace" in Dracula's face indicates. For that reason, Mina finds comfort in the thought that no matter what would have happened; the others would have done what's best for her. According to Locke, such sensitivity as displayed by Mina, which is based on genuine concern for our own person, is indispensable for attaining a personal identity. It's what allows us to develop a sense of ourselves which stretches over time.

Mina—the Golden Middle

Mina's in a unique position to pity the Count, and also to convince others to feel likewise. She's not yet vampire, but she's turning, and so must sense what it's like to be him. But she *hasn't* turned yet, and is actively resisting. As a result, she's self-consciously midway between vampire and human, and a person in both respects. She's thus a ready vehicle to generate pity—not only for herself, but for the Count—in those with much less in common with him, that is Harker and company.

Stoker roots Mina's pity, in its later expression, in a sort of inter-personal relation new to the lexicon in Stoker's time—that of *empathy*. He reflects this in her unique ability, under hypnosis, to experience at least in part what the Count experiences, as Harker describes initially in his October 4th diary entries. Because of her newfound status, that is, midway between vampire and human, she's able to empathize with the Count, in much the same way as she continues to be able to empathize with her endangered companions. They are able to pity him in turn, as a result of their empathy for her.

The "campaign against the Count" is not properly sanctioned, Mina insists, as a *morally righteous* campaign, unless in terms *not only* of "all the right and justice of reward and punishment," *but also* in terms of moral sentiments such as empathy and pity, which she insists on as well. "I am bold to think," Locke boasts in his *Essay*, "that *morality is capable of demonstration*, as well as mathematics," and so is mostly, if not entirely, the business of moral reasoning, not of sentiment. No surprise, then, that in searching its pages for the likes of Mina's empathy and pity, or similarly for sympathy, compassion, or most anything of the sort, we find them almost entirely absent. Like his views about personal identity, controversy also came up in response to Locke's views about morality, as to whether it derives altogether from reason or from sentiment. Mina's perspective seems to reflect helpfully a *middle ground*.

And this is not just middle ground regarding morality, but regarding personhood as well. The sentimental perspective that Mina brings to the morality of the campaign *is* what allows her to relate to the Count more *personally* than Harker and company seem to be able to, even while she's leagued with them against him. "You must destroy," we remember her saying to Harker and company, "even as you destroyed the false Lucy so that the true Lucy might live hereafter"—*even as*, she says, explicitly comparing Lucy and the Count. What's more, she continues to refer to him as "the poor soul," with a "better part" still, which, however obscured by his worse part one, makes him worthy to be both murdered *and* saved.

Harker responds badly to this with white-knuckled rejection of her point of view and also with confusion. Sharing Mina's reference to the Count's "soul," he is eager to commit it "for ever and ever to burning hell." But he'll settle for less. "May God give him into my hand just for long enough to destroy that earthly life of him which we are aiming at," he says—not "him *who*," but "him *which*," suggesting, grammatically at least, that he clings to the idea of the Count as something other than a person.

He does come around finally to Mina's more personal way of thinking of the Count, though, in light of the empathy she brings forth in him and the others, which leads to all the weeping. And there's definitely a cause for tears, as it "may be that God will let them fall in gladness," gladness for the opportunity to struggle to the death with a *person*, and not merely an animal—one *who*, however monstrous, is worthy of the unique respect we're able *as persons* to show one another.[1]

---

[1] I'm grateful to Sue Zemka for her help and support in the process of writing this essay. It's part of a broader effort to understand Gothic literature as reflecting new and interesting perspectives on personal identity, among other issues.

13
Who's the Ideal Dracula?

IVAN WOLFE

There are so many different versions of Dracula—and I don't mean different vampires, I'm talking about different *Draculas*. When I began writing this chapter, I mentioned it to my mother, and she started talking about *Twilight*. I had to clarify I was writing about Dracula and not vampires in general; she didn't seem to get the difference at first. I don't mean vampires are different from each other (which is much easier to see)—I mean one Dracula can be wildly different from another Dracula, yet we still call them all "Dracula" (except when we call them "Drake" or "Dracul" or even "Alucard"—but everyone knows those are just cover names). We may think "Oh, well, they all have enough in common that they can all be seen as basically the same"—but that's not true. But before we go into that, we first need to consider whether Dracula has a mustache.

I Mustache You a Question

Originally, Dracula had a mustache. In Bram Stoker's original novel, the first time we see Dracula, the book states the Count appeared "clean shaven save for a long white mustache," which is later described as "heavy." The novel also states that Dracula had "massive" eyebrows and "sharp white teeth" that "protruded over the lips" (fangs, basically). Very few movie adaptations of Dracula show Dracula like that, though. Bela Lugosi's Dracula has no mustache and somewhat thin eyebrows. Christopher Lee's Dracula also has no mustache, thin eyebrows

—but does have fangs, which Lugosi's Dracula lacked. Stoker's Dracula could walk around in sunlight and was killed by a bowie knife to the heart rather than a wooden stake. Lugosi's and Lee's Draculas could be killed by sunlight and would likely laugh at a bowie knife.

So, how can we call these various versions of Dracula "Dracula"? Is there something like an "essence" of Dracula? Well, each version we've mentioned so far are vampires, drink the blood of the living, have castles in Transylvania, and have some sort of connection to the historical Vlad Tepes (a.k.a. Vlad Dracula—Dracula means "son of Dracul" and his father was "Vlad Dracul"). Perhaps that's all we need to make something or someone "Dracula" (hint: it's not). Dracula seems a flexible enough character that we could strip away the window dressing of facial hair, styles of clothing, and other aspects like a "foreign" accent and still have Dracula. What would that essential, ideal Dracula look like? Plato had a few thoughts on Dracula . . . well, not Dracula specifically, but the idea of true, perfect ideal shared by all things that have the same label.

Plato's Thoughts on Dracula

For one possible way to reconcile various versions of Dracula, we can look to Plato and his theory of ideal (or perfect) Forms. The problem is that one term can refer to many things, such as "love" or "green" or "bed" (or "Dracula"). Imagine a chair in Castle Dracula. It's pretty easy to imagine that it would be ornate and large, likely made from some kind of ancient wood. There are many other things though, that can be called chair. Not all of them have four legs, some don't have a back, some have arms, but no back, what about beanbag chairs? What makes them all chairs like Dracula's chair? Maybe because they can be sat upon? But all things we can sit on aren't chairs. And there are chairs (like chair in museums or art chairs) that we aren't supposed to sit in! So what makes them all chairs?

Like with Dracula, individual instances of a word like "chair" sometimes bear little resemblance to each other, Plato argued that there had to be some eternal, perfect essence that all versions of a particular thing or idea shared, even if we can't perceive what that Form (the perfect, ideal essence) is. As we create versions of Dracula, or chairs, whether they are any good or not, we somehow participate in and draw inspiration from these ideal, perfect essences—the "Forms"—that exist outside our perception (and perhaps outside our reality—Plato was never consistent on exactly where these Forms were).

Look at a few examples: An "I love Dracula" T-shirt has a different "love" than someone saying "I love my spouse of seventy-five years" or "I love my dog" or "I love to vote"—yet, to Plato, they would all share in some eternal, ideal "love" that exists outside our perception. Someone could refer to Dracula's green skin (which he has in some adaptations), green energy policies, green slime, and green envy, yet it's clear that none of these are really the same type of "green. " Or, we could mention the guest bed in Dracula's castle, call a hammock in the trees a "bed" (because they slept in it), and refer to a blanket on the ground as a "bed" (because they used it to have some intimate time with the spouse)—but it's hard to claim Dracula's guest bed, a hammock in a tree, and a blanket on the ground really have much in common, yet all can be called a bed (though only one gets you attacked by vampire brides).

As for our beloved count, we have multiple versions of Dracula, all of which seem to have some features in common at first glance, yet when we compare two versions together, we sometimes find very little (if anything) in common, and even the traits shared by those two can seem hard to find in other versions. Yet Plato would insist that in each case, there is some perfect Form that all of these seemingly different and disparate examples share.

Can You See the Reflection?

Take a look at the superhero Dracula from Dell Comics, the one that lasted three issues in 1966 and 1967. While deservedly obscure, this Dracula does not get his powers from vampirism (though he claims to be a descendant of the vampire lord), but from science gone wrong. He tries to cure brain damage with bat blood and instead gains the power to change into a bat. He decides to, Batman-like, train his body to peak physical perfection and fight crime.

Now, compare that "Dracula" with the one played by Morgan Freeman on the old PBS children's show *The Electric Company*. That Count Dracula drank vanilla malts instead of blood and even offered to split a malt with a reporter. When asked if there were some other Count Dracula, he admitted there were six of them in the phone book. At this point, we're leaving behind the idea of evil, undead bloodsucker, and seeing characters labeled Dracula that have little resemblance to the Stoker original, if any at all. If we compare just these two Draculas to each other, we find almost nothing in common, except that they don't drink blood. However, most other versions of Dracula do drink blood.

For Plato, each particular thing was a reflection of a universal Form that existed outside the world of sense perception (the five senses of sight, touch, taste, hearing, and smell), in a reality truer than the one we think of as real. These Forms are self-existent, do not change, and can only truly be perceived by the mind (perhaps just intuited by or briefly glimpsed in the mind). They do not require our world to exist—our world, the world of physical senses, merely reflects them. However, whatever ideal Form exists in that ideal realm will be mirrored in particular things or concepts in our realm. Instances of love, green, and chairs all reflect the eternal, unchanging Form behind them.

But these particular instances don't share just all (or only) the elements of the ideal Form. They also have characteristics of their own, which sets them apart from Plato's ideal. A particular instance of Dracula may claim to be immortal and eternal, but all versions of Dracula we can perceive exist in our world and so they only reflect the ideal Form. They aren't the form, they are a reflection of that perfect idea.

How Do We Find 'Dracula'?

So, since we can't directly perceive (see, touch, or smell) the Forms, except possibly in the mind, how do we even figure out what they look like? The most obvious idea is to compare all the individual particulars you can, and then see what they all have in common. This can be quite troublesome. Still, let's give it a try and look at a few different aspects of Dracula, and see if we can gleam any universal qualities they all share.

First, look at Dracula's origins. Where does he come from? Stoker based him on Vlad III, a.k.a. Vlad Dracula, aka Vlad

Tepes (the "Impaler"), though no ancient vampire legends exist around Vlad's personal history. As mentioned above, "Dracula" means "Son of Dracul"—his father was called "Dracul" either because he was considered a Devil or because of his membership in the order of the Dragon (a religious order of Christian nobility who were noted for their defense of the faith); scholars disagree on the meaning of "Dracul." Many versions of the Count claim he really was Vlad III, either cursed by God or turned by another vampire. In the *Dracula: Origins* videogame, Dracula sought out his existence through research. However, in *Wes Craven Presents: Dracula 2000*, Dracula is Judas Iscariot, cursed to live for two thousand years for his betrayal. In *Blade: Trinity*, Dracula is called Drake, dates back to at least ancient Babylon and was born as the first vampire.

None of these origins are compatible. What seems like the only possible common thread "human becomes vampire through supernatural means" doesn't work with the more naturalistic and pseudo-scientific vampires of the Blade movies. We could say that, well, in all of these cases, he wound up sucking blood. However, that runs into the problem of the Dell comics or *The Electric Company* Draculas discussed above, who don't drink blood.

Even looking at Dracula's blood sucking causes some issues, especially his attitude toward it. In most instances, of course, Dracula drinks blood and loves it. Even setting aside the Dell comics superhero (who doesn't drink blood), we have Fred Saberhagen's *The Dracula Tape* (and its sequels), where Dracula tends to feed off animals (mostly rats) and only engages in consensual biting with humans. In *Hotel Transylvania*, Dracula prefers "near-blood" since human blood is gross.

Hotel Transylvania also provides a good contrast with another aspect of Dracula: his motivations. In *Hotel Transylvania*, Dracula's motivation for all he does is protecting his little girl. Conflicts with humans are caused by our prejudice and ignorance; a similar problem occurs in Saberhagen's works, where Dracula has extraordinarily bad luck in dealing with humans, and they tend to react with horror rather than attempt to understand those who seem different. In *Bram Stoker's Dracula* (a movie that needed its own novelization, despite the title), Dracula is partially motivated by his dead wife's reincarnation, a theme carried over in the recent NBC television series.

In all these aspects, it's easy to spot some characteristics carried over into several incarnations, but nothing that can be found in all incarnations. Plato would likely say we're going about this all wrong, though. He pointed out that there's no perfect way to figure out the Forms. So my first hunch was correct: Comparing all instances causes more problems than it solves.

Blade: Trinity Explains It All

For Plato, Forms are perfect. All particular instances in our reality are just distortions, and some instances will have more distortion than others. Dracula (Drake) in *Blade: Trinity* can illustrate this point fairly well: In one scene, Drake enters a vampire shop and is disgusted by the kitschy merchandise in the store—one of the employees even acknowledges how lame it is, by stating: "It makes you want to cry, doesn't it?" when showing him a bottle of "Drac-cola." Drake is the original vampire, the true Dracula, yet all of this kitschy junk is somehow ultimately derived from him. At best, they are pale reflections, at worst outright distortions with only the barest possible connection to the original. Such is the case with all versions of Dracula that exist in our world, when compared with whatever ideal Form exists outside and originally.

So the question isn't so much, What do all versions of Dracula have in common? Instead, we should ask ourselves: "What initial Form could have inspired them all?" In this case, it becomes easy to state that perhaps the Dell comics superhero contains too much imperfection, and that perhaps the Dell comics superhero, the outlier that seems to invalidate most attempts at comparison, is too distorted and too far removed from the ideal Form.

The danger with this approach, however, means we might too easily toss out a particular instance of Dracula, just because it doesn't fit with our notion of what Dracula is or should be. Forms exist independent of us and our imperfect reasoning, so if we declare any particular form too distorted or too far removed from the original, that idea might just come from our own distorted, imperfect reasoning.

And Now for Something Completely Different

Another possibility is that Dracula doesn't have an ideal Form. He might just be the reflection, or the particular instance, of some other Form, such as vampires or the undead or even "strange foreigners." To explore this idea further, let me modify one of Plato's allegories somewhat. Let me tell you the "Allegory of Dracula's Dungeon."

Dracula has several human cattle in his dungeon; he uses them for food. In fact, they've been there so long they've formed families and had kids for several generations, and the current occupants have never seen the outside world (let's say Van Helsing managed to kill Dracula, but never checked the dungeons for occupants, but somehow there's plenty of food). In fact, it's pretty dark down there, all they have is torchlight and not much of that. So, all they can see are the shadows on the wall, and all of them have become convinced that the shadows are reality. One of the prisoners accidentally manages to escape and sees the outside world (with Dracula's death, all the other vampires have left). Returning, she tries to describe the outside world, but no one believes her. They have no frame of reference to even comprehend her words, since all they can refer to are the shadows on the wall and she's talking about trees, wolves, and angry villagers with pitchforks.

For Plato, the world we see are like the shadows on the wall, and the ideal world of Forms is like the outside world in this allegory. We see the shadow of a vampire on the wall, but we have no comprehension that there is a real vampire behind us, ready to suck out all our precious blood. So, it's possible that Dracula is just one of the shadows on the wall, but he's being cast by some other ideal Form we can't comprehend and won't have the frame of reference to truly see.

Never Mind, This Is All Crazy! Dracula Can't Have a Form at All (Or Can He?)

Assuming Plato (or Socrates) wasn't Dracula (it's plausible that either of them might have been, I guess, if we believe Dracula started in ancient Babylon, as the Blade movies claim—fanfiction writers, get on that!), then Plato might decide that our entire effort is futile, because it's impossible for some-one or some-thing to have a Form. In Plato's *Republic*, Socrates expressed two principles that undermine the idea that Dracula might have a Form of his own.

First is the idea that the Forms only represent "The Good." "The Good" (which is another philosophical concept that would take another chapter to explain) created this world based on the Forms. In this world, we need to strive to understand and align ourselves with the Forms to achieve true goodness. So, the idea that there would be an ideal Dracula that "the Good" would create and that we must learn to align ourselves would seem, on the face of it, utterly absurd.

Second, Dracula is a fictional creation. Even with the histor-ical Vlad Dracula, the Draculas we're most concerned with are fictional creations. Socrates condemned all art, especially fic-tion, because it cannot lead us to truth. Art is an imitation of an imitation: a painting of a coffin is an imitation of a coffin, which itself is an imitation of the ideal coffin. So, looking at art or reading fiction (which would include viewing Dracula movies or TV shows, or reading this book) moves us further away from the ideal Forms, not closer. Since Dracula really only exists in the fictional realm, it's unlikely he has an ideal Form at all.

It's All in Good, Blood-Sucking Fun, Though

If I had a vampire at my neck, threatening to suck out all my blood unless I came up with my own views on what the ideal Form of Dracula might look like—well, I'd likely rise in a few days and start terrorizing a small rural town until Buffy or Van Helsing came and staked me. However, I guess I could give it a stab (in the heart with a wooden stake or bowie knife) anyway:

To me, the essence of Dracula boils down to three aspects that could have infinite expression: First, he's an outsider. Wherever Dracula comes from, whatever his motivations, ori-gins, or powers, he comes from outside the society. Sometimes he invades society (as in the original novel) and sometimes he sits himself outside (as in *Hotel Transylvania* or the backstory to Saberhagen's Dracula series). He may set up residence in society and behave himself, but whatever the case, he does not belong and either he must go or society must change to accommodate him. This works whether he's a space alien, a Romanian count, or an ancient Babylonian.

The second crucial aspect is that Dracula is an aristocrat. He's not just outside, but above. He's rich, or sees himself as above the common lot of humanity (or even all of humanity). Even in positive portrayals, such as Saberhagen's books (did I mention I really like that series?), Dracula tends to lapse into a snobbish attitude that indicates he sees himself as one of the "betters" of humanity (as in, "respect your betters" or "don't talk back to your betters").

The third aspect could be seen as related to the second: Dracula feeds off of others in some way. It doesn't have to be blood, though it usually is. However, versions where he feeds off spiritual energy, sex, or even spinal fluid could be fine. Even a metaphorical "feeding" off others (as aristocrats historically have done) could work.

Outside of those three aspects, almost anything is fair game. These criteria exclude the Dell comics Dracula and cause some problems with Wes Craven's *Dracula 2000* (and several other adaptations I could mention), but those three aspects could have almost infinite kinds of variety. I could see a time-traveling alien from an advanced species that must drain time energy from people in the past being a Dracula.

And if you don't agree with me, and think something else defines the true ideal of Dracula? That's fine with me. Dracula has proven a versatile enough character that he can take whatever modifications, debates, or crazy ideas we might have. You might even find yourself closer to his ideal Form than I could conceive—just keep him away from your ideal neck.

14
There and Bat Again

RICHARD GREENE

Count Dracula comes in many forms. There is the historical figure, Vlad the Impaler, who was a Romanian nobleman of the fifteenth century (VtI, as the kids call him, was also called "Dracula"). There is, of course the title character of Bram Stoker's masterpiece, and the numerous movie and television Draculas based closely on Bram Stoker's novel. And there are numerous film and television Draculas, based not so closely on Stoker's work, but more on a popular characterization of The Count. Dracula's identity is pretty flexible, to say the least.

These latter versions of Dracula are a kind of "meme"—kind of like a gene, but instead of a biological trait, a cultural one passed on through society. These Dracula memes mostly owe their existence to parodies of Bela Lugosi's version of The Count and then to subsequent parodies of those parodies. Versions of this Dracula are virtually everywhere, although they go by a variety of names. We have, for example, The Count from Sesame Street, Count Blah, from Greg the Bunny (Blah was a brilliant parody of a parody of the parody of the meme described above!—he looks like Dracula, is a puppet, and ends every sentence with the word "blah"), the breakfast cereal spokesperson, Count Chocula, the hilariously suave, over-the-top Dracula who appeared in an episode of *Buffy the Vampire Slayer*, not to mention tens of thousands of children and adults dressed up as Dracula each Halloween.

There's a different sense in which Count Dracula comes in many forms. According to the various books, plays, movies, television programs, and legends, Dracula could take the form of a young man, an old man, a gruesome looking man with sharp teeth and pointy ears (think of a man with certain bat-like facial features), a bat, a wolf, and mist (to name a few). Dracula is a shapeshifter extraordinaire!

But how is it possible that something that is a wolf, a bat, a scary-looking dude with pointy ears and really sharp teeth, etc. can all be the same thing? In what sense is Dracula the same person when he's a wolf as he is when he's a bat or when he's mist? How does he continue to be the same person when he changes from a man into a bat? Dracula's problem of identity will reflect deeply on our own!

What's at Stake?

To persist (that is, to continue to exist) through change is to be the same thing even though you have changed. To see what this means, let's consider an ordinary human being like Vlad the Impaler (well . . . as "ordinary" as a man who sits people on spikes can get). Vlad the Impaler was born Vlad III, Prince of Wallachia. He died some forty-five years later. Like everyone, he started off in life quite small. At the time of his death, he was a full-grown man. So, at minimum, throughout his life he changed in at least one respect: he grew. Presumably, he underwent a great number of other changes as well: he lost his baby teeth and had his permanent teeth come in, his voice likely got deeper as he aged, at some point his hair line may have receded, and his vision likely worsened as he aged. Throughout his life he certainly also underwent a number of less permanent changes: he sometimes had a cold and at other times didn't, he occasionally suffered minor injuries, like cuts or scratches, he likely occasionally experienced a sunburn or a rash, and sometimes his hair was longer and sometimes it was shorter.

If the right thing to say about Vlad is that he was always Vlad, then it must be the case that despite undergoing all these changes (and many more!) he was always the same thing—he was always the same person. This is what we mean when we say that he persisted through change.

Not all philosophers agree that Vlad the Impaler persisted through change. A number of philosophers embrace a view called "mereological essentialism," which holds that things are just whatever properties or parts they are composed of. So according to this view, the first time Vlad the Impaler changed even a little bit, he became a different person. Imagine that baby Vlad the Impaler (at age three months) gets his fingernails clipped. He's now someone else entirely. Not all philosophers find this view satisfying. For one thing it just doesn't sound right. This, of course, is not a good reason for rejecting a view (if it were, we'd have to get rid of many of our best scientific theories, like relativity).

So instead of just tossing out mereological essentialism because it doesn't sound satisfying, let's consider issues relating to justice. Vlad the Impaler didn't get his nickname by helping elderly people cross streets or by volunteering at the soup kitchen. He was a really bad guy! He was so called because, as a warrior, he impaled his enemies on stakes, and then left them hoisted pointy end up for all to see. He also tortured people and forced his enemies to eat the body parts of their deceased loved ones. For his acts of cruelty, Vlad was imprisoned.

It's not hard to believe that justice was served by imprisoning him (or at least partially served—the eye for an eye crowd will certainly want more). If the mereological essentialist is correct, then the person imprisoned was not same person as the one who committed the atrocious acts. That person underwent numerous changes prior to being imprisoned (for example, many of his body cells died and were replaced, his hair grew, perhaps he cut himself shaving, the pigment in his skin faded slightly while he was in a dungeon awaiting sentencing, and so on). While this is not a knock down argument against the mereological essentialist, it certainly provides us a reason to go on as if mereological essentialism is an incorrect view, if we want to be able to lock up people who do bad things in the hopes of preventing them from doing it again and serving justice. So what we need then is a theory that accounts for the fact that persons, like Vlad, and other things (such as non-person animals, plants, and rocks) undergo change and are still the same thing after the change.

A Puzzle that Drives Metaphysicians Batty

Well, why not just say that things that undergo change are still the same things after they change, and then give that theory a fancy philosophical sounding name so that folks will take it seriously? The problem is that philosophers tend to want to say more about objects and change than that, and not all of the things they want to say are compatible (or at least without some clever tweaking and reinterpretation).

As Roxanne Marie Kurtz points out in her introduction to the book *Persistence: Contemporary Readings*, philosophers who think about these things usually accept the following three claims:

1. *Consistency*—objects can't have incompatible features;

2. *Change*—Change involves incompatible features, and

3. *Persistence*—Objects persist, even when they change.

Each one of these three claims looks good at first. Each of them seems like common sense. Yet it turns out that any two of the above claims strictly logically require that the third must be false. If Dracula cannot have incompatible features (for example, cannot be both in Transylvania and not in Transylvania, or cannot be in human form and in bat form), and change involves having incompatible features (for example, when Dracula changed location) that would appear to mean that Dracula did not persist. It must not have been the same Dracula that was both in Transylvania, and was not in Transylvania. If the consistency and change claims are correct, then the thesis that objects persist when they change must be false.

Similarly, if Dracula did change, and persisted when he changed, then the claim that nothing can have incompatible features must be wrong. Finally, if nothing can have incompatible properties, and objects persist through change, then it must be false that change involves incompatible features.

These three claims generate a puzzle for anyone who wants to hold that objects undergo change and are still the same thing after they change. Some highly intuitive, long-held philosophical belief has got to go. To assert something as simple, and seemingly non-controversial, as that Vlad the Impaler was the same person when he was born as he was the day before he died, will involve letting go of something that makes sense to us.

Why Dracula?

We might wonder how Dracula could possibly be relevant here; vampires don't really exist. A couple of things are worth keeping in mind. First, we want explanations of persistence and change that apply universally. This means that we don't just want an account that applies to things that currently exist or have existed; we want an explanation that would apply to all possible objects. If we worked out an explanation of persistence that applied to everything but unicorns, and then unicorns came into existence, we'd be screwed. It would be straight back to the drawing board!

Second, Dracula provides an ideal test case because he gives lots of different kinds of change to take into consideration. In addition to all the changes to Dracula described above—the changes from man to bat to wolf to dog to mist, and so forth—we also get the kinds of changes attributed to Vlad the Impaler—the changes in size, appearance, location. In addition to these two types of change we get a third type. When Dracula becomes a vampire he changes in a very fundamental way from being a human. Vampires are different kinds of creatures from humans. So any successful theory of persistence will have to account for each of these types of change.

A final reason for testing theories of persistence by seeing how well they account for the kinds of changes Dracula undergoes is that it's just a lot more fun to do it that way. It beats considering the example of what happens when the philosopher David Lewis bends over as opposed to the situation in which he doesn't—an example that is everywhere in the philosophical discussions of this issue!

Getting on with Your Bat Self

The traditional response to the puzzle about persistence is to embrace something called endurantism. Endurantism is roughly the view that objects persist through changes and over time by being completely present at any point in which they exist. So Dracula is Dracula at birth, on his sixteenth birthday, when turned into a vampire, when he changes into a bat or the mist, and at every point in his existence. So which of our three claims does the endurantist give up? She has to give up consistency. The endurantist must find a way to hold that Dracula is both a wolf and a bat, and these are incompatible features (for example, things that are wolf-shaped are not bat-shaped, and vice versa).

The endurantist doesn't want to embrace contradictions by holding that Dracula can be both a bat and a non-bat, or can be in Transylvania and not in Transylvania, so they say that having features (such as being a bat) is always a matter of having features at a certain time. Dracula is not just in Transylvania; rather, he is in Transylvania on Tuesday at 4:30 pm. Dracula is not a just a bat; rather, he is a bat all-day on March 23, 1874, and so forth. Notice how this avoids the contradiction. Being a bat and not being a bat directly contradict one another. Being a bat on Thursday and not being a bat on Saturday do not contradict one another.

By abandoning consistency (in the strict sense defined above), the endurantist can say each of the following: Dracula persists over time, while changing, and change involves incompatible properties. So far endurantism looks pretty good.

Critics of endurantism point out that the endurantist has redefined, in an unfortunate way, what it is to have a feature or a property. Typically when we think of what it means to have a property, for example the property of having really pointy fangs, this has nothing to do with what time it is. We say that Dracula has pale skin. Even though Dracula also has black hair, we don't define what it means to have pale skin in terms of having black hair. The two things don't have anything to do with one another. Similarly, says the critic of endurantism, why would we want to say that having really pointy fangs has something to do with what time it is. But to avoid the charge of inconsistency, this is precisely what the endurantist must do— since the endurantist doesn't just talk about properties, she talks about properties at certain times (the time becomes part of the property!). So, while endurantism, initially looks good, it has its problems.

What Part of the Bug Does Renfield Like Best?

Given our worry about endurantism (along with some other criticisms), some philosophers have embraced perdurantism.

Perdurantism is the view that objects persist through changes and over time by having temporal parts that exist at every instance in which the object exists. This may seem a bit tricky at first, but let's see what it means . . .

Things have parts. Dracula has arms, legs, fangs, a widow's peak, really long fingernails, and so on. These parts are spatial parts (Dracula's hair is in one place, his fangs are in another . . .). According to the perdurantist, change over time is like change over space. So just as space has parts (again, think of Dracula's different parts), time also has parts. So Dracula would have both temporal parts and spatial parts. Only one temporal part exists at a time. A moment later a different temporal part exists, and then a moment later another temporal part exists. So Dracula has the temporal part that exists at 3:00 P.M. on March 7th, 1893 and the temporal part that exists at 3:01 P.M. on March 7th, 1893, and the temporal part that exists at 3:02 . . ., and so on.

The perdurantist is able to solve our puzzle by holding that Dracula changes over time (different temporal parts have different and incompatible spatial features), and persists, because he survives changes. For example, at one time Dracula is in bat form, and at a later time Dracula is in wolf form. There is no contradiction, because it is the different temporal parts that have the different properties. Also, properties are not defined in terms of time, so the perdurantist avoids the main criticism of endurantism.

Critics of perdurantism raise the worry that according to perdurantism, no whole object ever exists at any single time. If only temporal parts of Dracula exist at any one time, then Dracula never fully exists. This is analogous to holding that only the left side of Dracula exists, or only Dracula's insides exist. For any object that hasn't had part of it destroyed—say, Dracula's coffin—we feel that we want to say that the whole thing is there. But according to perdurantism, we can never say that. The whole of Dracula's coffin is the sum of all its physical parts *and* all its temporal parts.

A second worry about perdurantism is that it doesn't really allow for change as we normally understand it. Suppose that Dracula gets staked (heaven forbid!). Our ordinary take is that Dracula has changed because he was altered in some way—he went from not having a hole in his chest to having one. On the perdurantist view nothing has actually changed. One temporal part lacks a hole in its chest, a completely different part has one. Many take these consequences to be a deal-breaker for perdurantism.

Crap! There's a Whole Lot of Vampires All of a Sudden

So with endurantism, objects always exist in full, but we get the odd result that things don't just have properties; instead, they have time-referenced properties (again, these are properties that make reference to a time, such as the property of being bat-shaped at 4:30). With perdurantism objects have normal properties (as opposed to time-referenced properties), but they don't exist in their entirety, at any one time. So it would be great if there were a theory of persistence that gave us both regular properties, and held that objects fully exist at particular times. Exdurantism is just such a theory.

Exdurantism is roughly the view that objects persist through changes and over time by having temporal counterparts that exist at different times. This view is similar to perdurantism in that objects are made of temporal parts, but is different in that the temporal parts wholly exist. It is similar to endurantism in that the parts wholly exist, but does not define the parts in relation to times. So, according to exdurantism, Dracula has temporal parts, which have different properties or features, such as having black hair, long fingernails, and fangs, and these parts (both spatially and temporally) fully exist at various points in time.

So what's the problem with this view? Well, if the temporal parts wholly exist, and are distinct from one another, then the different temporal parts must be different things altogether. This yields the odd consequence that Dracula is made up of a bunch of different things—not a bunch of different properties, but a bunch of whole things! He's the thing that is the temporal parts plus spatial parts that exist at the moment he is born, plus the thing that is the different temporal parts plus the spatial parts that exist a moment later, plus the . . . well, you get the idea.

This idea that Dracula's made up of a bunch of different things is a pretty counterintuitive consequence, especially if what one is trying to show is how Dracula can be the same thing over time. It has us saying that Dracula is the same thing over time, but at the same time being a bunch of different things, none of which exist at other times. A second worry is that just like perdurantism, because exdurantism embraces a metaphysics of temporal parts, it doesn't allow for change as we typically think of it. There is nothing that actually changes. Change is just different counterparts having different properties.

Putting Too Fine a Point on It

So none of our three theories comes out unscathed. Is there any reason to favor one over the others? Like I said earlier, Dracula provides a good test case because he undergoes different kinds of changes from humans, animals, and inanimate objects. Dracula, upon being turned into a vampire, undergoes a change in kind. He goes from being a human to something that is decidedly non-human, but doesn't cease to be the thing that he is—he is still Dracula. He's the same thing (even though he's a different kind of thing) when he's a human and when he's a vampire.

Endurantism can account for this fact. Since endurantism holds that objects exist in full at any point in their existence, and rejects a metaphysics of temporal parts, it can embrace the notion of an object that has undergone a change in kind. Dracula, on this view, is the guy who was born human and became a vampire later, in the same way we might be inclined to say that he's the same guy who was born short and grew to be tall.

Neither the perdurantist nor the exdurantist can embrace that belief, as each is limited to discussion of the features of temporal parts. They can assert that some temporal parts are human parts, and others are vampire parts, but they can't assert that Dracula, in full, was both a human and a vampire. There's no thing (or guy) on these views who was fully at one time a person and at another time a vampire.

Perdurantism fares a little better here, as it holds that Dracula was both a human and a vampire, but never fully one or the other. While this is not a knock down argument for endurantism, nor does it create a decisive refutation of perdurantism or exduantism, it does give us a strong reason to favor endurantism over its competitors. Endurantism is easier to swallow—like a nice glass of warm blood! Blah!

15

More Things in Heaven and Earth

MICHAEL VERSTEEG AND ADAM BARKMAN

Many of us well remember the times when as children we tried, in some way, shape, or form, to fly: pieces of cardboard duct-taped to our arms; home-made wings slapped together from feathers and glue; or just the good ol' fashioned superman jump off of our parents' roof and into the pool!

Through our limitless creativity we tried to imagine ourselves as having the capability to fly—a capability which, in the end, gravity seemed to conclusively disprove. But despite gravity's cruel reminder, as kids we simply wanted to know what it was like to experience something foreign to our own experience of the world. Now this curiosity we had as children raises an interesting question: can we as humans know what it's like to be something *other* than human? Can we know, for instance, what it's like to be a bat?

This question may not be too hard for Count Dracula to answer since he himself can transform into a bat and merely experience what it feels like for himself. But what about those of us who still aren't vampires? Can we know what it's like to be a bat on our own? This rather odd and unique question was asked by contemporary philosopher Thomas Nagel. But this is a much more difficult question for Nagel since he not only lacks Dracula's affinity for fresh blood but also the ability to change into a bat.

Now, this question of what's it like to be a bat may make you sneer at first—probably in the same way our parents did when they witnessed our futile attempts to fly. Why ponder such a petty question? Have philosophers nothing better to do? But what if we told you that this very question is one of the most important ones you could possibly ask yourself? Shocked? Surprised? Maybe even a little skeptical?

Here's what it comes down to. From that simple question we realize that although, perhaps, Van Helsing's tendency toward the religious seems a bit extreme, he may not be entirely batty. What if there's more to the world than just what we can experience physically?

What's It Like?

In his famous essay "What Is It Like to Be a Bat?" Nagel raises the deceptively simple and perhaps peculiar question of what it might be like to experience the world from the perspective of a bat—How does a bat perceive the world? Now, what's most important for Nagel here has really nothing to do with figuring out what a bat's experience or perspective of the world is like. In fact, his essay's title can be somewhat misleading since Nagel spends little time actually discussing what a bat's experience of the world is like! (Sorry, Dracula.) Instead, the real consideration for Nagel is *whether or not human beings themselves, from their own perspective, can know or observe what a bat's conscious experience of the surrounding world is like.*

An odd question, perhaps, but do you see the difference? It's not about demonstrating what it might actually be like to experience the world from a bat's perspective. Nagel wants to find out whether or not human beings can know *for themselves* that perspective. He focuses on our human ability to figure out the conscious experience of a bat rather than demonstrating what such experience might be. So, then, Nagel's question of what it's like to be a bat focuses on our ability to provide that answer, not on the answer itself.

So, if you were hoping to learn how a bat perceives and experiences the world, a chiroptologist (someone who studies bats) rather than a philosopher (someone who studies . . . well, something of everything) might be of more use in this case. But don't worry! The question of whether or not humans can know what it's like to be a bat may not be too difficult for one endowed with Dracula's powers to answer. After all, they could simply transform into a bat and experience for themselves what it's like! Surely this would solve Nagel's question, right?

Well, first things first: we doubt anyone other than Dracula has the ability to change into a bat. So we must then consider whether or not those of us (presumably humans) without Dracula's powers are able to come to know just what it's like to be a bat. Is it really that difficult? After all, just look at all of the advances within our knowledge of neurology and the brain! Surely science would be able answer Nagel's simple little question, right?

A Bat's-Eye View

Nagel begins his essay by pointing out that every living organism perceives the world according to its own unique and particular conscious experience. This includes humans, bats, yourself, and even Dracula. Now this seems rather clear since, in the case of humans, we have a particular experience of the world, which differs from that of bats and from any other animal for that matter, which non-human organisms do not experience for themselves. Humans have a particular mish-mash of sensory perceptions and qualities of conscious experience which, although not exclusive to humans, form our own particular "human" experience of the world. That's because we experience the world through our five senses: taste, touch, smell, sight and hearing. Drinking coffee, holding someone's hand, smelling a barbecued steak, reading Bram Stoker's *Dracula*, or listening to an orchestra—all of these senses come together to form our own unique human experience of the world.

But Nagel goes even further. He adds that, along with our unified and particular mish-mash of sensory perceptions, there is what we might call the quality of "human-ness," or the conscious quality of what it's like to actually *be* a human being. But if this is true in the case of humans, then it seems clear that bats (along with every other conscious organism) must have this unique quality as well. In the case of bats, we again might call this the quality of "bat-ness," or what it's like to be a bat. After all, bats see the world through echolocation rather than human eyesight and maintain a steady diet of mosquitoes, things which we don't typically experience for ourselves. And even if humans could have these experiences, such would be a *human* experience of echolocation or eating mosquitoes, and would still lack the quality of "bat-ness."

Though Nagel doesn't address this in his essay, you could go even further still and show that there is even a unique quality of conscious experience present *for every individual member of a species.* It's not just that a human or a bat has the conscious quality of "human-ness" or "bat-ness," but there's also a quality of individuation; "*this*-human-ness," or "*this*-bat-ness." So, we could take Nagel's question even further and ask "What Is It Like to Be Dracula?" or "What Is It Like to Be Van Helsing?"

So can we, as humans, know what it's like to be a bat? Let's re-phrase the question a little. Can a non-bat organism know what it's like to experience "bat-ness"? In other words, can non-bat organisms, like ourselves, really know and experience the foreign and unique quality of being a bat? Now, this is, in essence, what Nagel's question really boils down to: can humans, from *our own* unique perspective and "human-ness," actually come to know and observe "bat-ness," or the unique quality of being a bat?

Now before you object, please note that this is quite different than *imagining* what it would be like for me or you to be a bat or behave as a bat does. You need only read *Dracula* or watch the movies to figure that out. Indeed, as human beings we can very well imagine ourselves as having a kind of webbing on our arms, seeing and navigating the world around us through echo-location, consuming insects as our main diet, or even spending the day upside down by our feet in someone's attic. But when we do this, we are imagining being a bat from a human perspective. Think about the echo-location. Even if you had some sort of echo-location helmet on with a heads up display that helped you navigate the world around you, you wouldn't know what it is actually *like* to have echo-location. In other words, there's only one way to know what it's like to have echolocation . . . well, *having* echo-location. It's kind of like seeing colors. If we have never seen any color we could try to imagine it and other people could try to describe it, but unless we actually see in color, we'll have no clue what it's like. So in the case of being a bat, to just *imagine* things only tells us what it would be like for a *human* to be a bat. What we really want is to find out the direct conscious experience of a bat, like that of what Dracula could experience as he becomes one. As Nagel says, what we are really after is "what it is like for a *bat* to be a bat."

I Spy a Corpse

To really understand what Nagel's getting at, we should keep in mind a crucial difference between two different types of conscious experience—what we might call *objective* and *subjective* experience. Now, for our purposes, the word "objective" should be understood as referring to something that *is not* dependent on (or exclusive to) the unique conscious experience of a particular organism.

Imagine that both Dr. Van Helsing and Count Dracula happen to be in the same room at the same time and both stumble upon the dead body of a girl and see her simultaneously. Got it? Now, even if Dracula was in the form of a bat, both he and Van Helsing would still be looking at the same dead body, albeit in their own unique conscious ways; Van Helsing would perceive the dead body in accordance to his "human-ness," while Dracula would perceive the same dead body in accordance to his assumed "bat-ness." But, regardless of their differing character of conscious experience ("human-ness" versus "bat-ness"), both Van Helsing and Dracula would still have what we would call the same *objective* experience of seeing that particular dead body.

So, then, we can say from our scenario that the perception of the dead body is an objective experience for both Van Helsing and Dracula since it can be, as Nagel says, "observed and understood from many points of view and by individuals with differing perceptual systems." The body doesn't change itself according to either Van Helsing's or Dracula's particular points of view or experience of it. Though experienced in different and unique ways by both Van Helsing and Dracula, the body of the girl is something which itself exists *outside* of the mind, and therefore independently of any one particular organism's experience of it.

To make things a little easier, let's now consider the other form of experience, that is, subjective experience. That's the sort of opposite to objective experience, at least in the sense that "subjective" refers to what's *inside* the mind, rather than outside. So again, if we return to our previous scenario, it's certainly true that both Van Helsing and Dracula see the same thing: the girl's body. But even though they might objectively see the same thing, both Van Helsing and Dracula are two different organisms, human and bat. They hence experience this body according to their own unique quality of conscious experience—that is, "human-ness" or "bat-ness." Even though Van Helsing and Dracula see the same body, they still see it from their own *subjective* points of view.

So, the word "subjective" here concerns something that *is* dependent or exclusive to a particular organism's unique experience of the world. Or to put it plain and simple, "subjective experience" is what it's like to be *that* particular organism.

So What Are We Lookin' at Here?

Now before we get too far ahead of ourselves, let's just try to put all of these pieces together. We've seen that an organism's subjective experience is the same as that particular organism's own unique character of conscious experience—what's called "bat-ness" or "human-ness." And on the other hand, we've seen that objective experience is something which two different organisms, even from their own unique points of view, are able to experience. So, Dracula, Van Helsing, you, or any other conscious organism can observe certain things objectively, like a wooden stake or a silver crucifix. But these things are also experienced subjectively according to those particular organism's unique quality of experience (which probably is why Dracula freaks out at the sight of a crucifix whereas you wouldn't). Now at this point you might just ask yourself: "What's the deal, then?" How, exactly, is any of this an issue at all?

Well, according to Nagel, there seems to be a disconnect, or gap, between objective and subjective experience. So again, let's recall our beginning question: What is it like to be a bat? The issue of knowing what it's like to be a bat shouldn't be too much for our favorite blood-sucking vampire to tackle. After all, to solve Nagel's question Count Dracula would merely need to transform and experience first-hand what it's like to be a bat—in other words, to experience "bat-ness" for himself. Then he could change back into a human form and he would now "know" what it was like to be a bat.

But mind you, Dracula is, in a sense, cheating a little bit here. The whole point of Nagel's essay is to ask whether or not humans can know *objectively* the particular *subjective* conscious experience of a bat. But in Dracula's case, though he might be human—or at least, some kind of human creature—in order to experience "bat-ness" for himself, he must still make the effort to transform and become a bat, so yes at that moment he is *subjectively* experiencing bat-ness *as a bat*. But as you might have guessed at this point, this is clearly not what Nagel's after. When he transforms back he will reflect on his bat experience *as a human*. So in other words he will be experiencing bat-ness through his human-ness, which really isn't like being a bat at all. As a human, Dracula might be able to recall certain memories or thoughts he had while he was in bat form. But any experience he recalls will be remembered now filtered through a human point of view. As a human, he can't directly experience a bat perspective. To truly experience or know what it's like to be a bat, Dracula must himself become a bat. But that is equal to saying that only bats can know what it's like to be a bat, which isn't very helpful.

So is there any way that we as humans can know, from our own point of view, the subjective experience of a bat? According to Nagel, that's impossible ("What Is It Like to Be a Bat?", p. 437). Even if we all had Dracula's ability to transform into a bat, as cool as that may be, it still seems that we would be incapable of knowing a bat's subjective experience directly from a human point of view. Any attempt to do so will ultimately fail. That's because, as Nagel indicates, subjective experience, by its nature, is impenetrable from objective experience.

The problem for Nagel then is that there really seems to be an insurmountable gap between a particular organism's subjective experience, and the ability for humans, or any other conscious organism, to objectively experience it. Now, this is not just a problem for fans of *Dracula* who fanatically hope to one day experience "bat-ness" for themselves. Indeed, as we hinted in the beginning, the problem raised here by Nagel suggests some quite provocative and uneasy philosophical implications.

Beyond Mind and Body

The discrepancy Nagel sees between objective and subjective conscious experience touches on what philosophers of mind call the mind-body problem. Put simply, this problem is about the unclear nature of the relationship between the mind and the physical body. But just what is the mind? Is the mind just as much a part of the physical body as an arm or a leg, being merely composed of physical and material parts? Or is it *beyond* the physical and material, characterized by what has historically been referred to as the soul or spirit? These are good questions to ask, and they help in particular to indicate an important point worth noting: mainly, that the way we understand mind and consciousness is closely related to how we understand reality.

According to Nagel the inability for us to know the subjective experience of another conscious organism, like a bat's, has troubling implications for one particular understanding of reality, which he refers to as *physicalism* (p. 437). This view basically holds that everything that exists can ultimately be reduced to and explained by elementary particles and mass-energy, that is, by what is *physical*. Simply put, bats, humans, brains, and even Dracula himself are ultimately reducible to mere physical compositions such as molecules, atoms, electrons, quarks, or superstrings. In this view, even consciousness itself can be reduced to something physical. This means that your conscious experience of the world, as well as Dracula's, can be explained in physical terms, or be shown to be physical itself. This is why Nagel accuses physicalism of a "psycho-physical reduction." Followers of physicalism believe that an organism's conscious experience is equal and identical to physical or material things (p. 444).

If physicalism's right, then, as we've seen, everything that exists can be reduced to physical states. But if that's the case, we as humans should be able to *objectively experience all of reality,* since all of reality would be physical. If physicalism is true, to know what's it like to be a bat would be child's play. And here's why: remember that "objective" refers to something which *is not* dependent on or exclusive to a particular organism's unique conscious experience. Recall our earlier scenario with Van Helsing, Dracula, and the girl's dead body. As we saw, both Van Helsing and Dracula were able to see the same body (objective experience) while also perceiving it in their own unique conscious ways (subjective experience). Now, if the body could only be experienced by Van Helsing and not Dracula, we would suspect that such would be a subjective experience. Maybe in such a case Van Helsing had a little too much to drink, or he had taken some drugs which caused him to see something which actually wasn't there. But since both Van Helsing and Dracula experienced the body, we can conclude that it was an objective experience.

Someone could argue that they were both hallucinating, and therefore seeing the body was just two subjective experiences occurring simultaneously. Although such an event would be extremely rare, we should therefore conclude that such an occurrence for Dracula and Van Helsing was, at best, *probably* an objective experience. But for the sake of the argument, let's just assume that the body was, in fact, present in the room.

In this same way, we can also understand physical states. Physical states are objective since they can be experienced from various points of view. They are *independent* of a particular organism's subjective experience. Just think about it: atoms, molecules, a bat's wings, this book, Dracula's cape, and all the rest that "physical states" encompass can be experienced or observed from different conscious points of view. And that's precisely the point that Nagel wants us to recognize. If all of reality is expected to be objectively experiential, then given the gap between subjective and objective experience, physicalism runs into a problem.

If all of reality, your body as well as your mind, including thoughts, beliefs, and the senses through which you experience the world, are identical or reducible to physical qualities, like atoms or molecules, an organism's consciousness (subjectively experiential) is equal and identical to physical states (objectively experiential). Basically, your own personal conscious experience or the world *should be* objectively experiential and observable by other organisms from their own points of view. But as you might be able to tell by now, this is exactly where the problem lies. As Nagel has demonstrated for us, this implication of physicalism leads to an impossibility: the subjective experience of a conscious organism *can't* be experienced objectively.

A Conscious Dilemma

This implication of physicalism raises an interesting dilemma. If physicalism is true, all of reality should be reducible to physical states, and could therefore be experienced and known from various points of view. But from what Nagel has shown, what we find runs counter to the claims of physicalism. Indeed, it seems to be the case that the subjective experience of an organism—what it's like to *be* that particular organism—is *beyond* a physicalist's reductive understanding of reality, suggesting that consciousness itself cannot be reduced to mere physical states.

But, you might ask, what about neurology and recent scientific advancements in researching the brain? Don't they demonstrate that the brain and the mind (consciousness) are the same? Not really. Far from proving that the mind is itself physical in nature, neuroscience has shown a *correlation* between what you might be thinking and what's going on in your brain. But such a fact itself is miles away from a proof that the mind and the brain are identical. Though we may know which kind of brain activity correlates with which thoughts or emotions, this is not the same as saying that we can reduce those same thoughts or emotions themselves to something physical, and therefore observable. Neuroscientists observe neurological activity within the brain which correlates to certain thoughts and emotions, but they don't see such conscious thoughts or emotions *themselves*.

So where does this lead to? Well, Nagel is certainly right in saying that this doesn't prove physicalism to be false. To settle the issue of whether everything that exists is "just" physical or not would take a lot more—more than any philosopher has been able to provide so far. Perhaps an organism's subjective experience seems not to be reducible to the physical simply because *it isn't reducible to the physical?* To say that the mind, or consciousness, is non-physical, would open the door for potential religious or spiritual implications. For someone like Van Helsing, who clings so strongly to the idea of an afterlife, the existence of an enduring immaterial and conscious soul would support his religious beliefs. If there should be such an immaterial (or supernatural, meaning "more-than-natural") aspect to the world, the implications for our understanding of reality are, quite literally, divine in proportion.

Yet we shouldn't jump the gun and assume that Nagel has proven the existence of the soul, or the existence of the supernatural. He hasn't. Though, it still remains reasonable to suspect that, if physicalism cannot account for conscious experience, then rather than deny the existence of conscious experience, perhaps we need to at least change the very way we think about consciousness. Indeed, what Nagel *has* demonstrated is that's time to reconsider how we understand consciousness and even reality itself.

IV

Why We're
Afraid

16
Dracula in the Age of Mechanical Reproduction

JOHN V. KARAVITIS

After Bram Stoker's *Dracula* was published on May 26th, 1897, readers throughout the British Empire agreed that the novel represented a fascinating tale of horror. Although it wasn't a runaway bestseller, a number of book reviews in newspapers at the time praised Stoker's novel and its place in the pantheon of gothic horror novels.

- *The Daily Mail*, June 1st, 1897: **The recollections of this weird and ghostly tale will doubtless haunt us for some time to come. . . . Persons of small courage and weak nerves should confine their reading of these gruesome pages strictly to the hours between dawn and sunset.**

- *Pall Mall Gazette*, June 1st, 1897: **Mr. Bram Stoker should have labelled his book "For Strong Men Only" . . . It is for the man with a sound conscience and digestion, who can turn out the gas and go to bed without having to look over his shoulder more than half a dozen times as he goes upstairs.**

- *The Bristol Times and Mirror*, June 8th, 1897: **To those who are fond of the ghastly and the gruesome, "Dracula" will be welcome reading. The story is cleverly constructed and brilliantly told . . . Mr. Bram Stoker sets forth the mysterious and the awful.**

- *The Stage*, June 17th, 1897: **Mr. Stoker's brilliant tour de force . . . all who are attracted by the supernatural in literature will find fascination enough in Mr. Stoker's *Dracula*.**

I remember reading *Dracula* while in grammar school. I had seen Dracula movies on television, of course, but I wanted to read "the real thing" for myself. I remember reading Stoker's gothic tale and being periodically frozen in terror, yet propelled onward to the end by my curiosity. I found the story of the confrontation between Dracula and his adversaries as terrifying as most readers must have in 1897.

Recently, I re-read Stoker's *Dracula* in its entirety. After I finished, I laid down my e-reader, and stared off in disbelief. Where was the terror that had captivated me as a young child? I now found *Dracula* to be positively tame, mawkish, repetitive, and, in all honesty, boring! But I know that the novel remains as Stoker wrote it in 1897, unchanged, word for word. Could it be that all the thousands upon thousands of copies that had been printed over the decades had drained the novel *Dracula* of its power to captivate and terrify the reader?

But that's nonsense! Just making copies of a book doesn't dilute its power! No way! The fault must lie within me, right? Well, then . . . What had happened to me in all these years?

The Three Rs—Reading, Writing, and (Mechanical) Reproduction

The short answer could be, "Well, you grew up." But that answer is unsatisfying. If a person's view of a novel, or any work of art, can change over the decades, can the same be said for how people in general have viewed works of art across a long span of time? According to philosopher Walter Benjamin (1892–1940), the answer is "Yes."

In "The Work of Art in the Age of Mechanical Reproduction" (1936), Benjamin looks at how advances in technology, by allowing people to mass-produce and distribute works of art, have changed the function of art in society, along with how people respond to it. Art's original purpose was to aid in ritual and religious ceremonies. It wasn't copied or reproduced—it couldn't be and still remain the same work of art. To view a work of art, one had to go and see it in person. Because of that, art had an aura of authenticity, and it was from this aura of authenticity that it derived its function and power. Authenticity can only exist in an original work of art. It can't be reproduced.

Advances in technical skill led to the reproduction of works that we today would view as having artistic qualities or merit. Benjamin starts by looking at ancient Greek works of art: bronzes, pottery, even coins. But the level of reproduction available to the ancient Greeks was limited, costly, and time-consuming. Art used in ritual or religion still had to be experienced in person, and this meant that the legitimacy and importance of the original work of art—its authenticity— remained intact.

Further technical advances, like the printing press and lithography, led to certain works of art (pamphlets and books) becoming more widespread. Everyone is aware of the marked change in society that resulted from the invention of the printing press. Books, no longer laboriously transcribed by hand, became more easily available. Everyone could now, at least in theory, own and possess a copy of the Bible, and read it for themselves, whenever they wanted. The Bible was emancipated from the ritual of being read during a church mass, and being interpreted solely in terms of that day's church sermon. The same can be said of *Dracula*. The fact that Stoker could tell Dracula's story by print meant that he could reach more people at one time than if the story were verbally narrated in ritual, as in an epic poem, at specific times of the year. Benjamin understood that producing multiple copies of a work of art means that it no longer depends on a specific ritual or special circumstances to make it a part of people's lives. The work of art has been made free. Subsequent technical advances in the mechanical reproduction of art, first with photography, then movies, have continued to impact contemporary life by changing how people react to and understand works of art.

In Benjamin's time, the impact of technological advances on art was most evident in the emerging technology of movies. Benjamin compares the effect of a stage actor in a theater, in front of a live audience, to a movie of the same play in a movie theater. In America, *Dracula* was presented on stage before it was transformed into a movie (both times starring Bela Lugosi in the title role), so we can directly compare the effect of the two media formats in light of Benjamin's ideas. In a stage theater, the performance is offered at set times, and the audience at any given performance is limited in size. For a movie, both the performances and the audience are potentially unlimited in time and space. The stage actor sees his audience as he reads his lines, and he can adjust his presentation based on the audience's reactions. The movie actor can never do this.

Given its limited existence, the stage play remains the province of the playwright, whereas the audience is left only with its fading memories of the performance. These memories will also tend more toward emotional reactions felt during the performance than to any analytical afterthoughts. Movies, because they can be watched anytime by the audience, are more readily subject to analysis and critical comment. This means that movies can be dissected, analyzed, and critiqued from many different points of view, which is something that can't be done as easily with stage performances.

Benjamin also looks at how changes in technical expertise have affected works of art in terms of economics. Going back to the comparison of stage theater to movies, Benjamin saw art becoming more a form of economic product, and no longer merely an object of ritual. But if art is no longer subservient to ritual, religion, or tradition, and instead is subject to economic forces, it becomes a tool only valuable in terms of money.

Given that the act of reproduction means that there is no original work of art to point to (which print of a photograph or movie is the "original" print?), the very idea of authenticity, and the art's creator, no longer have any relevance. Benjamin also believed that because of this loss of authenticity, there could no longer be any distinction between an author of a work of art and the public. For Benjamin, technical advances in the mechanical reproduction of works of art, from printing to lithography to photography to movies, had radically transformed not only all of the arts, but society as well.

How the Undead (Mechanically) Reproduce— For Adults Only

When *Dracula* was published in 1897, novels were still printed on mechanical presses, and most people would have had at least a passing familiarity with the vampire legend. Stoker wasn't exposing his readers to anything new. In that respect, his novel would have reinforced the vampire legend in people's minds. The readers would have merely been passive receptacles and the novel a form of entertainment.

A daring few might have proposed at the time that the novel stood as an allegory for threats to the British Empire. For example, the successful conversion of Lucy Westenra to the ranks of the Undead, and the attempted conversion of Mina Harker, could have been seen as a metaphor for a colonial threat to the purity of British blood. The subsequent challenge to and pursuit of Dracula, orchestrated by Dutch physician Abraham Van Helsing (a foreigner, no less!), could have been seen as a clarion call to British patriotism. But that is more than likely as far as any analysis would have gone in 1897. Also, depending on the novel's availability, its cost, and the general level of literacy in the markets where it was sold, the social impact of the novel could not have been as widespread then as it would be today.

What has changed in the last century? Benjamin's answer would be that the technology eventually developed that would allow for an even more widespread distribution of Stoker's novel, and in more than a single medium. Benjamin pegs 1900, just three years after *Dracula* was published, as the year when the technological expertise for creating movies was enough to change the world's perception and reaction toward all works of art. (The first public exhibition of "motion pictures" occurred in New York City in 1896, although 1900 is typically given as the year when movies as we now know them first came into existence.) In our age of mechanical reproduction, Stoker's novel doesn't stand frozen in time. Far from it. Today, strictly from a print perspective, different people reading the novel will look at it through different cultural lenses. So, we can get a feminist reading of *Dracula*, a sociological reading, a critique of Marxism versus capitalism, imperialism, race relations, slavery, just to name a few. The novel, as any work of art subject to reproduction, becomes more plastic; and the audience becomes more active in its relationship with it. Proof of this is in your hands right now.

Stoker himself must have had a premonition that the future would be different for readers of novels. First, *Dracula* is written in an epistolary format. That is, it is written in the form of diary entries (of multiple individuals), letters, telegrams, and memoranda. So, each character has his take on the events that transpired, given what was individually witnessed and experienced. (Except for Count Dracula; but please read my other chapter in this volume, where I tie up this loose end of Stoker's.) Everyone's experiences will of course be different. In a sense, the way Stoker wrote *Dracula* inadvertently heralds the twentieth-century philosophy known as postmodernism. The simplest definition of "postmodernism" is "All viewpoints are valid." The diary entry format of Stoker's novel, where each character writes the story of Dracula from his point of view, foreshadows the world of today, where every reader can in turn become an author. Mina Harker's transcription of everyone's diaries, and the survival of this copy subsequent to Dracula's alleged destruction of all of the original documents, also point to the idea of postmodernism. Here, with the destruction of the source documents, all we are left with are allegations of what happened. There is no supporting evidence; so, by default, every viewpoint must be equally valid.

Second, the action in *Dracula* explicitly expresses the idea of the new chasing away and replacing the old. It's no great stretch of the imagination to claim that Dracula can be said to represent the ideas and customs of an older, darker, and more violent age, whereas Van Helsing and the others who oppose Dracula represent the enlightened, forward-thinking, modern age. Given the way he wrote *Dracula*, and the overall theme, Stoker turns out to have, perhaps unwittingly, been as much of a philosopher and a prophet as he was a novelist.

Owner's Manual—How to Understand a (Mechanically Reproduced) Work of Art

Today, art no longer supports ritual or tradition. Art no longer exists for its own sake. It can't. The response to a work of art now becomes a collective, political response instead of an individual response. As Benjamin predicted, art has become a vehicle for politics. By promoting a postmodernist environment, technical advances in mechanical reproduction have inadvertently created an environment of increased political awareness and call to collective action. With the advent of the Internet, blog posts and tweets have joined the television news sound bite and the thirty-second political commercial to this end.

We can see this increase in political awareness and social consciousness applied in the various movies and movie parodies made about Dracula and vampires. Although novels and other books are still as popular as ever, nevertheless, movies allow for a story to be told to a larger, wider audience, at the same time, and with more emotional impact. Benjamin saw film as providing the most powerful tool that mechanical reproduction had for destroying the hold of ritual and tradition on art.

In leveraging the original story of Dracula to explore political and social issues, every genre is represented, in movies too numerous to mention: comedies (*Abbot and Costello Meet Frankenstein,* 1948; *Jesus Christ Vampire Hunter,* 2001); warnings about the excesses of science in the nuclear age (*Blood of Dracula,* 1957); race relations in America (*Blacula,* 1972; *Scream, Blacula, Scream,* 1973); homosexuality and lesbianism (take your pick of any Jean Rollin film); feminism (*Byzantium,* 2012); and the perils of drug addiction (*The Addiction,* 1995). The political agenda of art can also be extended so that art ends up serving capitalism. Here, Dracula is used symbolically in various non-political domains. In advertising, Count Dracula sells cereal to children (as Count Chocula, of course). Dracula also teaches young children how to "count" (*Sesame Street*). I'm sure Stoker would have marveled at how far we've come from Castle Dracula in the Carpathian Mountains!

In 1897, Dracula gazed at the reader through the novel, and transfixed him. In the twenty-first century, the reader's gaze captures Dracula and transforms *him*, with each reader seeing something different, perhaps something different with each successive reading. Through technical advances in the mechanical reproduction of works of art, we've arrived at a view of art that French literary theorist and philosopher Roland Barthes (1915–1980) held for novels. An author's intention in writing a novel is irrelevant to understanding it. A novel doesn't say what the author wants. That's the old way of looking at a novel. Rather, the novel says what each individual reader decides it says. *Dracula* needn't be just about vampires and their victims. It doesn't have to be just about good versus evil. It can be about whatever you read into it. A fragment of the novel can surpass the entirety of the story in importance and relevance.

By being able to read and re-read a novel, and being able to criticize it and re-form its story to support a political angle or social cause, we become authors in our own right. Like it or not, technical advances in the mechanical reproduction of works of art have resulted in our living in a noisy, crowded, chaotic, politically-charged, socially conscious, postmodern world.

From (Mechanical) Reproduction to (Spiritual) Resurrection

So, what, if anything, has happened to me in all these years since I first read *Dracula*? The answer I think lies in comparing my growth as an individual to what has happened to our world as our technological expertise in producing and reproducing works of art became more advanced over the centuries. A traditional work of art was experienced by one or a small number people at a single time. This allowed time for contemplation and deep thought, both of which were centered on each individual. This is sort of what we experience in childhood. It's the way I remember reading novels—being so engrossed in the actions of the characters that I forgot myself and my world. As a child reading what I wanted to in the dead heat of a Chicago summer, I was able to enjoy in solitude the experience of becoming one with a novel. As with art in days of old, art that was locked in aspects of ritual and tradition, there was opportunity for deep thought and "free-floating contemplation," as Benjamin called it. The work of art absorbed me. As I read *Dracula*, I didn't finish it in one fell swoop. I had to put the novel down at times and walk away. It was *that* vivid to my imagination. But I was *there*, with Van Helsing and the others, squaring off against Dracula!

Now, the child's way of quiet contemplation is lost to me. As an adult, I read critically, even when I read fiction. I also read fiction with a much broader and deeper knowledge of how the world works. I don't turn that switch off when I read—I can't. This means that I am not just a reader, but also a critic. The work of art doesn't absorb me; I now absorb the work of art. I capture it in *my* gaze and transform it to *my* expectations—not unlike Dracula with his prey. And any conclusions that I come to won't be the conclusions that many others will come to. This is a social phenomenon because the novel isn't all just about me or my reading and my particular point of view. Our ability to look at a work of art as individuals, to take it apart, and, if not find meaning, then to imply it, in a social setting, is a mark of a more mature understanding of how complicated the world really is. I didn't just grow up; the world has, too.

In a sense, the evolution from contemplation to criticism is a form of "dialectic." In dialectical thinking, we start with a thesis—a statement about the world. This thesis is challenged by an antithesis—an apparently contradicting or contrasting statement about the world. Understanding both, we hopefully can reconcile the two opposing views, and arrive at a new thesis—a synthesis. This synthesis takes the best of both theses that preceded it, and provides a deeper understanding of how the world works. In terms of the dialectic that we find in technical advances in the mechanical reproduction of works of art, the transition from passive acceptance of art (thesis) to active social critique of art (antithesis) can in fact be reconciled. These two opposing theses are reconciled because we can now, each and every one of us, become authors in our own right—by actively creating a new interpretation of a work of art, instead of just passively contemplating it. As I have done with *Dracula*, twice, in the book that you now hold in your hands. As Walter Benjamin predicted, the line between the author and the reading public has become blurred. "At any moment the reader is ready to turn into a writer."

Think of this deeper understanding of how the world works as a beneficial consequence of our age of mechanical reproduction. Art is no longer tied to ritual or tradition, for neither ritual nor tradition can survive if the work of art is critically examined. But we can still have art tell a story: your story, my story, everyone's story. We can now aspire to achieving a form of "resurrection" of our youthful, contemplative, soul-searching selves, one which doesn't require any black magic or getting "turned" by one of the Undead. Ironically, all it takes is just a bit of growing up . . . and daring to think critically, and deeply.

17
Letting Dracula Out of the Closet

Ariane de Waal

The DVD cover of Cole Haddon's new *Dracula* television series shows the typical vampiric scenario: a red-eyed, white-faced male vampire is getting ready to stick his teeth into the flawless white skin, or rather the blue pulsating vein, of the neck of a beautiful female victim reclining her head as if yearning for the bite. The sexual dynamics of this cliché scenario seem pretty clear: The vampire story appears time and again as an erotic heterosexual encounter between the handsome evil man and the ravishing (and ravished) innocent woman.

And yet things are not as straight(forward) as that. One of the reasons why Dracula is so scary is because wherever he appears he causes "gender trouble." You might say, "Of course he's scary. He wants to suck our blood! What more explanation do you need?" Sure, Dracula comes in the night to suck our blood, but Dracula holds a place much higher in hierarchy of monsters than most fiends of the night. Dracula's bite is more terrifying and lasting because of his power to cause mayhem in the orderly world of manly men and womanly women. Dracula drives healthy gentlemen like Jonathan Harker into brain fever and respectable old men like Van Helsing into hysteric fits. And the women . . . well, he turns chaste Victorian ladies into wanton vamps like Lucy Westenra or "stained" vampire mistresses like Mina Harker.

What's even scarier is that the vampire himself is a frightening shape-shifter, switching not only between the forms of bats, dogs, and wolves, but also between genders. In Bram Stoker's original description, he appears as a tall, strong man with a long white moustache. But does he act like a man? Remember the scene where he makes Mina suck blood from a wound in his breast? He feeds her like a mother (somewhat violently) breastfeeding her child—what's that all about, then? Let's find out by hunting down the Trans-sylvanian Count and looking at all the different ways in which he causes "gender trouble."

So Let Me Show You Around Gender

"Gender trouble" is an idea that contemporary philosopher Judith Butler came up with. Butler argues that gender identity—masculinity, femininity, and all the shades of gray in between—is neither natural nor completely imposed by culture, but that it is (re)produced all the time by our behavior. So gender is not a thing that we *have* or *are* but that we *do*. That's why Butler calls gender "performative"—it's by constantly acting as a woman or a man that we are perceived as feminine or masculine. So you can already see why Dracula is a tricky case: he certainly *looks* masculine, but he doesn't *do* what the other men in the story do, such as pursuing a manly profession, going hunting, or worshipping, protecting, and proposing to women.

Why would Dracula's rule-breaking be problematic? Well, even when we think of gender as performative, this still doesn't mean that we have complete freedom regarding what gender we perform and how we act the role. We can't exactly pick our gender like clothes from a wardrobe or food from a menu . . . "What's the gender of the day? I'll have female, please!" So why aren't we as free to play different gender roles as Dracula (or should I say "Drag-ula"?)

There are at least two reasons for our lack of freedom: First, there is the issue of "citationality." Literally, this means that in our gender performances we cite, or quote, previous performances. In other words, what's not okay at school becomes a rule here: only when you successfully "copy" other gender presentations will people think that you're "doing" your gender properly ("S/he's such a typical fe/male"). And although the range of available genders may nowadays seem great and increasing—just think of Facebook's recent move to introduce fifty-six gender options for its users' profiles—acceptable gender options are always culturally and historically limited. The fact that Van Helsing lauds all of Mina's contributions to the vampire hunt with exclamations about this "so clever woman" shows that, no matter how untypical Mina's behavior may be in gendered terms, she will always be perceived as a typical woman—or, in today's jargon, a "cis-gendered female," a woman by birth and by identification.

Second, gender presentation is not a one-off show, but Butler calls it "an *incessant* and *repeated* action of some sort" (*Gender Trouble*, p. 152, my emphasis). It's made up of everyday acts and rituals that we repeat over and over again. The drag queens at the Swinburne Club that Dracula visits in Episode Two of the TV series do not become women for the night just because they sing with higher voices or wear elaborate dresses, wigs, and makeup. They do it repeatedly, ritualizing their gender and rebelling against the typical gender roles. For Butler, drag is an excellent way to rebel against gender norms.

Drag queens do not imitate "real" women, but they exaggerate the way in which (some) women "do" gender. This is why Butler sees drag as a parody, or satiric imitation, which reveals that the supposedly original gender act (the "real" woman) is itself a repetition of previous acts, the copy of a copy of a copy. Through those gender parodies like drag, or by "doing" gender in ways that do not conform to conventions, we can cause gender trouble. If *Dracula* is a story about gender trouble, it must contain acts and behaviors that go against the gender grain. And if gender is performative, then why not rethink the original *Dracula* novel as a play? I'd say, curtains up for *Drag-ula*, a Trans-sylvanian drag show in five acts.

Act I: The Dude in Distress

The first act is set in Dracula's castle, where all the gender trouble begins. The way it slowly dawns on Jonathan Harker that Dracula doesn't mean well is inseparable from various transgressions of gender boundaries—how a "real" man or a woman should and should not behave. Although Harker is somewhat frightened from the time he enters the castle, he starts to freak out only when he notices that he's a prisoner. And I think the reason why this upsets him is that it forces him to play the unmanly role of the captive who's at the mercy of the villain.

Bram Stoker uses the common plot device of the "damsel in distress," with an obvious twist. Normally, a female character must be rescued from a dangerous situation (she's often trapped in a tower, dungeon, or castle) by a male hero she will eventually marry. Whether Sleeping Beauty in the classic fairy tale, Ann Darrow in the movie *King Kong*, or the princess in the *Super Mario* video games, the damsel in distress is, by definition, a young woman.

Now Harker, our dude in distress, feels uncomfortable in this twisted situation because it makes it hard for him to act like a "real" man. There is nothing much he can do other than sit down "at a little oak table where in old times possibly some fair lady sat to pen" (*Dracula*, Penguin edition, p. 49). Captivity forces him into a passive *feminine* role.

What makes matters worse is that Dracula also takes on a role that was reserved for women in nineteenth-century England, which explains why Harker's realization that Dracula does all the housework in the castle is the other great source of his horror. In Victorian times the private and the public spheres were meant to be separated, the one reserved for the domestic work done by women, the other for the "important" business done by men. The stereotypical (middle- or upper-class) Victorian woman would stay indoors and cater to her husband's and children's every wish. This ideal woman has been labeled the "angel in the house."

That Dracula prepares all the meals for Harker (and excellent meals at that, as the latter notes in his diary) and takes care of all other chores (including carrying Harker to his bed and undressing him at one point) freaks Harker out because it makes Dracula both his captor and angel—er, vampire—in the house. This confusion of gender roles even causes some homoerotic tension.

Stoker describes Dracula during one of the Count's long talks with Harker: "He grew excited as he spoke, and walked about the room pulling his great white moustache and grasping anything on which he laid his hands." The sexual undertones of this passage are obvious enough: the man gets excited, stroking his "great moustache"—I'm sure a double meaning is intended here—and grabs everything in sight (including, perhaps, his visitor). It seems that the vampire scare has a lot to do with homophobia.

The gender trouble unleashed at Dracula's castle culminates in Harker's encounter with the "weird sisters." As if under a strange spell, Harker dispenses with the moral codes of the Victorian gentleman and almost gives in to the thrilling voluptuousness of these temptresses. I think it's no coincidence that this first act of our drag show closes with a comment by Harker that actually shares some of the insights of Butler's *Gender Trouble*. The encounter with the weird sisters makes him question what it means to call someone a woman, and how this label cannot apply to everyone of female shape: "I am alone in the castle with those awful women. Faugh! Mina is a woman, and there is naught in common." A hundred years later a similar thought prompted Butler to draft her theory of gender performativity, because she realized that if "one 'is' a woman, that is surely not all one is" (*Gender Trouble*, p. 4). So Harker and Butler would agree that one word isn't enough: some women are vampires, some are chaste young ladies, and not all "do" their gender in the same way.

Act II: The Lady Is a Vamp

In his second challenge to gender, Dracula manages to transform Lucy, this paragon of Victorian chastity and beauty, into a wanton vampire lady. At the outset Lucy performs her gender in an extremely desirable manner, at least by Victorian standards: she is constantly described as appearing sweet, sensitive, and pure, and the fact that she has three proposals made to her in just one day leaves no room for doubt as regards her good looks (a 'must-have' of a damsel in distress!). Admittedly, Lucy has a little bit of gender trouble even before the vampire arrives: she is a "horrid flirt," as she confesses to Mina, and finds it difficult to settle for one man when she can have three. But marriage solves lots of problems (besides causing new ones, of course), and becoming Arthur's wife would surely have tamed this young lady.

And yet the vampire's bite disrupts Lucy's passage from innocent betrothed to faithful wife. In the scene set at the cliff's edge at night Mina obviously catches Dracula and Lucy in the middle of . . . something: she finds Lucy "half-reclining," with parted lips, breathing "in long, heavy gasps," even "moaning and sighing occasionally"—so there's all the evidence of a summer love gone naughty. That's why Mina is so concerned to get Lucy home as soon as possible. There's a reputation at stake here! Mina's worst fears seem confirmed when she discovers that Lucy's skin has been "pierced" and when she detects "a drop of blood" on her nightdress—obvious hints at a loss of virginity.

Due to the gender trouble caused by the vampire's bite, Lucy cannot effortlessly play the role of charming young lady any more. This is why Dr. Seward in his diary repeatedly takes note of how Lucy has to wear a mask, how she keeps up pretenses in front of others, and how hard she has to struggle to make a cheerful impression. The role of charming young lady becomes a drag performed by the vampire-to-be, the copy of a copy!

The gender trouble intensifies with Lucy's transformation. The voluptuous vamp makes her first appearance on the deathbed, where she bids Arthur to "kiss" her—clearly a way of "doing" gender that makes Lucy more akin to the weird sisters than to her faithful friend Mina. And Lucy's not the only one whose gender performance changes. Her death sends the composed old professor Van Helsing into hysteria—which was considered an exclusively female condition in the nineteenth century—as soon as Van Helsing discovers that Dracula, by forcing him to infuse Lucy's body with the blood of four men, has made a "polyandrist" of sweet Lucy and a "bigamist" of him. It seems that the threat of vampirism is inseparable from the threat of sexual promiscuity, which was, like homosexuality, a taboo subject and a great source of anxiety in Victorian society. So far we could say that Dracula's scare factor indeed increases with the gender trouble he causes.

Act III: From Vampire Hunter to Vampire Lover?

Mina is, from the beginning, an interesting case. She starts out as a fairly unconventional Victorian woman who aspires to more than being the angel in the house. At the outset she is an assistant schoolmistress, practices shorthand, and wants to be a "lady journalist." Even before the vampire trouble begins, her gender performance is already at odds with the stereotypical domestic role reserved for Victorian women. In some ways, she embodies the late-nineteenth-century idea of the "New Woman" who gets an education, works, and takes charge of her own life.

But the men surrounding her do not exactly encourage her independence. The more Harker comes on the scene in her life, the more she focuses all her activities on him. *Dracula* makes it very clear that Mina's professional life is a thorn in Harker's side: in the second episode they have a big fight after she over-hears Harker boasting in front of his mates that, as soon as Mina marries him, "she'll forget all this silliness . . . and settle down, and dedicate herself to more natural, womanly pur-suits." Thanks to Butler, we know that there are no such things as *natural* womanly pursuits, but we could say that Harker's hope is that Mina will stick to a more conventional way of behaving as a woman, or a more perfect copy of the copy.

Easily the worst decision the men make is to exclude Mina from the vampire hunt. She's useful to them as long as she copies all the cylinders into type and puts all the evidence in the correct order (here's the forerunner of the modern-day sec-retary), but when it comes to the real hard job of chasing down the vampire, that's "no part for a woman" (or so Van Helsing says). So they leave her home alone with a vampire hell-bent on sucking sweet female blood roaming about—that's the male genius for you.

Dracula's assault on Mina gets her into gender trouble in the sense that it thwarts the gendered plans the other men (and Victorian society) have made for her. Let us quickly run over that scene:

> the Count . . . held both Mrs. Harker's hands, keeping them away with her arms at full tension; his right hand gripped her by the back of the neck, forcing her face down on his bosom. Her white nightdress was smeared with blood, and a thin stream trickled down the man's bare breast, which was shown by his torn-open dress. (*Dracula*, p. 336)

The bloody scene into which the vampire hunters stumble here surpasses Victorian gentlefolk's wildest dreams. Not only is it a threesome situation with the second male lying in a stupor, but the sexual act in which Dracula and Mina engage is also far from conventional: the woman is sucking body fluids from a fresh wound in the man's breast.

Butler has some interesting things to say about this scene. For her, "sexual practices . . . that open surfaces and orifices to erotic signification or close down others effectively reinscribe the boundaries of the body along new cultural lines" (*Gender Trouble*, p. 180). This is precisely what happens in the scene above: the sexual encounter between Dracula and Mina opens the new orifice of the man's breast; it is hence an act that shifts the boundaries of the body (the way we're used to seeing, using, and feeling our bodies). In nineteenth-century Victorian society the "cultural lines" that Butler speaks about would have Mina "lie back and think of England" (rumor has it that this advice was given to newly married Victorian women) while Jonathan, her lawful lover, would legitimately penetrate that one permissible orifice to make babies. But, as Butler would have it, by opening new orifices to an erotic encounter that certainly doesn't produce babies, Dracula turns Victorian rules and morals upside down. The gender trouble caused by this transgression is immense, and the "mark of shame" which Mina has to carry after the encounter is visible evidence of that—and a fair warning to all other young Victorian ladies.

Is Dracula's unconventional gender performance a bad thing, then? Not in Butler's view. Her theory can help us see Dracula and Mina's bedroom encounter as a "parody" of the conventional heterosexual act, a raunchy drag show that breaks the rules of the gender game. Of course, Mina has to disown the pleasure this little fling may have given her in front of the jury of men. But Dracula is, in fact, a liberating influence. He teases her out of the home to which the men would like to confine her and disturbs her performance as angel in the house and prospective mother. His appearance interrupts the endless gender game of copying the copy. And we are left to wonder whether the path to becoming the vampire sidekick wouldn't have been the more exciting biography for Mrs. Harker.

Act IV: Sterilizing the Vampire

Running parallel to Dracula's assault on Victorian sexual morals inside the bedroom is another, larger scheme to wreak gender havoc. Act Four of the drag show is about Dracula's attempt to procreate. Keeping Mina from having nice human babies with her husband by turning her into his sidekick is just part of that plan; producing a new generation of vampires is the bigger picture. Again, it's an unconventional gender performance—procreation without female help and without sexual intercourse (well, of the usual kind)—that is part and parcel of the Trans-sylvanian's terror.

The vampire hunt that takes place in London in the novel is actually not very spectacular. In fact, it's a far cry from catsuit-wearing Lady Jane Wetherby taking out vampires with guns, knives, and martial arts moves in the television series. For the most part, the purpose of the original vampire hunt is to "sterilize" Dracula's lairs, as Van Helsing calls it. I would argue that the language used to describe this procedure is no coincidence. There were already experiments with male sterilization, or vasectomy, in the nineteenth century, so the double meaning of the word may have been obvious to readers at the time. In addition to the long-term objective of killing Dracula, sterilizing his boxes of earth is of ultimate importance and is mainly a symbolic act to sterilize the vampire, that is, to keep him from uncannily producing new creatures.

If compulsory sterilization is the response to Dracula's power as the potential "furtherer of a new order of beings," then what does this say about society? The nineteenth century saw the beginning of the eugenics movement, which was concerned with the "improvement" of the human species. Male sterilization was among the measures discussed to keep "undesirable" parts of the population from reproducing. So, Dracula must be counted among those whom the eugenicists considered mentally, physically, or morally unfit to become parents. If, at the same time, he stands for all those who cause gender trouble, then people who are "nonconforming in their gender presentation" as Butler calls it apparently belong to this group of "undesirables" ("Your Behavior Creates Your Gender").

The act of sterilizing the trans-vampire can then be seen as a drastic form of punishment for people who don't fit in the gender boxes. It's an extreme example of how, in Butler's view, society's "police function" controls and discourages nonconforming gender presentations. And we still see traces of the Trans-sylvanian hunt in today's controversies surrounding same-sex marriage and adoption. Butler's theory challenges us to overcome the police function en route to a society that accepts unconventional ways of "doing" gender. As a first step, we should grant the Trans-sylvanian Count the freedom to cause a little gender trouble.

Act V: Winning the Gender Battle

Unfortunately, this is not what happens in the original story. Killing Dracula spells the end for the Trans-sylvanian gender trouble. The most visible symbol of this defeat is the disappearance of the stain on Mina's forehead, which is left as pure and white as ever. In the end all the characters go back to "doing" their gender properly. Lord Godalming and Dr. Seward marry happily (but not each other, of course), Mina eventually becomes a mother and forgets all about those silly plans to be a journalist, and Van Helsing remains their benevolent mentor, rejoicing in all this conjugal bliss.

Could we imagine otherwise? What if Dracula's scheme had been at least a little more successful and wanton, voluptuous vamps would still be stalking the streets of London at the end, men and women would share in hysteric fits, and no one could predict what might happen inside Victorian bedrooms? Wouldn't that have been more exciting?

The *Dracula* series is actually a little more daring when it comes to that: Mina and Dracula are united and have great sex at Carfax, in a scene that makes Mina's earlier pre-marital escapade with Harker pale in comparison. But then again, we are still dealing with a conventional ending in terms of gender relations: the very final scene has Van Helsing and Harker team up to fight against Dracula and retrieve Mina, who has conveniently been turned into a damsel in distress—this eternal excuse for men to act like action heroes.

Are we still waiting for that completely gender-troubled transgressively Trans-sylvanian *Dracula* story to happen, then? Maybe all the ingredients are already there. Even though Stoker lets the good guys win, it's a rule in horror stories that the monster will be back. The gender troublemaker may be killed at the end, but this doesn't necessarily mean that we put down the book—or close the curtains on the drag show—satisfied that boys will be boys and girls will be girls. I think the ongoing fascination with Dracula and the plethora of spin-offs is a clear sign that the Trans-sylvanian keeps haunting us. Which could mean one of two things: a. we love writing and reading ever new stories about Dracula because we cele-brate gender trouble, or b. Dracula still does such a good job of scaring us because the fear of nonconforming gender perfor-mances is as great as ever. In either case, if society's police function is about keeping everyone in their gendered place, then getting Dracula out of the closet—or coffin—can only be a good thing.

18

The Empire's Vampiric Shadow

Tim Jones

Bram Stoker's *Dracula* is not the tale of pure good triumphing over pure evil that it first appears. The sheer desperation of Jonathan Harker and his friends to eliminate any trace of Dracula from the face of the Earth might be the result of a motivation that's a little bit morally murkier than it seems at first glance.

Sure, it's true that Dracula is a pretty monstrous individual who totally deserves what's coming to him. After terrorizing Transylvania for a few centuries, he heads over to Britain, seeking to make its capital his playground. He feeds on its citizens' blood, stealing from their bodies a vital resource they need to stay alive. He doesn't just drink his fill and move on, but drains them to lifelessness. And, what Stoker's non-vampire characters clearly regard as most horrifying of all, he uses his powers to transform the bodies of his victims into something *other* than human, so that they're doomed to live on after death as monsters themselves. So why might I say that Jonathan and his friends driving a stake through this guy's heart is anything other than an awesome victory over the forces of darkness?

The answer lies within the nature of the British Empire, which formed a sprawling backdrop to the historical context in which Stoker, his audience and his characters would all have been immersed. Dracula *is* a monster. But whatever Dracula wants to get up to in Britain, British people in the nineteenth-century were busy getting up to in foreign countries themselves. Not literally, of course, unless the British Empire had a few extremely well kept secrets. But each of the crimes that Stoker's characters charge Dracula with has a pretty gruesome parallel within the workings of the Empire.

Britain rocked up in other countries and acted like it totally owned the place. Britain stole the resources that these places offered, taking them back to the mother-country for its own sustenance much like Dracula gorges himself on other people's blood. And while Britain never publically sought to create an army of the undead to do its evil bidding, it nonetheless worked to shape the identities of the people who lived in these countries in some pretty dehumanizing ways. If Dracula could see his reflection in the mirror, it might look something like the face of a British imperialist. And a British imperialist might see that his own reflection looks a little too much like Dracula for his comfort.

Somebody's Casting a Shadow

Stoker's novel is *actually* the story of a bunch of white people destroying a physical manifestation of colonialism's true, monstrous character. Dracula is the "Shadow Self" of British colonialism. A deeper explanation of this concept can be found within the psychological theories of Carl Jung (1875–1961). As the founder of what he called analytical psychology, Jung was interested in how the stuff we're getting up to on the surface (avoiding making a difficult phone call; procrastinating on writing a book chapter; fighting vampires) is the result of stuff going on beneath our conscious awareness. He believed that our actions are the result of drives and needs that we're not even aware of, unless we take a long, hard look at where exactly our actions are coming from.

This area of investigation led Jung to the idea of the Shadow Self, which is basically a bundle of all the negative aspects of our personality that we'd rather not admit to owning, thank you very much. Because if we *did* admit we have those negative aspects, it would cause some pretty big upsets to our sense of ourselves. What Jung calls the Ego is the sense of our self that we *want* to believe in. In the case of the Empire, this might involve the image of a benevolent parent nation reaching out to and improving the lives of less fortunate nations, purely out of a sense of charity. The Shadow, by contrast, is the darker truth about the Empire's true nature. The bit that looks a lot like Dracula. The bit that the Ego denies having.

Jung argues that we don't only deal with the Shadow side of ourselves by burying it deep within our own personalities. We also project it onto other people, who then end up embodying all the bits of ourselves that we don't want to own up to. If you're ever truly, deeply pissed off at someone else, then a therapist following Jung's model might suggest that you have a good think about whether or not the bit of him or her that so annoys you doesn't actually represent a part of *yourself* that you're not wholly happy about possessing. If that guy across the room from you right now is being frustratingly loud and you're finding that he's more annoying to you than his actions really deserve, then think for a second about whether *you're* ever inappropriately raucous when people around *you* would rather be quietly reading thought-provoking stuff about Dracula.

Projecting a Shadow Self onto other people can actually be pretty useful to the survival of the Ego. Disowning the qualities that make up the Shadow in this way is what allows the view of the self preferred by the Ego to remain safe from the facts that contradict this idealised image. But sometimes the image we project onto another person can just be too vivid a reminder of what we long to deny in ourselves. The logical endpoint of Jung's thoughts on all this is that if you actually got angry enough to attack this supremely annoying other person (or maybe even stake them—but don't do that), then perhaps what you're actually trying to destroy is the disliked aspect of your own self that this other person has come to embody.

So I'd charge Jonathan and his friends not with loathing Dracula himself, as much as the aspects of their own society that his presence continually rubs in their imperial faces. Their attempts to destroy Dracula are actually the attempts of people who live within and benefit from an Empire to eradicate a reflection of the Empire's true nature. They want to drive a stake through the heart of the Empire's Shadow Self, so that they don't have to look at it anymore.

Vampiric Empire

The cliché goes that the sun never set on the British Empire. This would make it a pretty inconvenient place for a guy like

Dracula to live, if it didn't refer to the fact that the Empire was so geographically large that in one place or other it was always daylight. From the eighteenth century until as relatively recently as the 1950s, the British Empire was the largest grouping of territories in the world, covering swathes of continents as far apart as America, Africa, and Asia. At its height, its subjects totaled a fifth of the world's population. The sheer thoroughness of the Empire's colonizing activity makes Dracula wanting to buy a few houses in London seem pretty small-time by comparison.

Apologists for the Empire, then as now, have plenty of justifications for Britain's activities during this period. As a supposedly morally superior Christian nation, it could deliver natives of non-Christian countries from their heathenism and bring them into a proper relationship with the true God. These natives might also feel the benefits of superior British education and technology, such as the telegraph and railway lines that soon criss-crossed colonized landscapes. And by being brought into the folds of the Empire, countries that were imagined by the colonizers to be a disparate collection of peoples fighting amongst themselves would be brought into harmony, as loose and fractious "tribal" identities were replaced by an allegiance to a single mother-country.

To be fair to the Brits, then, they didn't exactly go into all this imagining themselves to be the straightforward villains of the piece. Just as we might picture Dracula being very able to list the benefits of letting him turn you into a vampire, any number of British people would have been able to rattle off a whole host of reasons why the peoples of the Empire should be much happier as colonized subjects. They could even explain why others should be grateful to Britain for taking the time and effort to bother conquering them.

So you might be forgiven for thinking that the British Empire emerged through a sheer sense of goodwill towards the colonized territories. But Britain's aims were a little more self-serving than this picture shows us. It's pretty easy to point out that Britain itself was the prime beneficiary of its "helpful" colonization, particularly if we think about the financial advantages that Britain got from the resources that it discovered in foreign countries. Tea from Canton in China became one of the most valuable exports, paid for by goods taken from Indian territories, at first cotton but, increasingly, opium too. Goods seized from one country became the means by which to take advantage, in turn, of goods taken from another.

And all the while London itself, as the economic center of the Empire, gets increasingly fatter on the proceeds of what was discovered abroad, these foreign resources as vital to London's own economic growth as the blood of other people is to a vampire. And like Dracula himself, Britain never seemed particularly guilty about drinking its fill.

Riot Club

The prospects provided by the Empire's new territories were not only economic. Civilized life in Britain at the time could be pretty boring for those lucky enough to be near the top. The vast new opportunities granted by the colonized lands abroad seemed the perfect antidote to this boredom—so much so that Scottish essayist James Mill, as quoted by Ashley Jackson, described these lands in 1817 as a "vast system of outdoor relief for the upper-classes" (*The British Empire*, p. 30). Botanists and anthropologists had whole new species of plants and animals that they could now go and study at their leisure, while people more interested in sport than in discovery could indulge in a safari or two.

Again, this doesn't sound like a radical departure from Dracula's own behavior. He hunts creatures he regards as lesser than himself across the streets of Whitby and London, as British people hunted game across foreign lands like the Serengeti. And like the British leisure class, Dracula also has far too much spare time to fill. In the opening chapters of Stoker's novel, you get the sense that Dracula suffers from something of an existential boredom of his own, much like what drove game hunters from their comfy armchairs in Britain over to Africa.

It's obvious from Count Dracula's lengthy speech to Jonathan Harker that he's extremely proud of the struggles faced by his nation during its history, but beyond the grandeur that bleeds from his words there's an impression too that the *present* he sees around him can't really offer anything like the same opportunities anymore. If he wants similar glory or excitement then he, too, will have to seek it abroad. Only in this case the "abroad" that he chooses turns out to be Britain. Bad luck for the British. You might be thinking by now a little like it was probably their turn.

So it's safe to say that Dracula's attitude actually resembles the British mindset at the time pretty closely. He searches abroad for opportunities he no longer has at home, and also views the resources he finds there as ripe for providing his own sustenance, which is pretty much what the British were doing to other nations. But there's a further, still more insidious way in which Dracula's plans weren't that far removed from the workings of the British Empire, one which might be particularly unsettling for a respectable Brit like Jonathan if brought out into the open.

Bodily Transformations

While Britain had a ready list of supposedly benevolent excuses for the activities of its Empire, in actual fact British people were just as (if not more) interested in the opportunities the Empire provided for themselves. These opportunities highlight motivations closer to Dracula's own reasons for claiming territory in a foreign country than the average British person at the time would probably be comfortable admitting. Let's look also at the attitudes of the British colonizer towards the people of the colonized countries themselves; these attitudes show a further, even darker way in which the men of the Empire are pretty similar to Dracula.

The British colonizers carried with them impressions of the subjugated races that were far from flattering. Each of these races was, to the British, the opposite in some key way of the rational, responsible, and powerfully masculine white man. Professor of Imperial History Ashley Jackson outlines some of the ways in which imperialism "constructed" the very shape of the natives in each country, be it the "child-like" or "lascivious" African, the "inscrutable" Chinese man, or the "effeminate" Bengali (p. 42). These highly problematic and homogenizing characterizations of foreign identities are not just neutral descriptions of how the British saw the people they encountered, but became part of the very justification for continuing the Empire's expansion. Through Britain's influence, supposedly inferior peoples could be shown better ways of living. If Britain wanted to continue benefitting from the Empire in these various ways, then, it had a vested interest in keeping these somewhat offensive characterizations in circulation.

The novel's opening pages provide some telling examples of how these sorts of problematic descriptions of foreigners come so easily to the mind of a man growing up within an Empire that specializes in such moves elsewhere. Look at how readily Jonathan describes the Slovakian peasants as "barbarian," as though they're a completely self-identical group with something intrinsically wild in their natures; or how his narration frames the elderly female keeper of the Golden Krone Hotel at Bistritz, whose clothing is "too tight for modesty." Even older women from these unfamiliar cultures can't escape being described in overtly sexualized terms by the white, Western European male intruding in their country, just because they don't follow the models of propriety he'd be used to seeing back home.

The relationship between these characterizations made by British colonizers and Dracula's own activities goes something like this: we might simply dismiss such characterizations of foreign peoples as *wrong*, and for perfectly good reason. In straightforward factual terms they obviously *are* wrong, based on prejudice and ignorance about cultures that differed in key ways to Britain's own. Through these descriptions, every difference between the British citizen and the foreign culture is read as a sign of inferiority, or even immorality, while every trace of complexity or nuance existing within and between each of the individual people from this culture is erased.

But what's worse, the word we've seen used by Jackson, "constructed," points towards these suspect characterizations being a little more sinister. They're actually much more than mistaken descriptions. These characterizations aren't simply describing something and getting it wrong, but have the potential to actually *transform* their subjects. And these transformations weren't perhaps entirely accidental. The more that foreign cultures were successfully twisted into something in desperate need of British intervention, the easier it was for the Brits to justify marching into other countries in order to "help out." And then, "Oh look, some diamonds! . . . Might as well take them while we're here."

Making Things Come True

How might these transformations actually have worked upon their targets? Think about the stereotype of a young vampire being told repeatedly by his sire that he'll never amount to anything—who, decades later, has indeed never amounted to anything. He hasn't even managed to turn his first human or get hold of a mortgage for his first spooky castle. People can be pretty good at fulfilling the expectations about their lives and identities that are put before them by those in authority.

Descriptions rooted in prejudice and ignorance regarding the vibrant realities of what they're attempting to describe can, in time, become a self-fulfilling prophecy. In some cases, colonized subjects begin to genuinely believe that these characterizations of them must be true—that the foreign invaders must know their true nature even better than they do themselves. Natives were given the tribal identities and allegiances that the British considered them to hold, but which *before* the arrival of the British absolutely did not exist. And then these enforced, artificial identities would dictate not only an individual's access to jobs, but also what parts of his or her own country he or she would be allowed to travel to.

False ideas about other people's identities, then, don't necessarily remain false forever. Through the ways in which they influence people's behaviors or dictate their future opportunities, they can take on a reality that moves them beyond their initially fictional nature. Colonial ideas about identity can actually change the people they're targeted at into something other than what they originally were.

What Dracula achieves with his fangs and his nocturnal blood transfusions, British colonizers proved just as capable of doing with words and propaganda. Their way of working perhaps makes them even more powerful and efficient than the vampire himself, since they didn't even need any physical contact in order to kick-start the transformations of their own victims.

Staking Shadows

So given all these sinister points of contact between Dracula's behavior and that of the British colonizers, what exactly might a guy like Harker see when he looks at Dracula?

Perhaps someone who is planning to do exactly what Harker's culture has already been up to for the last few hundred years, only this time with Britain herself as the target rather than the conqueror. But not *only* that. The physical descriptions of Dracula made by the narrators who encounter him constantly stress the ungainly, awkward or otherwise aesthetically unappealing aspects of his appearance. Mina describes his face as "hard" and "cruel," while her descriptions of his "big white teeth" point out the nightmarish prominence of the tools he uses to bleed his victims dry by taking from them what he needs. Jonathan notes the look of hatred that is often scrawled across Dracula's lips and his eyes. And, after feeding, he appears "gorged with blood . . . like a filthy leech, exhausted by his repletion" (p. 59). After taking what he wants from those he regards as his natural inferiors, he appears glutted on what he has stolen in a way that makes him physically repulsive.

He's not just a reflection of a man of the Empire, then, but a reflection with its grotesque nature vividly on display. Dracula acts in a way which is uncomfortably similar to how British people were acting themselves. But while they were busy putting a lovely veneer on their own desires to colonize other countries, drain them of their resources and reshape the identities of their natives, there is no such veneer over this man's own appearance.

Unlike the supposedly gentlemanly British and their supposedly noble plans for other countries, Dracula looks exactly like the monster he is. He is, therefore, more than a reflection. He is what Jung would describe as the Empire's Shadow, revealing the monstrous nature of the Empire so vividly that it becomes impossible for the onlooker to ignore or deny.

So while it's worrying enough that Dracula wants to turn the table on the British by doing on their soil exactly what they're busy doing elsewhere in the world, there's something about him that's likely to be even more horrifying to the colonizers than his plans could be on their own. What's truly horrifying about Dracula is that he *is* the colonizers, but with the pleasant veneer stripped bare. As long as he exists, he highlights to them their true nature, mocking the delusion that their activities could ever be anything other than as monstrous as *he* openly is.

And that is why he must be not only chased out of the country, but completely eradicated. The flight across Europe to bring him down is the ultimate example of wanting to hurt someone who embodies your own most despised qualities—your Shadow.

He's Not Alone

Dracula was far from the only example of a story about a foreign visitor arriving in Britain with the intention of starting a bit of a ruckus. There was quite a flood of these "reverse invasion" stories in the second half of the nineteenth-century, with the typical plot having a monster from one of the colonized countries crossing over to the British heartland and making life hell for the invaders.

Sometimes there's rampaging Egyptian mummies, like in Sir Arthur Conan Doyle's brilliant short-story "Lot No. 249." And published in the very same year as *Dracula* itself was H.G. Wells's *The War of the Worlds*, which shows London destroyed by Martian invaders from a civilization that clearly reckons it's superior to humankind, just like the Brits would have reckoned themselves superior to their colonized subjects. It's almost like there was some recurring concern preying on these Victorian writers' minds. . . . Live according to the logic of the Empire, then die by it too, these stories appear to be warning their British audience.

And considering the inhuman shapes that the invaders usually take in these stories, they might even suggest a collective guilt about the monstrous nature of the Empire's activities—guilt made visible through these writers (whether consciously or subconsciously) creating characters who perform a fantastical version of the stuff Britain was doing abroad, while, like Dracula, being literal monsters. Maybe these authors sensed or even knew the real nature of what their country was getting up to, but could only safely work through their guilty feelings at a fictional distance from the real world. The characters they created and the stories that they told about them would then see these authors making their own versions of the Empire's Shadow Self via their writing, and then destroying them much like Jonathan and his friends destroy Dracula. The value that Jonathan gets from killing Dracula, so too might Stoker himself.

And maybe these stories were so popular with their Victorian readers because they provided them too with a similar sort of satisfaction—the satisfaction that anyone with a problem acknowledging troublesome bits of their personality might get when they see their Shadow Self hurt or even destroyed. Readers got to see the most morally problematic aspects of their political, economic and cultural surroundings brought to life via monstrosities that need to be eradicated. By reading these books, the colonizers watched the staking of their own Shadow Selves with the added convenience of not having to chase them all across Europe first.

And How Does That Make You Feel?

This might even explain why stories like *Dracula* remain so popular today. The legacies of the British Empire ensure that countries created from its collapse, like modern India and Zambia, are still suffering from the after-effects of colonization and the identities Britain forced onto its subjects. The worst effects of the Empire aren't over and done with. And other countries than Britain have much more recently demonstrated a keenness in intervening in affairs abroad, supposedly to help out the people there, but arguably with the main goal of helping themselves to their resources.

Renfield is very fond of telling anyone who'll listen that "the blood is the life." But considering the criticism that's often thrown at our own modern interventions in places like Iraq and Afghanistan, then if Renfield were around today he might talk instead about "the oil" that we're so happy to take advantage of in these lands. Just like the Brits back when *Dracula* was published, maybe we're still in need of an externalized Shadow Self that takes on the more monstrous aspects of our own country's behavior *right now*, so we can avoid owning up to them.

Except that thanks to Jung, we now have a means of understanding and engaging with the Shadow Self that the nineteenth-century did not. Stoker's characters missed the introduction of analytical psychology by a few decades. A much healthier way of dealing with our Shadow Self than hunting it down and staking it comes from learning to recognize the presence of the darker aspects of our own behavior—to admit to them being there and dealing like grown-ups with the difficulties that those dark aspects create, rather than disown them. Imagine Jonathan lying back on a therapist's couch and slowly coming to understand that much of what he hates in Dracula is reflected in his own country's behavior. He might then own up to and shoulder responsibility for the wrongs that Britain inflicted upon the world that *he* like Dracula benefits from!

If we followed such a lead ourselves today, then we might shout a far louder challenge whenever our own nation's foreign policy gets all vampiric.

19
Vampirism and Its Discontents

JANELLE PÖTZSCH

On the face of it, Count Dracula seems a pretty polished person: He speaks several languages, is impressively well educated, and while catering for Jonathan Harker or moving in high society, he displays more than a rudimental knowledge of decorum. Still, calling Dracula civilized or even decent might be a bit bold.

Between keeping people captive, feeding toddlers to creepy vamps, and preying on other people's blood, Dracula isn't doing a good job of being all that decent. But strangely enough, these less than likeable traits of Dracula don't weaken the appeal he has on deluded (and tasty) mortals like us. We are both repelled and captivated (sorry, Jonathan!) by Dracula. His fancy cape might be one explanation for this, but I think key to Dracula's strange attraction is his reckless attitude. It's like with the hip teens at school that did all the stuff you and I didn't have the guts to do. Very much like our childhood bullies, Dracula doesn't give a damn about basic social rules. Put differently, Dracula seems pretty cool because he does what he wants. And he's scary as hell precisely for the same reason.

The fascination we feel about Dracula is an odd mixture of envy and fear. What's more, Dracula reminds us of an aspect of human nature we don't like to be reminded of. I mean, let's be honest about it, there's a little bully in all of us, someone who just waits to play havoc with the other children, as Dracula does with the people in Whitby and London. For that reason, it takes more than the kind of smattering of history and literature Dracula demonstrates in his conversations with Jonathan to deserve the label "civilized."

Learning to keep our internal bully at bay is much more important than such superficial learning, as Austrian psychologist and philosopher Sigmund Freud (1856–1939) noted. Culture, or civilization, is not about talking with a stiff upper lip or reading smart books, but about finding ways to deal with our most basic (and also most powerful) urge: Our inclination to violence. Unlike most of us, Dracula doesn't shy away from living this disposition. He embodies the primitive impulses we as humans still possess, but no longer (well, let's say "seldom") dare to act upon. The unease we feel about Dracula, as well as our crude admiration for him, tells a lot about our relationship to culture—or, more precisely, how awkward this relationship actually is.

Culture Vultures

The starting point of Freud's classic *Civilization and Its Discontents* from 1930 (Yeah, *that's* where I got the title for my chapter from) is a puzzle you might have come across sometimes yourself: Despite technological advances and rising living standards, people still feel dissatisfied with their lives, as if something they need to be happy is being withheld from them. And aren't they right?

True, we do have nice innovations and gadgets like the Internet and cell phones (as well as cell phones with access to the Internet, I mean, wow!) which make our lives much easier and more comfortable (or at least less scary) than they used to be. Thanks to laptops, home office and stuff like this, I can work wherever I want to and don't have to clock in at a special place from nine to five. Also thanks to these latest technologies, as well as to ever faster trains and planes, it's no longer a big deal if your sweetheart or close family members live thousands of miles away from you. We can easily keep in touch via email and Skype, and even (depending on the depth of your purse) regularly meet them in person.

But as always, there's a drawback to everything: If planes wouldn't make traveling so damned easy, I may not have left my family in the first place. And without laptops and an ever faster Internet connection, my boss probably wouldn't expect me to be available 24/7. Our lives may have become more comfy thanks to these innovations, but they are no less complicated.

People in Freud's time felt very much the same way—and even to such an extent that a busybody like Freud bothered to write books about it. What we can gather from this widespread attitude is that technological advances actually have little, if any, effects on human happiness (try to sell that to Tim Cook!). Sure, they do make life more pleasant, but that's basically it. Happiness takes other things. Now, this chapter isn't about telling you to free yourself from the charms of our modern consumer culture in order to achieve some form of satisfaction with your life. This is something Freud couldn't have cared less about.

As a psychologist and social philosopher, he was concerned with the *reasons* for this negative attitude towards culture, not its possible cure. He simply was baffled by the fact that people can become so hostile to something of their own making which has made their lives so much easier. Thanks to culture, we can travel through a neatly paved London (or Vienna, in Freud's case) to our cozy house and shop for dinner while on the way; we don't need to fight our ways through the hinterlands of an underdeveloped Transylvania (unless you're poor Jonathan Harker). Given the immense comfort modern civilization offers, what could be the possible reason for people's frustration with it? Before we go into to that, let's briefly spell out what Freud actually means by "culture."

So You Think You're Doing Great . . .

The term "culture" usually brings to mind things like operas, museums, and other highbrow stuff your parents thought they'd do you a favor with. But culture is actually much more down-to-earth. It's essentially everything which eases our life. One of the characteristics of culture is the invention of tools. Basically everything humans have created served (and does serve) the task of making up for our own shortcomings as regards our physical strength and abilities.

Dr. Seward and Mina Harker wouldn't have to use journals and phonographs if human memory weren't as bad as it is (remember your written tests at school?). Thanks to our inventions, we're able to overcome most of our shortcomings. Don't you feel like a god when you race along in your brand-new sports car? (If you don't have one, just pretend you do). And how must Jonathan Harker and Quincey Morris have felt after they've plunged their knives into Dracula? Powerful? Maybe even invincible? Well, neither you nor they should get carried away by this feeling. For what would they have done if they didn't have their weapons with them? (Jonathan to Quincey: "I thought *you* were going to bring the knives!"). As strong and great as we might feel when supplied with our gadgets, this mood shouldn't blind us to the fact that it's not *we who* are powerful—it's our cool gizmos.

That's why Freud argues that although we might feel like God, none of us is an actual, real God, but only a "prosthetic God" (*Civilization and Its Discontents*, p. 39). We're pretty awesome once (or as long as) we're equipped with our fancy devices. But sadly, these cultural inventions are no genuine part of us: artificial limbs have the nasty habit of *not* growing together with your body, which is why we're so helpless without them. A crucifix for example is a very handy thing when you come to think about it (and you should think about it after you've read Stoker's novel), but if you don't have it with you when Count Dracula's approaching—well, close your eyes and think of England.

So in a nutshell, culture is about making life easy and enjoyable. According to Freud, that's why we have such harsh guidelines when it comes to order and personal cleanliness. From a certain cultural level onwards, we consider some things as just intolerable. Recall how Jonathan recoils from Dracula's bad breath on his first night at his castle. This lack of personal hygiene is somewhat at odds with Dracula's posh appearance, which makes him seem a highly civilized person (at first).

Freud holds that civilization consists in both making up for our bodily limitations as well as leaving behind our animal nature. To achieve this, though, Dracula would need to do a tiny bit more than brush his teeth regularly. This becomes particularly clear when we turn to what Freud believes to be the most important feature of culture: It provides guidelines for our relations with other people.

Might Makes Right

Dracula and his babes give a very good idea of what a community without any binding social rules would be like. Thanks to their superhuman strength, they feel free to treat people as they want to. In other words, theirs is a group where only the rules of the strongest are valid. Everything is subject to their interests and inclinations. If they feel like setting wolves on someone or kidnapping children, they just do it.

According to Freud, the first step to civilization, and to a functioning living together, is when people form a majority which is "stronger than any separate individual and which remains united against all separate individuals" (p. 42). Civilization arises when the power of an individual is replaced by the power of a group. Every member of such a group accepts that its liberties will be limited. This is reciprocal, so that no one has to fear of being cheated. In this regard, culture has a lot to do with common sense: I forego some of my impulses and desires to make sure that you do the same.

Dracula, who is not only physically powerful but who can also command over wolves and rats and God knows what, would simply deride this idea. Why bother about other people? He doesn't need anybody; he doesn't even have a single servant in his whole bloody castle. Freud would probably point out that the advantages of culture would be lost on a person like Dracula. Civilization did arise only after people realized that they *needed* others, and that life could be much easier if they co-operated with each other instead of smashing their heads (or sucking their blood).

Give Me Liberty . . . And Give Me Death

So somewhere at the dawn of time, humanity faced two options: they could continue to lead the life of hermits and sociopaths, who are free to live out just any of their nasty inclinations without ever bothering about another living being. The drawback of this scenario is that all people would very likely behave in much the same way. This makes the other option, the building of rule-following groups so appealing. But as always in life, this choice comes with a downside: Dracula would angrily observe that such an arrangement simply sets too much limits to what he can do. And he's certainly correct. Culture does severely restrict a person's individual freedom. But according to Freud, that's precisely the point.

A person's freedom was indeed boundless before the beginning of culture. You could've behaved more or less like good old Count Dracula. But before complaining about this missed opportunity, just keep in mind that the liberty of everyone else around you was similarly unlimited. This made your total, Dracula-like individual freedom quite an empty promise because you could hardly defend it against all the other little Draculas who were as free as you. As weird as it may sound: life, liberty and the pursuit of happiness can be achieved much easier when people are at least somewhat restrained in how to realize them. Without some rules, all it takes is an assertive ass like the Count to make you wish you've never been born.

Civilization demands people to check their selfishness in order to make life a tiny bit more agreeable for everyone (that's why Arthur Holmwood, Quincey Morris and John Seward follow the rules of courtship instead of just—well, I leave that to your imagination). Essentially, we're asked to give up our impulse to have everything we want and to beat out at those who don't do our bidding (remember Dracula's outburst when his brides tried to have a go at Jonathan?). Freud claims that it's exactly this aspect of culture which makes people so dissatisfied with it. We're unhappy not despite, but *because* of civilization and all the nice accessories it offers. They simply can't make up for the uneasiness which comes with the need to restrain ourselves all the time.

Love Thy What?!

Because of this discomfort we feel in culture, Freud thinks that culture actually runs counter to our nature. The denial culture expects from us covers two essential human instincts. One of them explains why we envy Dracula for going scot-free when entering strange women's boudoirs. Culture has it that we should be a tiny bit more choosy (and constant!) about the people we share our bedroom with, thank you very much. But defining how we're supposed to live our sex lives is just half of the cultural story. Another rather annoying human trait Dracula embodies (and lives out) so nicely is our inclination to violence. It is first and foremost because of this tendency that culture takes great pains to control our sexuality (and if you don't believe me, just shut up and read on, you filthy little . . . see what I mean?).

If it weren't for this, civilization might also work without bothering about what we do to whom in the boudoir. But according to Freud, aggressive behavior is hard-wired into us. This is why our relations with other people are always prone to disaster. As Dracula doesn't content himself with just drinking people's blood (turning them into vampires seems to be much more fun), we don't like the idea of sparing the other person if doing so is not useful for us. Freud maintains that every human feels deeply hostile against all other humans. To get a better idea of just how ingrained that feeling is, he asks us to consider one of the cornerstones of our culture: The good old plea to "love thy neighbor."

Let's play dumb and pretend to hear that demand for the very first time. Freud believes that we'd be flabbergasted by it. Why on Earth should we love just anyone around us? And how is this supposed to be possible? Love is understood as something exceptional, something people have to deserve. That's why Dracula falls for an outstanding woman like Mina or for a hottie like Lucy. Why bother about an ordinary person like Renfield, or about a total stranger from whom I have nothing to expect? (Your mom didn't warn you against strangers because you can expect something nice from them!) Besides, I'm pretty sure the reply of that stranger to this stupid request of "love thy neighbor" would be quite similar to mine.

Freud argues that this distrust we feel towards others touches on something we'd rather ignore: all of us are actually far from being good guys. It's wrong to think of ourselves as gentle, obliging creatures that only defend themselves, but never attack. In case you've ever been looking for an in-yer-face illustration of the famous adage that "man is the wolf to man," here's Freud's view on humans:

> Their neighbor is for them not only a potential helper or sexual object, but also someone who tempts them to satisfy their aggressiveness on him, to exploit his capacity for work without compensation, to use him sexually without his consent, to seize his possessions, to humiliate him, to cause him pain, to torture and to kill him. (p. 58)

So we might think of ourselves as nice guys, but we're actually quite some jerks. We don't socialize to simply enjoy each other's company. What we really strive for is to make others do our bidding—no matter how hard to accept or creepy that might be.

Little Wolves

As Freud's gloomy portray suggests, there's a little Dracula in all of us. That's where culture comes in. According to Freud, culture's request that we shall love our neighbors is justified by its being so contrary to human nature. The demands of civilization are at odds with people's desires, which is why they feel so strange and frustrated. And really, the options we face don't make you cheer: if you live out your inner vampire you have to live with with other people doing the same. The possible result of this decision is very likely a cut, or otherwise injured, throat.

Everyone living out their inner vampire is likely not a freedom we would enjoy, not for very long anyway. Alternatively, you and other people may agree on some basic guidelines to ensure at least some kind of physical integrity. The problem with this choice is that we have to go without fulfilling our most basic urges, which is a bit like forbidding the Count to drink blood.

It's simply impossible for vampires to follow such a ruling. And neither are we as humans able to love our neighbors. But culture demands precisely this from us. And strangely enough, it seems to work. Freud was writing in the 1930s, after thousands of years of human civilization. So, somehow, culture manages our social awkwardness quite nicely. Which might make you wonder: how the hell does it do that? The answer Freud offers touches on the very keystone of his theory. It is also a nice consolation for all those who envy Dracula for being able to change his forms: He may turn himself into a wolf, or a bat. But Freud holds that we humans consist of three different types of personalities. Now who can keep up with that?

Me, Myself, and I

Like a Van Helsing, culture needs to find ways to prevent us (or Dracula) from doing harm. For Van Helsing, crosses, garlic and knives do the job quite well. But culture works in a much more subtle way. Freud explains that civilization functions such that we internalize our aggression. Like Van Helsing and Arthur checking on Lucy's tomb, culture sees to it that we restrain ourselves by appointing a little ...—well, I can find no other word for it than "spy":

> Civilization . . . obtains mastery over the individual's dangerous desire for aggression by weakening and disarming it and by setting up an agency within him to watch over it, like a garrison in a conquered city. (pp. 70–71)

Civilization makes sure that we follow its rules by installing some kind of internal supervisor in us. This inner agency Freud talks about is nothing but the moral demands the group we live in has on us and which we've internalized.

We develop a so-called "super-ego," an inner Van Helsing who tells us what we might and might not do—a conscience, basically. And from what you remember of your good old childhood days, what's the trouble with that thing called "conscience"? It makes you feel bad even in cases when you haven't done a thing (or at least something Mom doesn't yet know about). Other people may think you as a nice person because you don't live out your aggressiveness and hence have never ever done anything "evil". But you might have *thought* about doing so. And you can't hide these thoughts from your inner Van Helsing. Your super-ego knows what you've been pondering, which is why you feel guilty.

Jonathan shows this feeling of guilt when he confides the spine-chilling encounter with the vampire chicks in his diary. He tells that he felt "a wicked, burning desire" to be kissed by them. Something about the blonde was both "thrilling and repulsive." In anticipation of God knows what, Jonathan lay on the couch "in a languorous ecstasy and waited—waited with a beating heart" (Palgrave edition, p. 62). If these aren't the words of someone torn between his own sexual desires and the cultural guidelines on how these desires ought to be dealt with, I don't know what they are.

Freud would point out that Jonathan faces a conflict between his super-ego and his "Id." That's the name tag Freud puts on the least refined part of our mind. "Id" represents our pure, unrefined desires and urges (Just think of a demanding infant and you get a pretty good idea of what this means). But there's still more to human consciousness than the "Id" and the super-ego. I'm talking about a kind of mediating factor, which bears the simple name of "I." Its task is to reconcile the needs of the "Id" with the demands of the super-ego (a bit like a referee between Dracula and Van Helsing). Sadly, this job is no piece of cake, as people's unease with culture makes plain.

Killing Me Softly?

As important as culture is in making our lives more agreeable, Freud thinks that it actually does little for human happiness. We've exchanged happiness for security. But as the behavior of Dracula shows, to refrain from this bargain isn't an option either. Basically, we're in a kind of catch-22 situation: If we wouldn't embark on the path to civilization and the restrictions that entails, we'd be dead sooner than you can say "garlic."

In spite of that, culture can make us experience another, annoyingly slow sort of death. According to Freud, the demands of culture are simply too strict to be followed. Our super-ego doesn't care whether we can fulfill its requests. "Love thy neighbor" isn't so much a friendly advice as more of a cruel denial of human nature. Culture tends to be quite unrealistic when it comes to whether and to what extent we act upon its claims. Because we can't hide our sentiments from our inner Van Helsings, we feel guilty for not living up to the cultural mark. It's this quite constant feeling of guilt which makes us turn hostile against civilization.

What's worse, culture doesn't even *really* succeed in curbing our aggression. Like Dracula, we've learned to smile and bow and be polite, but things can change awfully easy (and quickly) once we're feeling our oats (or a taste for blood). Thousands of years of civilization have had only little if any effect on our true, rather nasty disposition. War and murder are no things of the past: throughout our history, we're accompanied by violence as Dracula is by his boxes of Transylvanian soil.

This explains why we're just so drawn to Dracula. He makes us turn green with envy because he can (and does!) live out just any of his dirty little impulses. Yet, he also makes us aware of the dangers of such behavior. But as Freud pointed out so neatly: at the end of the day, it doesn't really matter whether you behave like a vampire or not—you're screwed both ways.

20
Dracula: The Shadow Archetype

CARI CALLIS

There are far worse things awaiting man than death.

—COUNT DRACULA in the 1931 movie, *Dracula*

There he was—bigger than life—shimmering in black and white on a silver screen in the Paradise Theater Sunday Horror Matinee, Dracula, the mysterious monster able to transform himself into a bat or a wolf and make a woman do anything under his hypnotic gaze—even drink the blood of children. A dangerous man, a man to be feared, he excited something in me that made me shiver with dread but also made me want to bury my head in his cape and let him sink his fangs into my neck. He aroused a tingle in my belly and somewhere else I couldn't quite explain.

The 1931 movie *Dracula*, directed by Tod Browning starring Bela Lugosi, was dated when I watched it in the late 1960s with my teenage cousins who reeked of patchouli and cinnamon gum. We made fun of the fake bat on wires and the cameo appearances in Dracula's castle of the armadillo, opossum, and Jerusalem crickets and the pencil spots directed into Bela Lugosi's eyes to cue the audience that Dracula was using his hypnotic powers. It all seemed better suited to the theater than the big screen. Even so, it was powerful. *He* was powerful.

The 1931 film puts us in the first-person perspective of Dracula, something the novel never does. None of the low budget production values really mattered in my first encounter with Dracula because from the moment he emerged from his coffin onscreen, Dracula drew us in, made us shiver in our red velvet seats and hold onto each other with delicious fear and sexual anxiety. In the 1931 black and white movie, there is no blood or fangs, just the sinister presence of our deepest fears. Yet we learn more about who Dracula really is as a *human*— despite his power to transform his physical body into rats, bats, and wolves, communicate telepathically and effectively hypnotize his prey into submission—than we ever do in the novel.

Shadow of a Dream

Dracula is what Carl Jung (1875–1961), the founder of analytic psychology, would call a Shadow Archetype. Jung was helping his patients to transform their lives from schizophrenia and other mental imbalances. And gradually his ideas about helping patients regain mental health changed the way he looked upon what it meant to experience life as a human. He believed that our dreams revealed the lessons that we ourselves needed to know. He unraveled psychosis by studying the recurring patterns in patient's dreams and helped them to understand the shadows that haunted them from their subconscious.

He defined those recurring characters, whether they were mentors or monsters, by equating them with aspects of the self. As individuals, we all have a multitude of experiences that we draw from and that make us who we are. We interpret our identity by the totality of those experiences and their unique meaning to ourselves. But some of these characters aren't exclusive to us as individuals. There are patterns within all of us that we love and which we tell over and over. They unite and connect us in the shared human experience. Jung called this connection that we all share the *collective unconscious*. And Dracula is definitely a part of this collective unconscious.

First and foremost, Dracula is the perfect challenge for *any* Hero to overcome, because he has the intellect and understanding of humans and the strength and cunning of an animal. And, he has something else—the ability to read our thoughts and know our deepest desires. Dracula is able to make us to do things that our morals would tell us otherwise not to. The story of Dracula and his desire for human blood is the single most often adapted book to date. There are adaptations of Dracula of everything from comic books to television mini-series. The vampire is something we come across in every culture, from Japanese to African. What is it that fuels our desire to create a mythical monster that feeds on the blood of humans? Jung would say that to defeat Dracula means to defeat the darkest parts of the human psyche. Beating Dracula will transform anyone who encounters him.

Jung studied the characters repeating themselves in dreams and stories and figured out that versions of the characteristics or archetypes provide an important way to understanding human consciousness. —And we see nearly all of the archetypes he defined in the story of Dracula but none are so compelling as Dracula himself. When he meets Mina, or Eva, as she is called in the Spanish version, he meets his match. His desire for this woman will become the "eternal" death of him, something we're never quite sure whether he welcomes or not in the movie. Dracula claims outright that "To die, to be really dead, that must be glorious." Seeing Mina shudder, he tells her, "There are far worse things awaiting man than death." Obviously, he has an awareness of death and a desire for the release of what he's doing in a moral sense. To be human and have such possibility to opt out would be better than his present existence.

The Shero's Journey

Mina is the "Hero" or "Shero" of the movie. She undergoes the transition from wanting only to stay in the normal or ordinary world to becoming possessed and obsessed by a romantic stranger, one whom she tells us appears as if in a "dream." At the beginning, Mina tells Lucy after the ballet that she wants only to marry her "normal" boyfriend and to stay in the "ordinary" orbit of John Harker She mocks the dramatic way Dracula speaks but Lucy confesses to Mina that she finds him fascinating. Lucy sees more in Dracula than a stranger with a weird accent. He's the "bad boy," the mysterious "unknown" that she wants to experience.

Lucy's interested in his big castle and the title that goes . along with it. There is no multitude of beaus for Lucy in the film as there are in the novel, for her, there is only that longing for adventure and social rising. A crumbling castle is better than no castle. Mina teases her when she says goodnight and calls her "Countess." Unlike her friend, Mina doesn't want to leave the comfort of what is familiar and *known,* and she likes the ordinariness of Harker and all that being married to him will represent. But she can't refuse the "Call to Adventure" (as Joseph Campbell calls it in *The Hero's Journey*) and she must take her Shero's Journey because to truly know herself she must defeat Dracula. She must confront her fear and come out better for it at the other end.

It's not Harker who is bitten, it's Mina, so he can't be the Hero of this movie the way he shares the hero's journey with Mina in the novel. And it's also Mina, by her ability to read Dracula's mind and reveal his whereabouts in the novel, who enables him to be found and ultimately staked by her men. But in the movie she takes no part in helping to find him or capture him; she's saved by her mentor, Van Helsing. The feminist side of me wants to argue that the film is weaker in its characterization of Mina because Van Helsing and John find and destroy Dracula without her involvement. And it is, after all, a story written and conceived by a male, and Mr. Stoker probably thought he'd gone far enough by Victorian standards. Just think of the raciness of Lucy and her many marriage proposals and the modern ability of Mina to type on that newfangled typewriter and document their story. But my ten-year-old self didn't agree, and still doesn't. Perhaps Mina's intellect includes getting men to do the dirty work of having to actually kill Dracula. And when he we see a part of Mina die as well. And let's face it, there is something to be said for a woman who can keep her hands clean and get men to take care of the messy details of killing a monster.

To fully understand who Dracula is as the shadow archetype to Mina, we need only look to Mina to see how he reveals her deepest darkest places. If John Harker is the "known", Dracula may be what she has not known. And by all accounts, in the beginning of the novel and for the entire movie—Mina is a virgin. No penetration has occurred. Poor John Harker, Dracula gets there first. His penetration of her with his bite provides the same swooning reaction as an orgasm and once penetrated, Mina is enfolded into his dark embrace. As she is enfolded in his cape, the two become one. And like a bad love affair, once bitten, *all* women succumb to the will of Dracula.

In the movie, Dracula doesn't even need to bite but can use his sexual energy and hypnotic power to get women to do his bidding, as the moment with the coat check girl at the beginning of the movie shows us. From the moment we first see Dracula emerge from his coffin back in Transylvania and ascend the stairs from his tomb, it's clear that his beautiful wives, no matter how stunning and seductively dressed, are of no interest for him. He doesn't even look at them. Yet, they follow him, helplessly.

I Am . . . Dracula

Dracula challenges Mina and her commitment to John Harker. She must defeat him or die. Jung's book *Man and His Symbols* makes clear that the appearance of the shadow doesn't just signal the appearance of "difficult and ethical problems." If the "Dreamer" is a man he'll discover a female personification of his unconscious called the *"anima,"* a woman will encounter a symbolic masculine figure called the *"animus"* in her dreams. The woman's animus is shaped by her father who provides "unarguable, incontestably 'true' convictions—convictions that never include the personal reality of the woman herself as she actually is" (p. 199). The shadow shows us parts of ourselves we don't want to admit.

Mina's animus is Dracula. Lured away from her human relationships, Dracula is the romantic fantasy that led Lucy to her destruction and tempts Mina away from the reality of happiness with John Harker into a desire for a dangerous fantasy that can never be. Jung would say that what she dislikes the most in her conscious self could be found in her unconscious self, manifested in the Shadow Archetype, "Dracula." One of her greatest fears must then be the betrayal of both John, her future husband, and of her mentor, Van Helsing, because she does exactly that when she hides her wound from them—the wound that Dracula inflicted upon her.

If Mina was on Jung's couch would he question her virginity after Dracula bites her? If Dracula is the dark reflection of Mina, then what kind of penetration is she hiding? Cinematically, she's in a flowing dress still knotted in a few strategic places for modesty, even after she's been penetrated by his teeth. And when Dracula arrives unexpectedly, she sees nothing else in the room but him and focuses all of her sexual energy upon him. When Van Helsing holds up the mirror from across the room, Dracula can't be seen in the mirror, meaning that he has no self-reflection, only Mina's reflection is there. Jung would say that Dracula is a reflection of Mina, and a manifestation of her psyche.

Once Van Helsing confronts Dracula about not being seen in the mirror, the evil vampire hightails it out of there. Harker looks out the window and sees a "big dog" or a "wolf" running away. Dracula's ability to shapeshift increases the level of fear and suspense: Dracula becomes not only the shadow for Mina but also what Jung calls a Shapeshifter Archetype that the Shero will often encounter on the journey to confuse her. How appropriate then that Dracula reveals himself as a "wolf," which is also a term for a womanizer. He expresses the masculine energy of the animus that will inevitably seduce and lure Mina into danger.

The only way we can bring out the best in Mina is to give her a worthy opponent and to put her in a life and death situation. If the Shadow Archetype represents not only our psychoses but also that which threatens to destroy us, we must wonder what emotion Mina has suppressed so deeply that it has manifested itself as Dracula. The obvious answer is her fear of her own sexuality, her fear of penetration, but perhaps that is too simple.

Dracula is a sexual being who seduced women rather than "attacking" them in the movie. Unlike in the novel, he makes them *want* to succumb to him. He is not the monster of the novel. Instead, he's handsome, upper-class, romantic, and mysterious. So does Mina actually fear her sexuality or does she fear and repress its power? Her gradual change of costume from a rather demure dress at the beginning of the movie to a flowing transparent gown when Dracula carries her into his tomb at the end, reveal that she's turning into one of his "brides."

In the final scene, Mina's dressed identically to what they were wearing when they emerged from their coffin in the beginning of the film. Perhaps Mina is not repressing her sexuality, but avoiding her future role as Harker's wife—the thing she says she desires most. She might simply be trying to avoid the restrictions that come with married life. After all, she's already being given a foretaste of the domesticated life by Seward and Van Helsing when they treat Mina as a child who must be told what to do, sent to her room and protected at all cost.

Crossing the Threshold

The strength of the vampire is that people will not believe in him.

—VAN HELSING

So maybe Mina actually tries to break free from marital slavery when she rushes into Dracula's arms. She disobeys her father and Van Helsing and leaves her room to cross the threshold onto the terrace when she sees Dracula waiting for her in the darkness. Jung might say that her secret desire is to defy them all and do as she pleases. Without hesitating, she walks directly into Dracula's embrace until she literally disappears and becomes one with her "shadow." She's overcome any fear she may have had of it, and she's committed to her journey. This is the beginning of her transformation into her brief life as a vampire.

Dracula Is in the House

In the final confrontation with Dracula, Van Helsing is told that Renfield's bars on his cell have been twisted to allow him to escape yet again. Van Helsing, Seward and Harker conclude from this that Dracula is in the house. As the others run off, Dracula confronts Van Helsing and tells him that he has mingled his blood with Mina's and that she will live for centuries to come. Dracula tries to hypnotize Van Helsing, who takes a few steps toward Dracula but then pauses. Dracula is much more humanized in the film because he interacts with all of the characters in a social environment. By making Mina's shadow more human and vulnerable we can more clearly empathize with her as she struggles with her desire to be with him.

When John goes to see Mina, he finds her physically transformed, and he tells her so. John is easily taken in by her assurance that she's fine and then she lures him out onto the terrace where she's tempted to drink from him. Just when she's about to attack John, Van Helsing rushes in with the crucifix and saves Harker. And Mina passes the final test of

her journey when she suddenly confesses that everything Van
Helsing said is true. She again sacrifices herself and her
desire to drink from John because love allows her to overcome
her desire for Dracula.

Dracula Strikes Again

Despite all their precautions, Dracula leads Mina from her bed
and takes her deep underground into the catacombs where his
coffin is hidden. As she descends the stairs, now dressed almost
the same as Dracula's brides, he follows behind her. She sleep-
walks, wearing the same expression as Dracula's unhappy
wives did earlier. As Van Helsing and Harker struggle to find
her in this inmost cave, this land of the dead and the undead,
they at last find the coffin where they will confront Dracula.
But when they find the Count, Mina is not with him.

As Van Helsing "stakes" Dracula and we hear his groans, we
cut to Mina who reacts as if she herself is being staked. The
audience is held in suspense as they wonder whether or not she
will survive the death of Dracula. Each blow of the stake
demonstrates that they are one and that her life without him
won't be the same. As Dracula dies, so does a part of Mina. And
which part might that be?

Jung would say that in this resolution and the final stage of
her journey, Mina undergoes a "resurrection" when she comes
to her senses after the death of Dracula and realizes the spell
she has been under. Her shadow has been brought into the
light. In the final scene, as she is reunited with John, she has
defeated death and her reward is to be with the man she had
wanted right from the beginning. And the final shot is Mina
and John ascending the staircase together with chapel bells
ringing, signaling their union and inevitable nuptials. As they
rise up from the catacombs and out of the darkness, Mina has
faced her shadow of her fear of being wedded for life. Her
dreams of freedom are dead, along with the dark shadow of
Dracula. She has defeated her greatest fear.

As a girl I sat listening to those chapel bells ringing for the
first time and even after the credits began to roll, I wondered,
as I still do, whether, given the knowledge that she returned
with, being bound in wedlock for the rest of her ordinary life
with Harker, was really a happy ending. As she walks down the

aisle, her expression is not one of joy, but of resignation. Mina may have confronted the deepest aspects of herself and brought them into the light, and this certainly would have pleased Carl Jung.

Mina faced her animus in the form of Dracula who tempted her away from her relationship with a "real man." And Jung would envision a happy ending for Mina, who faced this reality instead of remaining possessed by Dracula who may now be turned into an "inner companion who endows her with the masculine qualities of initiative, courage, objectivity, and spiritual wisdom" (*Man and His Symbols*, p. 208).

But back in the dark Paradise Theater as the credits rolled and the lights came up and my cousins stubbed out the cigarettes they'd smuggled in, I wondered whether Mina might not have been better off with her secret shadow, living out the centuries single and free to do as she pleased. It's surely worth fighting our shadows to learn more about ourselves, but maybe we shouldn't just forsake them after we're done.

V

From the
Dracula Files

21

Memoirs of the Prince of the Undead

JOHN V. KARAVITIS

Bram Stoker's *Dracula* is the Gothic horror novel that breathed life into the legend of the vampire, and it has given birth to countless retellings, adaptations, and interpretations. It presents the battle for survival and dominance between Count Dracula and a small group that, considering him a threat to all that is good in life, seeks his destruction. The novel itself is unique in that it is written as a series of diary entries, letters, and news articles, thus offering multiple perspectives. But still, there's one glaring omission in Stoker's novel: we never get Dracula's side of the story. Although the reader is presented with Dracula's actions and speech, this is always from the point of view of those who seek his destruction. That's a one-sided view of events, and I don't think that's trustworthy. I wouldn't trust anyone's adversaries to accurately present their opponent's side of the story or even just a balanced recitation of events.

I think that if we had some sort of access to Dracula's side of the story, I'm sure we'd be surprised at how much it would differ from what we've read in Stoker's novel. Maybe Dracula wasn't the evil monster that Van Helsing and others made him out to be. It could be that Dracula was just trying to live his life on his own terms, pursuing his own rational self-interest. Maybe he just didn't want to bow down to society's arbitrary rules. It does strike me as peculiar that, with all that he claimed about how evil Dracula was, that Van Helsing didn't just go straight to the authorities. I really believe that we'd have a clearer picture of what happened if we had Dracula's side of the story. I'm sure we'd be able to make a more informed decision about the events of 1893 if Dracula himself had kept a diary . . .

February 7, 2014—Email, John V. Karavitis to Editor Nicolas Michaud

Mr. Michaud:

Hello. My name is John Karavitis, and I am writing to you about an item that I recently had the good fortune to acquire at an estate sale in Washington, DC. It appears to be a diary, written in meticulous English longhand, by a gentleman whom I will only refer to at the present time as being of ancient Eastern European nobility. I am contacting you directly as the diary in question appears to involve two contrasting philosophical positions that readers of books in the "Popular Culture and Philosophy" genre might enjoy reading about, if they were properly presented. The manuscript appears to contrast the idea of happiness as the pursuit of one's rational self-interest against the mindless conformity of the collective. It's not as simple as "good versus evil," but it does appear to contrast the individual against the collective. Sort of like Ayn Rand squaring off against Karl Marx.

Your reputation as someone who is not unwilling to take chances on novel ideas and unproven authors has led me to contact you directly. Do you feel that this might be something that you or Open Court would be interested in?

February 14, 2014—Email, Nicolas Michaud to John V. Karavitis

Mr. Karavitis:

Thank you for reaching out to me. Unfortunately, I feel that your proposal is too far outside the Popular Culture and Philosophy genre for me to consider pursuing it. I'm sure you will find someone else, or you could self-publish on the Web.

February 17, 2014—Cutting from *The Washington Standard*

In what can only be described as a curious coincidence, the Washington DC Police Department released a report of a second woman having been found unconscious in the vicinity of the city's nightlife scene near Dupont Circle within as many weeks. The young woman was found slumped at the edge of the Dupont Circle Fountain, with a small wound on the left side of her neck. This incident matches an earlier one that occurred two weeks ago, however, police have declined to comment on the possibility that these two incidents are related . . .

February 17, 2014—Email, John V. Karavitis to Nicolas Michaud

Mr. Michaud:

The diary's contents allege its author to be Count Dracula, the same Prince of Darkness from Bram Stoker's novel. Apparently, Stoker's "novel" was more fact than fiction.
    Still not interested?

February 19, 2014—Email, Nicolas Michaud to John V. Karavitis

Mr. Karavitis:

Although I really think you've been the victim of a cruel hoax, and have parted with your hard-earned money unnecessarily, I am willing to oblige you.
    Please scan a few pages of this alleged diary in pdf format and send them to me via email. I'll get back to you as soon as I can, but I really am quite busy at the present time.

Dracula's Journal

1st May, 1893. Castle Dracula.—I am finally embarking on a new adventure in my long and lonely life. And a very long life it has been. From a nobleman who led armies into fiercest battle and defended both Europe and Christendom from the peril of the Turk, to my now solitary existence high in the stunning yet claustropho-bic mountains of Carpathia, I yearn for a change. It's time for a new chapter in my life; and, in keeping with the latest fashion, I have decided to chronicle my new adventure with this journal—a "diary," as the English call it.

A diary! How many such volumes would I have writ-ten had I done this from the very beginning! Suffice it to say, I am weary of this solitary existence. Who would have thought that discovering the secret of immortality would come with a burden all its own? And for a price that seemed so trifling at the time. Enough. I want to breathe fresh air, and to walk among people who are not afraid of new things, who are not afraid of tomorrow and what it may bring. To find myself among people who walk with vigor and look forward to the future. I am back again in pursuit of that ever-so-elusive quarry—my own happiness. My happiness is the focus, the purpose, of my never-ending life. I have plans . . .

I have looked toward this era's empire builders, the British, and have become enamored of and intrigued with their capital city, London. London! An ancient city, older than I myself, but now growing, re-born, re-vital-ized, and full of fresh, vibrant blood. Blood! For the blood is the life, and new blood, new *life*, is what I crave and seek. To discover new life, new opportunities, new expe-riences, new adventures, perhaps, even, new love! Yes! To dream, and to dare!

I have been corresponding with solicitors in London in order to acquire property which will ensure that I will have a firm base of operations from which I can strike out into that brave new world. Look at me! Always think-ing in military terms! The curse of the nobility! But in this brave new world, I do not intend on destroying, as I have had to do in the past. Rather, I shall build; I shall create; I SHALL ACHIEVE! I SHALL CONQUER! Soon, I expect the arrival of a solicitor from that ancient-yet-reborn city. Upon the arrival of this solicitor, with his assistance, I will review all the necessary deeds and legal documents. I will also have a chance to practice my com-mand of the English language. I do not wish to speak with so heavy a foreign accent that I repulse anyone by being "too" different. For this, I am sure I can impose upon the good graces of this solicitor to stay a while here at the castle, as my guest, of course. I have been assured by his employer that he has been instructed to be co-operative . . .

February 20, 2014—Cutting from *The Washington Standard*

The Washington, DC Police Department has announced that a third woman was discovered late last night, her throat completely torn open, as if by some savage animal. A taxi driver who was in the area claims that he saw a tall, slender, pale man walking with the woman in question shortly after midnight. Police stress that there is no immediate danger to citizens or tourists, although this reporter has spoken with area residents, who appear to be on edge . . .

Dracula's Journal

30th June, 1893. Castle Dracula.—It is done. All the preparations that I have made are being executed to plan. My planning has been as meticulous as my drive to succeed has been resolute. I am the author of my own reality. Would one expect any less from him who struck fear and terror into the minds and hearts of the Turks? My life is a work of art, as this diary shall itself become.

I must say that I am in no small way disappointed in the demeanor and behavior of the solicitor sent from London, a Mr. Jonathan Harker. Altogether too coarse, and somewhat discourteous. Too "green," I believe the word is. I have the distinct impression that he does not particularly care for me, indeed, that he fears me and staying at the castle! I pride myself on being a most gracious and courteous host. I cannot fathom his attitude. I have also been concerned about his state of mind. At times I found him wandering the halls of the castle, talking to himself, apparently oblivious of his surroundings.

Fearing that he would inadvertently come to harm, I forbade him to leave the grounds unescorted, and most definitely never at night, when the wolves were out in force. I hope that the English are not all so . . . strange!

Dracula's Journal

8th August, 1893. Whitby, England.—I have arrived. The trip by sea was tiresome, and not for a moment did it let me forget why I despise crossing open water. A man should be able to trust in the solid ground beneath his feet!

The ship was the *Demeter*, and it sailed under the flag of the noble Russian emperor Alexander III. After landing, I left the ship, knowing that my boxes of earth would be secured and forwarded to my new properties. And already, I feel as though fortune has smiled upon me, for I have met a most amazing young English lady. Her name is Lucy . . .

Dracula's Journal

20th September, 1893. Whitby, England.—It is done. I have finally brought young Lucy Westenra over. It is not an easy thing. The process can leave the neophyte disoriented and confused, and the master on the brink of exhaustion. But now I have someone here in England who is just like me, and with whom I can share my boundless life. Her family and close friends tried to interfere with my plans, but, to no avail. I am nothing if not persistent. Besides, young Lucy came to me of her own free will. Who were they to interfere? And this Van Helsing that they have brought into the picture. Who does he think he is? What business of his are my affairs? Neither he nor anyone else has the right to interfere with my life, my goals, and my plans. I owe no one anything. I shall pursue my own self-interest, no matter that others may disapprove. What do I care what other people think? Insufferable fools! My happiness is the purpose of my life, and my standards its moral code. What I earn by my efforts and my intelligence are my own, not for any-one to lay claim to. If Van Helsing wants to compete with me, I am ready for the challenge. But I refuse to let him, or anyone else, dictate the terms of my life!

Dracula's Journal

29th September, 1893. Whitby, England.—I write this entry with blood from my own veins! She is gone! Truly gone! This madman Van Helsing has convinced Lucy's former suitors, who once professed their love and admiration of her in volumes, that she had to be destroyed! For all the love that they proclaimed for her, they went and became willing accomplices in her mur-der. For murder it was! Foul, villainous murder of a defenseless young woman!

Unbeknownst to them, I caught sight of their move-ments as they skulked around the cemetery after hours. I saw how furtively they looked around and at each other as they progressed to their final destination. I was too unsure of their designs, however, and too far away to act once I had discerned them. I am in agony! Why was young Lucy destroyed? Why could I not have saved her? I am wracking my brains over this, and over the interference orchestrated by this monster Van Helsing. Did they object because I am a foreigner? Or was it my age difference with young Lucy? And if either I or young Lucy were in the wrong, for anything, why did they not involve the authorities? That they did not do so is proof enough that they acted as the craven scoundrels that they are. They skulked around the cemetery grounds, after hours, like ghouls! Foul, insolent villain Van Helsing! Oh, my dear, sweet Lucy! That I may avenge you!

February 24, 2014— Cutting from *The Washington Standard*

The Police Department has confirmed a fourth attack of a young woman in the Dupont Circle area, with wounds on her throat. In response to a call from the mayor for action, the police have created an official task force to investigate these incidents; but beyond that there is no official comment. However, sources within the police department have confirmed to this reporter that DC residents have expressed grave concern regarding their safety after daylight hours . . .

February 24, 2014—Popularcultureandphilosophy.com Call for Abstracts

Dracula and Philosophy CFA is here! Abstracts and subsequent essays *must* be accessible to a lay audience as well as philosophically substantial. All writing should be engaging and directly relevant to the original *Dracula* book, films, comics, or the TV series.

Kindly submit abstract (with or without Word attachment) and CV by email to: Nicolas Michaud . . .

Dracula's Journal

2nd October, 1893. Carfax, England.—My plans for revenge have been discovered. In my mad grief, I hatched a scheme to get back at Van Helsing and his group by visiting the woman who is now married to that bumbling idiot, Jonathan Harker! What a small world indeed this is, for me to have fallen in love with the best friend of that idiot's fiancée, now his wife. Regardless, it made for an apropos revenge, to visit Mrs. Harker and begin to convert her, with Van Helsing and his group being as powerless to stop me as I was to stop them from murdering young Lucy!

I have done no wrong in pursuing this act of revenge. This craven collective has sought to use blind force against me and my plans for a new life! To retaliate in kind is appropriate. I, having never done them any harm, nor ever having intended to, now do unto them as they have done to me.

Before visiting Mrs. Harker, I paid a visit to Renfield, in order to tie up what had become a loose end. A very loose end indeed. I also paid a visit to Dr. Seward's study. There, to my great amusement, I came across the journals of these meddling fools, and read some of their hysterical entries. Mawkish self-centered pabulum! Emotional drivel! Misplaced faith in their own righteousness, that they can determine the fate of someone like me! *Folie à plusieurs*! They refuse to believe their own eyes when it comes to *objective* reality. They prefer to rely on emotions and faith, "faith" in their feelings, and in their quixotic cause! Absurd! Subjective feelings cannot be a source of knowledge about the world! Would I, who have spanned the centuries, and fought innumerable battles, and eagerly took men to their deaths, not know this to be a fact of the real world? Reality is *objective!* If only they had seen what I have seen, with my own eyes! In disgust, I condemned all of their dim-witted scribblings to the fire.

More and more, I am finding that the English are as strange a people as I had feared! Not at all the forward-thinking people that I had imagined them to be. They openly pride themselves on their mighty empire, built upon capitalist ideals, and on the right of the individual to pursue his own self-interest! Rather, in their own way, they are as backward and superstitious as the peasantry back home.

I have also heard that inquiries have been made regarding my various properties throughout England. I can only presume that Van Helsing is pursuing his futile quest against me. I need to think . . .

Dracula's Journal

3rd October, 1893. Whitby, England.—It is over. England is no place for the new life that I desired. Today I discovered Van Helsing and his group at my property on Fenchurch Street in Piccadilly. They almost succeeded in killing me! Blind, foolish children! I later discovered that they had visited my properties in Carfax, Walworth, Mile End New Town, and Bermondsey. All but one of my boxes of earth have been made useless. What luck that I had made provisions to scatter my fifty boxes of earth around England! I am now left with only a single box to provide me refuge during the day, as needed. With such meager resources left to me, my plans are unsustainable. I cannot pursue my interests in this land. I am forced to withdraw from England as quickly as possible.

Van Helsing's interference in my affairs has been nothing short of maddening! Why is he doing this? What does he mean to gain? And again, his actions were clearly illegal. One of his group pretended to own my property on Fenchurch Street, and induced a locksmith to gain them access. Why the deceit and subterfuge? If I had done wrong, why not involve the authorities? Certainly I cannot, as they may just be the embodiment of their misguided society! Van Helsing and his group have acted as criminals, for criminals they are. They seek to thwart my plans and efforts, and to destroy me, if for no other reason than that they cannot stand anyone who does not fall into line with their proletarian beliefs. They have used deception and blind force to thwart my plans, indeed, to challenge my very existence! Do I alone have the free will to think for myself, for my own benefit? I exercise my free will, and I think. I accept and live in a world of *objective* reality, not subjective delusions and emotions. Why do they not do so for themselves? To remain alive, I MUST think! My mind is the only tool I really have for my survival, and use it I shall!

This craven collective of barbarians has been spouting the same sort of nonsense in their journals as I once read in a pamphlet a few years ago, while I was visiting the City of Lights. *"From each according to his ability, to each according to his needs."* Such outrageous drivel! And then what incentive to work and achieve would there be? This same kind of defective reasoning that the collective herd must believe in and espouse, which keeps them warm at night and assuages their collective guilt, places the burden on that one percent of us who think and act to make the future a better place! Are we to bend to their will?

Insufferable insolence! I, who commanded armies, and made Europe safe for Christendom, who scourged the Turk and laughed at them, will not be brought to heel by these cowards! My happiness is my own to make, and I craft it by pursuing my own rational self-interests. I believed that London, the capital of the mighty British Empire, would have been fertile ground for new opportunities and adventure. I can see now that I was wrong. They are in their own way still mired in the same superstitious mindset that the peasantry back home is, that the people whom I fought for centuries ago against the Turks were themselves mired in.

I will leave London, leave this constant interference, this collective herd mentality, and go home. There is no new blood here. No chance at a new life.

February 28th, 2014—Email, John V. Karavitis to Nicolas Michaud

Mr. Michaud:

It's been some time since I emailed you sections of Dracula's diary. Any comments?

P.S. I've noticed that you've put a call out for abstracts for a new entry in Open Court's Popular Culture and Philosophy series—*Dracula and Philosophy*. I hope that means good news!

Dracula's Journal—Three Years Later

31st October, 1897. Castle Dracula.—I sit here in front of a raging fire in my castle. I've been staring at my diary, unsure if I want to write . . . to continue with such nonsense as keeping a diary. When I first began to write, I saw it as being a work of art, a record and reflection of the high standards that I set for my life. Now . . .

But write I shall, if only this one last entry.

As one would readily surmise by having read this journal—if anyone else could ever read this journal!—I did not, as Bram Stoker put it, perish at the hands of Van Helsing's merry band of cowardly vermin four years ago.

Far from it. Do you really think that I, Vlad III, Prince of Wallachia, the Son of the Dragon—Vlad Dracula!—could have been so easily tracked, cornered, and dispatched? I, who led armies of warriors against the Turks, who saved Europe and Christendom for the ages, who casually impaled thousands on a whim, and dipped bread into bowls of their still-warm blood? I, who have lived through the centuries, and struck fear and terror in the hearts of my enemies? Do you really think that such a person would have the faculties of "a child," as Van Helsing so casually put it? That such a person as I could not outwit a superstitious, half-witted, bumbling old fool like Van Helsing?

I have a fundamental right to life, to live my own life as I see fit. I am responsible for my own happiness! To pursue my own happiness as I see fit, and the world be damned! I use my reason to understand the world, and I choose which values to defend with *my* virtues. It was my ability to reason that triumphed over the writhing, chaotic spasms of that imbecile Van Helsing's servitude to emotion and superstition. Clearly, it was Van Helsing, seeking to deny me the right to pursue my own happiness, who was truly evil.

Having placed Mina Harker under my control, I used that to my advantage, steering Van Helsing and his group astray at every step. *I make no apologies for having done so. They drew first blood!* They never did find me, nor would I ever have permitted it. But I did not think that the story of my misadventure in England would have been fictionalized by anyone. And the "happy ending," as it could be called by those insolent fools, was a complete and utter lie. I live, and I always shall live.

Perhaps I was indeed wrong in choosing England. As fervently as the English deny it, England is still so much a part of Europe, of the "old" world, that it could not possibly have provided new, fertile soil for my plans. No new blood. Perhaps . . . America holds the promise and opportunity that I seek. Perhaps America will give me the chance for new blood . . . for new life. Even, yes, for new love. Oh, Lucy . . . how I do miss you!

February 28th, 2014—Email, Nicolas Michaud to John V. Karavitis

Mr. Karavitis:

I've had a chance to look over the diary pages that you've emailed me. I must say, I can't believe that something so sophomoric could have ever been considered to have been an authentic diary from the end of the nineteenth century. I will say, though, that this has given me an idea for your entry in *Dracula and Philosophy*. I suggest that you write a chapter that shows how easily Ayn Rand's (1905–1982) work can be used to justify outlandish ideas. In other words, that when reading her work we realize her ideas—that everyone should be in it just for themselves—could be used to cast someone as villainous as Dracula in a good light. Her rejection of Karl Marx (1818–1883), and his idea that everyone should have equal access to the goods and services of society, regardless of their effort, seems reasonable until you realize that the extreme other end of her ideas justify profoundly selfish actions. In fact, her book could be considered a "manual for vampires"—justifying why you should take what you can, regardless of the impact on others.

I suppose you could take it in the other direction, if you wanted to, and your chapter could be read as a kind of "Randian" justification for why Dracula wasn't such a bad guy, and the rest of us are just keeping him down. You could leave it to the reader to decide, I suppose . . .

Dracula's Journal—Present Day

March 1st, 2014. Washington, DC—I was recently possessed by the idea that, after more than a century of people believing Bram Stoker's lies, after decades of being mercilessly mocked and pilloried in movies too numerous to mention, that it was well past the time for me to make an attempt to have my side of the story—that is, the *objective* truth—told. Of what really happened in England all those years ago. Unfortunately, it appears as though my story has fallen on deaf ears.

How can anyone doubt that I exist? If any single fact in this world can be self-evident, it is this: *I exist*. Those who have challenged me learned this the hard way, and fell before my will. They would indeed attest to this fact of *objective* reality, were they not at this very moment roasting in the fires of the damned.

I, of course, do not accept failure. I have *never* accepted failure. My will be done! Perhaps I can be more persuasive . . . in person.

I shall always prevail. I—AM—DRACULA!

22

Correspondences between the Count and the Stranger

MARY GREEN AND RONALD S. GREEN

Jonathan Harker's Journal

I have finally taken this collection of letters and diary entries from my vault so that whosoever dares might examine them. I could hardly ask anyone, even if I so wished, to accept them as proofs of the heretical exchange they document. These correspondences between the malevolent Count and a "Monsieur Meursault" reveal much more than the casual eye might perceive.

In particular, Meursault's letters express the conviction that any effort by *any* person to find meaning in life or death is ultimately doomed to failure. It is left to the reader to decide if this view is in line with the horrid life of the Count, as Meursault expresses. But if such is found to be true, may God show us all his mercy. For this suggests there may be a new Nosferatu amongst us even now, an archfiend who once again threatens to suck the founding beliefs from the heart of genteel society. I have collected the letters here, as well as two others that seem relevant, and, yet, they seem to make no sense . . . Perhaps a wiser man than I can decipher their meaning.

Letter, Count Dracula to M. Meursault

Monsieur Meursault,

I am writing as you come recommended to me personally by my long-standing attendant, R.M. Renfield. At my request, he researched the best shipping firms for my unique needs and interviewed proprietors accordingly. You see, I intend to purchase a home on the Mediterranean and must make firm arrangements to ship fifty important boxes with cargo that is dear to me. Mister Renfield has discovered that your company so routinely ships such goods that there is always a stack of freight invoices on your desk. Upon further interview, your boss insisted that I write to you directly as you are in a particular position to address certain fears I have, not only about the shipment but also concerning the details of my upcoming relocation. Your superior also guaranteed that you are extremely neutral in business affairs and indeed in all matters. With his assurance and recommendation, I will rely on you wholly without dread of betrayal of my endeavors to any living soul.

Although I have read much on the subject of French culture, I am certain that it is not enough for me to fit in seamlessly so that no one should suspect in any way that I am a foreigner. To do so, I realize that I must not only perfect my ability to exhibit the intricacies of your language, but also to inhale the charming aroma of your philosophy. Normally, I would insist that you vacation in my castle while this is to be accomplished, entirely at my expense, of course. However, such arrangements fell into corruption the last time I made them for purchasing a new home in a foreign land. Therefore, I ask this time that you will not disdain to honor my request to exchange a few correspondences. Please, be my friend and I will welcome you into my new home soon enough.

Forgive me for being forward under the assumption that you will not find this request absurd but will be agreeable to be in my service, since it is the duty of your employment. I am particularly interested in learning from you the thoughts and feelings of your people. Specifically, if it is not an inconvenience, I would like to know your beliefs about God or gods, your ideas about patriotism and society, and yes, your very feelings about love. I know these questions are horribly personal and I apologize, since we are strangers. But perhaps it is our mutual estrangement that will allow you to indulge me in this.

Truly your friend,

Dracula

Letter, M. Meursault to Count Dracula

Count Dracula,

I have no objection to being your friend, for the question of friendship means nothing. I should inform you now, since you are thinking of moving to the Mediterranean, that the weather is sometimes quite unbearably hot. The sky is often a blaze of light and the sun feels like it is beating down on your head. I suppose it is as good as it would be anywhere else though, such as Paris, where I used to live. Paris is a dingy sort of town, to my mind, masses of pigeons and dark courtyards. And the people have washed-out white faces (*The Stranger*, p. 54). As to the question of how to blend in with the people, since you asked, I guess what you should do is just nod your head at them. Personally, I find it easiest to not say anything at all, for usually I have nothing to say. I don't think it matters either way. As for one's identity as a stranger or an insider, I'm not really sure what to say for that as well. I don't think about it. I guess when I look in the mirror, I don't see anything.

As for my religion, of course I have wished there were an afterlife. Everybody has that wish at times. But such a yearning has no more importance than wishing to be rich, or to swim very fast, or to have a better-shaped mouth. It was in the same order of things (p. 150). I have grown tired of searching for meaning in this meaningless world, though I'm not sure I can help it. I know life is all-empty, devoid of meaning, yet still I try to understand it in those terms. So, it boils down to life just being one long task, unlikely to produce any pay-off of any kind. I think this would be the sentiment of all people, if they thought rationally enough. But I don't really know. It doesn't seem to matter either way and it certainly does not to me.

Love is just as frivolous. I am now engaged to be married to one Marie Cardona. Though I had no inclination either way, she asked if I would marry her and I told her I wouldn't mind. Pressing me further, she asked if I loved her. As with the matter of friendship, I told her that the question meant nothing, but that I supposed I didn't. I only agreed to marry her to please her. When she remarked that marriage was a serious matter, I answered with "No." She said she wondered if she really loved me or not. I, of course, couldn't enlighten her as to that. So I must give the same sort of answer to you, and tell you that I cannot enlighten you on matters of love either.

As to shipping your cartons, I'm sure this company can handle it about as well as can be expected.

Meursault

Letter, Count Dracula to M. Meursault

Monsieur Meursault,

Thank you for your admonition about the heat on the Mediterranean. I too have a bit of an aversion to direct sunlight. As for the situation you mention concerning the mirror, my friend, I find in it a quandary as well. But which of our situations is the most wretched: looking in the mirror and seeing no body or seeing there a physical presence void of purpose? For when you related to me your dispassion for your existence I thought, "Ah, sir, you dwellers in the city cannot enter into the feelings of the hunter" (*Dracula*, Chapter 2). Like you, I too have been indicted for being incapable of love. But unlike you, I do love, perhaps too strongly for the tastes of some. For this, it is no exaggeration to say, I have induced horror in genteel society for ages.

Indeed I feel your outlook on life is grim and bleak, which carries much sentiment when scripted by these hands. But I wonder if yours is not the understandable perspective of one who has suffered defeat in war. I myself, being the conqueror and victor time and again, live by a different set of metaphors. My soil has been fertilized by the decayed corpses of the Maygar, the Lombard, The Avar, the Bulgar, and the Turk, all of whom received the bloody sword upon trying to invade. Fools, fools! Of old, my countrymen and women, the aged and children too, waited on cliff tops for foreign trespassers, sending an avalanche of rocks down to crush their bones to earth. Had any been left to search for fallen allies, none could be found, so completely had their bodies merged with the soil. When I think of the blood of many brave races, who fought as lions fight, flowing through myself, my veins throb, knowing no limits, as if it will forever keep me alive. But forgive me, I sometimes become most invigorated when thinking of this.

I thank you for your advice about fitting into your society by nodding and saying nothing. I have a friend, however, about whom I ask your counsel as to how he should behave when visiting your country. My friend, it has been said, is as strong as twenty men. He is more cunning than an ordinary mortal, for his intellect has grown with the ages. He is called a brute and more than a brute; he is said to be a devil in his callousness. Such is the potency of his will that he can direct the elements, the storm, the fog, and the thunder. He can also command rats, owls, bats, and wolfs. I have also heard it said, "He can do all these things, yet he is not free. Nay, he is even more prisoner than the slave of the galley, than the madman in his cell. He cannot go where he likes, he who is not of nature has yet to obey some of nature's laws, why we know not. He may not enter anywhere at the first, unless there be some one of the household who bid him to come, though afterwards he can come as he pleases. His power ceases, as does that of all evil things, at the coming of the day" (Chapter 18). If even a portion of these things were true, what should my friend do to pass yet unnoticed in your land? It is his curse that he must continue to strive each night to survive being utterly different from his fellow beings, a most ghastly fate.

Very affably yours,

Dracula

Letter, M. Meursault to Count Dracula

Count Dracula,

I have experienced a great change in myself since I last wrote, although no one else is likely to see it. Do you know I actually yelled at the chaplain today in cries of anger and cries of joy for his certainties that are not worth as much as a one hair on a woman's head?

I am presently writing you from my cell in the county jail. I have been sentenced to death in a trial that was more about judging my character in the eyes of social expectations, that is, parading my unwillingness to pretend I felt things in the way the world deems fit, than it was about the murder I carelessly committed. I suspect you can relate to this in some way. Do not think my situation is so grisly, however, for as I was being questioned during the trial, I came to think about the human condition. Then, at dawn, as the time of execution drew nearer, I had my life-changing revelation and at that moment transitioned from a life of indifference to one of acceptance. I realize in saying this that it must seem to you a fine distinction, but I assure you it is a monumental one that you of all people might appreciate. That's why I have taken a moment of my last of such, now freed from the drudge of workdays and my related obligations to you, to write this fragment of explanation.

When you described the situation of your "friend" in your last letter, I surmised that you were likely speaking of yourself. If so, your words tell of an understanding that the great tasks fate has placed in your charge, are in fact rationally impossible. That is, you know that you cannot continue to uphold your hereditary position as a noble boyar indefinitely, for the time of feudalism has passed to modernity, which has usurped the values you hold dear. Foremost, the nightly struggle you narrated, which is no less than an effort for immortality, is doomed to failure. At the same time, by your own admission, you are bound to the fate like, as you say, a prisoner.

Let me interject something of my revelation here. Although your situation is as grand as that of any absurd hero (and please trust this is my highest compliment as I will explain below), it is also emblematic of the wider human condition. By this I mean that all people have only one meaningful decision to make in life, regardless of status or epoch, that is, whether to commit suicide or not. If the person chooses to not commit suicide, then he or she has chosen to live a meaningless life and is responsible for the consequences of that decision. This part of my revelation is fairly easy to see. However, you are in a particular position to appreciate the weight of the second part of my equation fully. That is, all absolutes are rationally impossible, yet people continue to believe in them in their longing for meaning. This irrationality may be called faith, "To believe in things that you cannot." I heard once of an American who so defined faith, "that faculty which enables us to believe things which we know to be untrue" (*Dracula*, Chapter 14). All of those absolute matters held before us, God, love, immortality, are all impossible or at least impossible to know, yet we continue to live as if they were possible.

In this, life is absurd and you are a remarkably absurd hero who exemplifies for the rest of humanity, the only way we can find a little piece of freedom: by accepting the absurdity of the human condition and choosing to live with it rather than commit suicide. We're all elected by the same fate, death, and everyone is equally privileged in this with the ability to accept the condition as it is or not. The realization of this reality is why I have moved from indifference to acceptance, why I have yelled at the chaplain rather than remained apathetic as before. Now there remains for me the further hope that on the day of my execution there should be a huge crowd of spectators and that they should greet me with howls of execration (*The Stranger*, p. 154). That would be a grand confirmation that I did not live by their absolutes but continued to speak only the truth to the end of my days.

In closing, as I march with readiness toward execution, I congratulate you on achieving the status of the legendary absurd heroes, joining the ranks of those other giants of literature: Don Juan, Don Quixote, and Sisyphus. Like you, the last was considered the wisest among us, the one who put Death in chains. Perhaps also like you, all absurd heroes share three traits: they reject suicide as an option, they reject help from a higher power, whether one exists or not, and they accept life as despairingly absurd.

Yours even in death,

Meursault

Letter, Count Dracula to M. Meursault

Monsieur Meursault,

I hope this letter reaches you before your untimely demise. I find it a desecration that healthy blood must be shed in such a wasteful way.

Allow me to express my gratitude to you, though admittedly mixed, for your charitable evaluation of me as one of your heroes along the lines of Don Juan, Don Quixote, and the Sisyphus fellow. You have correctly surmised that I was referring to myself when previously writing of "a friend." It is also true as you say that I share with your heroes two of the three major traits you suggest of the absurd creature: the rejection of suicide as an option and the rejection of help from a higher power. But the third trait, acceptance of life as despairingly absurd, I categorically reject.

Forgive me, my friend, but your philosophy of the absurd rings to the points of my ears as the words of a desperate man knowing he is at the end of his days, hoping to convince himself that in the life he has squandered by being barren of both love and hatred he might yet find a slight taste of happiness in the very realization of its meaninglessness. Such a philosophy would likely appeal to those who have been ravaged by war. But I am, as you know, the victor in countless campaigns and the active conqueror of those who have sought to take what I have built and more often tried to destroy me out of fear for what they imagine I am. In this I am also free of the imperialism of Western European philosophical traditions, which I have beaten back and impaled on sharpened stakes. I am from Transylvania. Our ways are not your ways nor are our worldviews your worldviews. There are many things you would find strange here.

Although I have disagreed with you, I have done so only meekly and only in contention of the suggestion that I am endowed with the third characteristic of an absurd hero. I am of the sanguine belief that if you were at liberty to act more widely on your newfound engagement with life, you too might come to join me in my nocturnal hunts. Perhaps in those expeditions you would have come to experience, as I have, that lust is only one characteristic of love and not its entirety, just as sex is only one characteristic of lust. As it is, I can but offer this small voice of variance to the howls of execration from the crowd that will give you serenity in the moment before death.

Yours in all sincerity,

Dracula

P.S., May you also rest in peace knowing that I will take eternal care of Mademoiselle Cardona.

Note

It has been years now since the swift blade of the guillotine glistened in the sunlight that Monsieur Meursault so hated, as it fell toward his stretched and restrained neck. Who would have imagined a World War would claim over fifty-two million lives, that horror and holocaust would spread the popularity of absurdism and existentialism in art, theatre, and philosophy due to a questioning of the individual's effectualness in swimming the turbulent tides of the social ocean?

In the case that you see Albert Camus's philosophy of the absurd as less a blessing in the cause of overcoming despondency and more a curse for perpetuating it, let the following be known to posterity, for I have now grown much older than Professor Van Helsing was during our fateful venture in Transylvania, so I now leave the matter in the hands of the youth. The professor recorded precise instructions for killing the vampires among us. They must be followed exactly, for as he warned, "The Nosferatu do not die like the bees when they sting once. He is only stronger, and being stronger, have yet more power to work evil" (*Dracula*, Chapter 18). I now repeat this as it is most important in the present. The vampire must first be impaled through the heart with a wooden stake and then beheaded with a silver blade. Only these two in exact combination are effective. Which of our absurd heroes was dealt the blow that would banish him from our world? And, has anyone noticed that only forty-nine of the fifty boxes of Transylvanian earth have been found to date? As I think of this now, I cannot help but wonder what treasure is hidden beneath that blue flame, the fiftieth box or *The Stranger*.

Make haste, you vampire hunters, for the dead travel fast!

Jonathan Harker

Appendix: Other Excerpts Found Folded in with Harker's Journal

From Sisyphus's Diary:

Dear Diary,

Stubbed my toe six more times today. Divine beings aren't caving on their oath to see me eternally rolling this rock up the mountain. Keeps rolling back down over and over. Guess that's the price for scorning the gods, hating death, and having a passion for life. So, here we go again.

Heard Camus cast me as an "absurd hero" or something like that. Says people can never find happiness if they keep looking for it by trying to escape the absurdity of their condition. Sees me as exemplifying the acceptance of that condition every time I start back down the mountain to get the rock. May be true. But if you ask me, the real absurdity is that he thinks I've found happiness by accepting this rubble. Oh, my aching back!

Note from Vampira

AAAAIIIIEEEEE!!!

Screaming relaxes me so. I have been quite unsettled since reading these eerie epistles. When I read Monsieur Meursault's dreadfully lifeless responses to the Master's requests in these letters of the poison pen, well, I rolled over in my grave! What I need is a Vampira cocktail to settle my nerves. It'll not only settle them, it will petrify them. A Vampira cocktail. You like it? It hates you.[1]

---

[1] The first sentence and the last five in this paragraph are quoted from *The Vampira Show*, which aired on ABC television in 1954.

23

Dracula's Quest for Enlightenment

CHRISTOPHER KETCHAM

From the Diary of Christopher Ketcham:

I write this with shaking hands and a trembling heart. I had always wondered about Dracula: Did he have a soul? What was his relationship to God? What does it mean to be undead? I made it my goal to discover the truth . . . Now I know it is too much for any mortal heart to bear. I do not know how much time I have left. I will relate my story to you to the best of my ability.

Tired of my requests for funding, my university refused any more assistance in my endeavor to discover the truth about Dracula, so I used my own resources to travel to Transylvania to find answers. I found something marvelous!

First, Dracula has been in his present state of undeadness since the twelfth century! From a loose stone in the wall of a long ago collapsed synagogue I discovered a chronicle, more like a journal really, of Dracula's journey to and meeting with Moses ben Maimon, also known as "Maimonides" (1135–1204; Jewish calendar 4895–4964). Scholars should recognize that I have discovered a long lost manuscript of an amazing conversation with this great Jewish thinker of the Middle Ages as related by a previously unknown "Rabbi Glilscescu." With some help from a local Jewish historian, the badly stained journal was translated. Alas, I cannot reveal the translator's name for he has since disavowed any assistance in this effort.

Before I found the journal, I had already known that Maimon wrote a text he called The Guide for the Perplexed *for a student of his. This fact is well known by most philosophers, particularly the ones who study philosophy of religion. Maimon intended this text to be an expansion on his own teachings about certain metaphysical topics and to explain key words primarily associated with the Bible (the Torah) through a set of thirteen principles. Two of Maimon's thirteen principles of faith were that there would be 1. a messiah, and 2. a resurrection. It appears that Rabbi Glilscescu, the man I've discovered, also read* The Guide for the Perplexed *for he expressed both agreement and concern with Maimonides's ideas in his description of Dracula's conversation with Maimon. I cannot even begin to fathom the dark implications of Glilscecu's journal, though. Therefore, I have included excerpts from it here:*

First Chronicle Entry Fourteenth Nissan, 4959 (April 19th, 1199, or thereabouts)

Blessed be the God of Abraham. May God grant you the light of day even as this is a tale of darkness and dread. For this is an account of a tragic being who wanders the Earth in a state not like you nor I. It is believed he comes from the people who first settled Sigh⸗⸗⸗ra in the mountains of our fair land (though this is not certain). His renown came from being a crafty warrior who long ago first forced the retreat of Roman legions. And he later fought the Vandals and dispatched them mercilessly. Some say he is as old as these hills. That he was a bastard child of one who shall not be named in the book of Genesis may or may not be the truth. But his existence, or what serves as such, has spanned at least as many years as the more venerable of souls chronicled in our sacred testament.

And, of course, there are some who say that Dracula was the subject of a book that was written to be included in our Torah but that God himself erased it for an unknown, unsaid transgression by Dracula. It is said that God's punishment, in addition to his erasure from history, is that Dracula will wander the world in the darkness but will meet his certain desiccation should he ever seek the sunlight. I have not seen him in the light of day but this just may be because his albinism produces such pain to his eyes even in dim candlelight.

Of course Dracula is a gentile and knows the Catholic faith. And because he had preserved this land's only abbey from the Mongols, he was celebrated, first with a feast, and then a private meeting with Father Przybilski, the Abbot from Poland. The Abbot had ambitions for higher office, preferably in Rome itself. So the Abbot was not about to ignore the spiritual needs of such an important person as the Count. Dracula gave himself this title of Count after he routed the Mongols at the eventide battle of the Abbey of Glad.

Dracula asked the priest whether Lazarus's raising from the dead and Jesus's subsequent resurrection were mere flukes or was it possible that there were more such persons as Lazarus, perhaps even alive today. The Abbot thought for a moment and said that it was up to God whether to let one return to the living after his final breath or to let him die and ascend to heaven. And what would such a resurrected person be like, asked the Count? Only God knows, the Abbot replied.

The Abbot then launched into biblical recitation. Dracula said that the Abbot spewed forth chapter and verse like blood from a cut artery. Dracula politely listened throughout the interminable repast and soliloquy, touching none of the meat stew as it was so hard cooked not a bit of pink shone through. And this went on as the Abbot drank more deeply from the flagon of abbey wine until he began to slur and forget which verse he was quoting and why.

Dracula asked the Abbot if he would hear his confession. The Abbot agreed and bent to hear Dracula. Dracula said he gave his confession factually and without leaving out anything of his affliction and his blood lust. He said that the Abbot sweated profusely and between Dracula's pauses began to mumble the rosary. By the time the Count had finished his confession the Abbot was quite pale and shaking. He stared at Dracula for a moment, and then ran from the room crying, "Cursed, cursed, cursed!" He offered Dracula no penance, no forgiveness. Instead he hurried to his cloister and shut himself in his tiny room. In that prison, he prayed until death released him.

The Abbot refused all food and drink, and expired with the rosary clenched in his fist and a grimace of abject terror on his face. His rigor in death was such that his arms had to be broken to fit his corpse into the pine box. Dracula said that on his way home after the confession, he met a drunken soul carrying a haunch of pink lamb who had also been invited to the feast in Dracula's honor. Dracula said that only then that his hunger was sated and added that it was a fitting end for the reveler's evening, and the meal left him pleasantly inebriated. But, otherwise, Dracula said, that the evening left him unsatisfied both with the Abbot's answers or the church's teachings in general.

Chronicle Entry 17th Nissan, 4959 (April 22nd, 1198)

Why would I, a rabbi of the Jewish faith, have anything to do with such a creature as Dracula? That is a very good question and one which I have prayed over for quite some time. It was Moshe the tailor who introduced us one evening after one Sabbath in Silvan, 4955 (May–June 1194) in our modest synagogue which is nothing more than a cleared out space in the Moshe's small hut. Moshe had said that the gentile known as Dracula, who called himself a Count, was having a crisis of faith. That the Catholic Church no longer served his thinking about life, death, and God adequately.

Moshe said that he told Dracula that he would introduce him to me, the rabbi, for I had great insight to God and the greatest scholar of our age Moses ben Maimon. Moshe is a flatterer, always seeking to maintain close relationships with Jews and gentiles alike to sustain work for his little business. Moshe said that it would not lead to anything like a conversion because he knew that was not something our small community had interest in. But Moshe said that he thought that I would be interested in hearing about another's faith and I could help Dracula through Maimon and ease his perplexity. And, of course, I also understood that having Dracula as a satisfied client was beneficial to Moshe. I agreed to see the man after Sabbath next.

Dracula and I spoke by candlelight. As he explained about his faith leaving him I saw that he was a thoughtful man, but so pale. He was dressed like a noble with sword at his side but Dracula had no hair neither on his head nor near his eyes nor any stubble for the growth of a beard as is customary among Jews and gentiles alike. He hinted at his affliction, his lust for the sight of blood . . . not only in battle as evidence of his prowess, but also even the beating of an artery in another's neck enflamed his passions.

Dracula asked about the faith of Judaism; he was curious as to what it offered that Catholicism did not. Dracula said that he knew that Jesus was a Jew and that other Jews had not seen fit to embrace Jesus as the messiah. I told him we were still waiting. However, I said, there was a great Jewish philosopher and physician to the Sultan of Egypt in Cairo. This philosopher, Moses ben Maimon, has confirmed with his publishing of the thirteen articles of faith that there will be a time when such a messiah will arrive and the dead will be resurrected.[1] I also explained that not all rabbis and Jewish scholars agreed with all of the teachings of Moses ben Maimon. However, I said that I felt strongly that these thirteen articles, if properly understood by our people, can provide us with a way of fighting back against the alchemy and magic that has so poisoned our faith.

In my research I discovered that Maimon wrote many letters, some in response to his critics and others which

---

[1] Sanhedrin, Chapter 10. As my translator explained, the Sanhedrin is a part of Book 14 of the *Mishneh Torah* written by Maimon. The *Mishneh* was an effort by Maimon to codify Jewish law. Comparing the *Mishneh Torah* with *The Guide to the Perplexed*, Leo Strauss writes, "The *Mishneh Torah* is primarily addressed to the general run of men, while the *Guide* is addressed to the small number of people who are able to understand by themselves" (*Persecution and the Art of Writing*, p. 94).

served as teachings in and of themselves. In one, The *Letter on Astrology*, he exposes astrology as a false science.

Dracula asked whether this resurrection would be for all dead or only the select few who were otherwise holy. I explained that forty years after the true messiah's coming all whose bodies that are dust will rise again and their souls will return to their bodies. And Dracula asked whether this would be only for the true believers of the Jewish faith. I replied it was God's choice and that I could not say whether some, even Jews, would be left as dust. I said also that I did not believe that, as with Christianity, some will be cursed to burn eternally in hell. But, Dracula asked, what if it is possible for someone to return from death to the living without there being a confirmed Jewish messiah? And if there was, would this give credence that Jesus was the true messiah?

Chronicle Entry 25th Nissan, 4959 (April 30th, 1199)

Oh, the difficult floods of spring! They challenge our small village but somehow we survive. I left off at the messiah question for which I am happy for the day's delay because my recollection of what was said has improved.

After Dracula's question, I thought for a moment. I replied that there are many who have shouted out that the messiah has come and lo, forty years later, the dead are still moldering in their graves. But what if there were a few who could, Dracula asked again? Perhaps, perhaps, I said, but without the messiah it is likely that the body alone would rise, without the soul returning which is not what the resurrection intends. Dracula thought for a moment and said, Well then that is it, I have no soul or it wanders the Earth without me. Perhaps I passed it on the way here.

At this point in time I did not know the manner or extent of his affliction other than his thirst for blood, and that I understood only metaphorically. So I asked, what happened to your soul? And also I said to Dracula that a crisis of faith does not mean that the soul departs the body.

It is that I am undead but not living, Dracula said. That your mystics and worshipers have always known that there are those among us who travel the dark places on the Earth existing as one who is alive. Dracula then explained his whole malady. I felt the coldness of his skin when he touched my arm and the mold of his breath when he leaned down so that he would not be heard by Moshe who toiled at his labors in the next room. But, he said, that he had not previously considered the possibility that his soul had been lost to him. And now it seems that it was and this seemed to disturb him greatly.

I explained that, yes, the mystics were deceivers and were likely to take the word of the Bible to be literal. I said that some who think this way see the finger of God as from a giant hand in the flesh. "Preposterous!" I told Dracula and that the explanation of the non-corporeal nature of God was one of the reasons why I so admired Moses ben Maimon's teaching. However, I explained, that I still had some difficulties with Maimon's ideas and one of these was the denial of the Bible's infallibility.

Yet to give Maimon some charity, I explained to Dracula that I also understood that the Bible can be metaphorical and not always literal. And while I understood Moses ben Maimon's thirteen acts of faith, I was somewhat skeptical and understood Dracula's concern that resurrection would apply to all, whether the most heinous of persons or true believers. But I did point out that Maimon himself wrote, "All Jews have a share in the world to come" (Sanhedrin, 10:1).

Dracula looked up and asked me to explain. I said that the souls of the dead before the resurrection reside in Eden. The resurrection will reunite them with their bodies. But, I said, what bothers me about this is whether this is a reward for the body if the soul is inherently evil. Dracula replied that he thought it is perhaps possible that in Eden the soul is reclaimed by God and this does purify the soul. That could be so, I said, but why resurrect the body as well? I said, of what use is a body in the afterlife where there is no need to eat? Then Dracula turned to me and said, So, you too are having a crisis of faith. Not a crisis, said I, but this will take a lot more thinking. Perhaps more thinking than for what I am capable as a humble rabbi from a small village.

Dracula pondered for a moment and I could see that behind his eyes he was scheming something. He asked whether I would be willing to travel to Cairo with him to meet this Moses ben Maimon so that we could both ask our questions about the resurrection. Dracula explained that he would undertake this with his own funds. My single responsibility would be to gain audience with the great philosopher. This, of course, intrigued me, for another opportunity to be able to speak with such a great scholar would not likely come again in my lifetime. I said that I would consider it and asked him to return the night after the next Sabbath. He agreed.

I have no wife and no family, and our small synagogue could take care of itself for the months that I was gone. The Count was not someone who would reflect badly upon me as a companion on a long journey because he was highly respected. And I knew that his skill as a warrior would keep me safe on the journey. I worried about the blood lust, but I decided that he needed my introduction more than my blood. I had decided by morning but waited until our appointment to tell Dracula I would travel with him to Cairo to meet Moses ben Maimon. I did fret about what might happen to me on our return journey when he no longer needed my skills of introduction.

Chronicle Entry 12th Tamuz, 4959 (July 15th, 1199)

We left the village on the fifth of Av, 4955 (July 21st, 1194). It was long and strange, the journey to Cairo. We drove the horses both day and night from two carriages, mine open and airy, Dracula's dark and blacked out. He joined me during the evening and retired to his funereal trap before sunrise. Ten soldiers, six on horseback, and four drivers in uniforms with red sashes, accompanied us on our journey to the Mediterranean. By and large we were unmolested by bandits but we did skirt most towns. Dracula preferred solitude and remained mostly within his own thoughts even at night. Eight soldiers left us after Dracula engaged a cramped merchant vessel for

Cairo on the 10th Cheshvan, 4955 (November 2nd, 1194). Two soldiers had ridden ahead of us the last few leagues and had long since departed to Cairo by another ship to prepare for our arrival.

Dracula said that he would have business to attend to before we departed, and I would go on alone but he would soon follow. He gave me a heavy bag of gold to use to obtain an audience with Maimon. What I have since learned is that he was lying in his sarcophagus in the belly of my vessel along with the rest of the cargo.

Chronicle Entry 20th Tamuz, 4959 (July 23rd, 1199)

It has been as warm this summer as I remember those in Cairo which is why I have not been in my study for a number of days.

I arrived in Cairo the 29th Kislev, 4955 (December 21st, 1194). The scents alone assault the senses and the mass of people and vendors shouting over each other in Greek, Arabic, and other tongues reminded me of the biblical Babel. But I soon got used to the cacophony and the bustle and dickering of the markets and narrow shadowy alleys.

It was not difficult to find the whereabouts of Moses ben Maimon. I had only to ask where the Sultan's palace was. When I neared the palace, a scruffy beggar pointed out Maimon for a piece of Dracula's gold. I stepped into Moses ben Maimon's path, bowed, explained who I was and where I had traveled from, and asked for a meeting. The learned man huffed and brusquely waved me away. I followed and pleaded politely. He kept walking. He said that he was busy with the Sultan's business all days but the Sabbath and on that day he was busy tending to the spiritual needs of the Jews in the city. "No time, no time," he said. I offered him a donation, "It will be enough to build a school, whatever school the great Maimon would want to build," I told him.

Maimon paused and turned. "One hour, one hour only," he said. "After Sabbath next at my home in Fostat—ask and you will be led to it. At the hour before midnight." He disappeared into the crowd. I hurried back to tell Dracula but it was mid-afternoon, so I waited.

Last Chronicle Entry 21st Tamuz, 4959 (July 4th, 1199)

Evening approached and I greeted Dracula with the news. Upon mentioning its price, my conscience flared in trepidation. And Dracula said to this sum, "I have forever to make my fortune but only a few moments with such a learned mortal. It's a fair bargain."

At the appointed hour we arrived at the modest dwelling of Moses ben Maimon. He looked like any other rabbi but wore a turban-like head covering popular with the Arabs. His beard was well trimmed and his eyes penetrating. He was draped in the garb of an Arab of Cairo. I introduced myself and Dracula and we each shook his hand. "Your hand is as cold as death," Maimon said to Dracula, "And yet the night is warm."

"You may soon understand why," said Dracula.

To me, Maimon asked, why are you here?

"For two purposes," I said. "For me a few questions about your work and for Dracula . . . well, he should explain."

Dracula smiled beatifically and began. "You see, Rabbi, I met your Moses near Sinai once during his long journey from this land to Israel. His power shone in his eyes . . . and, like you are probably experiencing at this moment, a shudder of cold went through him when I neared. We never spoke but he looked into my eyes for a long time and then took his leave from me. I believe he obtained two tablets from the mount shortly after our encounter."

"You cannot be that old," Said Maimon.

"Ah, but what is old?" replied Dracula. "The Bible chronicles many sages who lived far beyond that of ordinary men."

"Are you claiming to be immortal?" asked Maimon.

"What is immortal, Rabbi," asked Dracula, "if only God is immortal? I surely am not God before you. As you yourself have said, Rabbi, those who believe in the flesh of God will be idol worshipers. I certainly am not one of those. I am, as it were, undead but not living . . . And, as Rabbi Glilscescu has informed me with his teaching, soulless."

Maimon stared at Dracula for a moment and then looked at me. "Hear his story," I said, "I, like you, want to see an end to idolatry and alchemy and magic but this is something untoward that defies my understanding."

"Examine me, physician," said Dracula.

Maimon agreed, asking questions about digestion, habits, pains and the like. Maimon summarized his findings: "I find you to be an albino with an uncomfortably cold countenance and foul breath. Other than that, I cannot detect a difference in existence between you and your companion. Your habits of drinking the blood of humans, 'Thou shalt not eat the blood (nefesh) with the meat' as it says in Deuteronomy xii. 23, is blasphemy. But this affliction can be cured with proper care. You have intelligence and curiosity which for me is the essence of the soul."[2]

"It is of some consolation," said Dracula, "that you view the presence of intellect as being soul. Yet I am not yet convinced that my soul is still possessed by my body. Rabbi," said Dracula, "for those afflicted such as I there is no escape from the blood lust, for it is the essence of our burden. Like Job I bear it upon my shoulders and in my loins when I make of me the blood of others. But what of sacrifice? Your Bible speaks of sacrifices and God's vengeance. No great lightning bolts have pierced my flesh as I go about my ghastly business. I have received no personal rebuke from God for these things I do. It is the question of resurrection of which you have so eloquently spoken in your epistle, the *Letter on Resurrection* that concerns me. I have studied this letter in the Arabic."

"But this resurrection I have spoken of is forty years after the coming of the messiah," said Maimon, "and as of yet I am aware of no messiah amongst us."

"Perhaps yes, and perhaps no. Perhaps the Jesus you wrote of in your *Epistle to Yemen* as being an impostor," said Dracula, "may not be the truth even though the

---

[2] Maimon's *Letter on Resurrection* refers to the immortal soul but Sarah Stroumsa says he was referring to immortality of the intellect (*Maimonides in His World*, p. 181).

dead have not risen.[3] And yet I have become what I am long before the time of the Christ. But you yourself said, philosopher, that it is conceivable that the resurrection will occur and it is part of the articles of your faith. But you have no scientific evidence of the possibility of dust becoming flesh once again. And in your *Letter on Resurrection* you said, 'I thereupon announced very clearly that the Resurrection is a fundamental of the books of Moses our master but that it was not the ultimate goal, and that the ultimate goal is the life in the world to come.' And in the same letter you say that for those resurrected, 'there will be no food, nor drink, nor sexual intercourse.'"

Dracula leaned forward, "So, is it not possible for one like myself, whom God finds detestable, that God could suffer him into a soulless state where he must find nourishment in the foulest manner? Could not God have reserved for someone like me an existence without a soul to serve out a sentence for some transgression? You said yourself that my own habits are a blasphemy to your faith. And what form of transgression would make such a being as me possible? What penance might it be that I need to serve?"

I watched Maimon's eyes as he contemplated this explanation from Dracula. Then Maimon spoke. "God has his reasons for what he does. But it is unclear to me whether any of this could be from God . . . and that assumes I believe your story which I find borders on the fantastic and mystical. The logic of your argument is intriguing, but I am also of the opinion I am in the company of a trickster."

"The logic strains, I admit," said Dracula, "but my existence is as in the afterlife, without known end. Yet, I am on and of this Earth, not the beyond. And, if I could be thus as I speak, could you accept my arguments and my existence as without resurrection but akin to it?"

---

[3] Maimon has written the *Epistle to Yemen* to the small community of Jews in Yemen who, under pressure by the local Muslims were toying with apostasy (denying their faith). In this letter, Maimon said that Christianity and Islam are superficial imitations of Judaism.

Maimon frowned and shook his head. The discussion wound towards the dawn but did not resolve itself. Before sunup Dracula turned to me and said, "I see that my quest for knowledge must continue. My affliction is as mysterious as Ezekiel's vision of a chariot with its four-faced beings and winged wheels. The nature and whereabouts of my soul and my existence is beyond even the well-formed logic of this physician who has taken of his most precious time to see me."

"I bid you the greatest thanks Rabbi," Dracula said to Maimon. "And I have the highest regard for your insights. I know that I will not assuage your skepticism, so I will take my leave." And with that Dracula was gone, disappearing as always like a ghost, evaporating from the room.

I remained behind with Maimon. We spoke no more of Dracula for it was as if the conversation had become only a hazy memory. We discussed my questions about his work. Then I asked him what manner of school he wanted to build. He shook his head. I understood and returned the gold purse into my garments. I took my leave.

From the Diary of Christopher Ketcham Continued

Glilscescu then goes on to relate that he never saw Maimon again, though he remained in Cairo for just over three years. Nor did he see Dracula again. He had enough gold left to return home on 6th Elul, 4958 (August 29th, 1197). Much like Maimon's Letter on Resurrection, *Glilscescu ends his journal simply: "The chronicle is finished with the help of God, blessed be He and blessed be His name" (*Guide for the Perplexed*).*

What plagues me now is the realization that Dracula casts a dark look on the possibility of resurrection. What if the resurrection that Maimon describes is far more an "undeath" than a new life . . . one without food, drink or intimacy? What if Dracula is right about his curse? Far better to be left dead than to live his undead afterlife! But surely a man cannot live long spouting such heresy . . . will Dracula himself be sent to collect me? I can only pray that I will not be similarly damned to a resurrection.

24

Hoover and McCarthy Meet Dracula

TIMOTHY SEXTON

The most influential and longest-lasting effect of alleged Communist infiltration of the motion picture industry during the late 1940s and 1950s was the transformation of the Monster of horror movies—especially those science-fiction horror hybrids so popular on drive-in screens during the Eisenhower era.

What psychology has termed the Other—a monstrous threat to normalcy and the status quo that must be either annihilated or assimilated—underwent a truly revolutionary evolution during the period defined by the Hollywood Blacklist. Such creatures of fright as the mythic European aristocrat hiding his true vampire nature suddenly no longer seemed as terrifying as nondescript small town neighbors hiding their sinister intention to snatch bodies in the name of the Communist Party, monsters from outer space intent on propagating their socialist agenda by marrying homecoming queens and, of course, them giant ants, all the more frightening because of their single-minded purpose to protect the collective from the individual.

What follows may seem as much a piece of pure fiction inspired by modern-day folk tales as Bram Stoker's novel *Dracula*. In fact, the format, content, and even the language is based on a series of actual FBI files. All of the real-life Hollywood celebrities mentioned by name in this piece actually do show up in the real FBI files. While the specific events and dialogue attributed to these people may not have occurred in the context described here, those events are all based on historical activities described by FBI agents and undercover informants in the real-life files actually known as COMMUNIST INFILTRATION OF THE MOTION PICTURE INDUSTRY (COMPIC).

```
FREEDOM OF INFORMATION
AND
PRIVACY ACTS


SUBJECT: COMMUNIST INFILTRATION—MOTION PICTURE INDUSTRY
     (COMPIC)
FILE NUMBER: 100-138754-101962
SERIAL: 1003 (part 2)  dd: 222
PART: 101962: THE BRAIN OF FRANKENSTEIN
```

Retitled Abbott and Costello Meet Frankenstein SACNP

```
To: FBI Director Hoover
```

(RUNNING MEMORANDUM) *ORIGINAL COPY FILED IN:*   100=13875

```
IV. COMMUNIST INFLUENCE IN MOTION PICTURES
```

There is submitted herewith the running memorandum concerning Communist infiltration of the motion picture industry which has been brought up to date as of August 31, 1950. Part 101962 of file number 100-138754 deals specifically with "ABBOTT AND COSTELLO MEET FRANKENSTEIN" aka "THE BRAIN OF FRANKENSTEIN", with special Bureau attention on subversive activities of screenwriters Robert "Bobby" Lees and Frederic Rinaldo. Attached please find pertinent Office Memorandum regarding actor Sterling Hayden's recent decision to cooperate fully with the House Committee on Un-American Activities.

OFFICE MEMORANDUM   United States Government
To: Director, FBI   Date: September 1, 1950
From: SAC, Los Angeles
Subject: STERLING HAYDEN   100/33 DEPT. OF JUSTICE
         SECURITY MATTER (COMPIC part 101962) RE: HCUA 1951

As the Bureau has previously advised, HAYDEN was originally interviewed on August 3, 1950 by Special Agent R.B.
HOOD when he voluntarily appeared at his office. On August
10, 1950, he was re-interviewed by two Bureau agents at
his home. Subsequent to the second interview, HAYDEN was
contacted personally by representatives of the House
Committee on Un-American Activities who conducted a third
interview on the subject of Communist infiltration in
Hollywood at his home on August 17, 1950.

Please let it be noted that practically all of the
information and identifications relative to the investigation of suspected infiltration of subversive Communist
messages and meaning in "ABBOTT AND COSTELLO MEET FRANKEN-
STEIN" provided by Mr. HAYDEN to date have been largely
subject to verification from other past and present
sources.

Mr. HAYDEN has let the attorneys representing the House
Committee on Un-American Activities know that he is prepared to share all information he knows about ROBERT LEES
and FREDERIC RINALDO relative to their connection with
Communist Party propaganda in their work within the motion
picture industry. Relative to the specific inquiries
related to COMPIC part 1019561, HAYDEN has confirmed
through his interviews that LEES and RINALDO purposely set
out to transform the horror movie character of Count
Dracula into a symbol of Communist Party suspicion and
hatred of American capitalism.

As a preface to this section, it should be pointed out
that it has not been a function of this Bureau to review
motion picture production for political content as the
Bureau's representatives cannot be considered experts in
this field. However, the Bureau receives reports from
Confidential Informants and other sources that are considered to be experts concerning the tactics used by the
Communists in their attempt to influence motion pictures
and actual examples of Communist propaganda in motion picture films. Confidential Informants working in the motion
picture industry have passionately requested that the

Bureau maintain the confidentiality of those providing
information obtained as a result of access to restricted
studio documentation, including scripts, inter-office memoranda, production notes, archival records, conversations
and minutes of meetings related to films in any stage of
production by any motion picture studio in Hollywood, USA.

Analysis of Motion Pictures Disclosing Communist
     Propaganda Therein
"THE BRAIN OF FRANKENSTEIN" Retitled "Abbott and Costello
     Meet Frankenstein G.B.
To be released by Universal International Pictures on June
     15, 1948.
Producer—Robert Arthur
Director—Charles Barton
Screenplay—Robert Lees, Frederick Rinaldo, John Grant
Cast: Starring—Lou Costello, Bud Abbott, Bela Lugosi, Lon
     Chaney, Jr., Lenore Aubert.

Producer Robert Arthur developed the idea for this
Universal International Pictures horror-comedy picture in
1946. Scenarist Oscar Brodney created a story outline
based on Arthur's concept of having his Universal Studios'
comedy stars meeting up with Universal's lineup of horror
movie stars including not only Frankenstein's monster
character but also the Wolf Man, the Invisible Man, the
Mummy, Dracula and Count Alucard (aka the Son of Dracula).
On February 3, 1947 screenwriter Bertram Millhauser began
eleven days of work that expanded Brodney's outline into a
47-page treatment titled "THE BRAIN OF FRANKENSTEIN."
Robert Lees and Frederic Rinaldo were contracted to write
the screenplay based on Millhauser's treatment and began
work in earnest on April 1, 1947. Shortly thereafter, our
undercover Confidential Informant ███████████ filed the
first of a series of increasingly alarmed reports concerning the development of the script for "THE BRAIN OF
FRANKENSTEIN" by Lees and Rinaldo.

Filed April 3, 1947

"An Abbott and Costello movie matching them up with
Universal's cast of horror movie figures is exactly
the kind of studio offering that the Bureau and House

UnAmerican Activities Committee needs to be focusing on.
While the Bureau and the Committee may see such a motion
picture as seemingly mindless entertainment devoid of
much opportunity for effective transmission of dangerous
Communist messages, you can be rest assured that those
operating within the People's Educational Center assuredly
do not."

Confidential Informant ███████████ has been filing a
running memorandum on meetings, lectures, courses and
classroom discussion taking place at the People's
Educational Center, formerly known as the Hollywood School
for Writers where screenwriter Robert Lees held position
as an executive board member and lecturer. The People's
Education Center acts as a subsidiary of the League of
American Writers and is known to be a transmission belt
whereby aspiring screenwriters are conditioned for eventual
membership in the Communist Party. In addition to offering
instructional curricula geared toward teaching aspiring
writers how to work within the motion picture, the
People's Education Center also routinely and often without
advertised notification has offered lectures on political,
social and cultural matters. Attached below are photostat
copies of typed notes provided by our informant citing
concrete examples of such propagandist content as it
relates specifically to the Abbott and Costello film.

Filed April 8, 1947

Hard as it may be to believe, Lees and Rinaldo have only
been working on the script for their Abbott and Costello
meet Dracula movie (which is how they refer to the story
they are basing on the treatment titled "The Brain of
Frankenstein") for a week, yet have managed in that time
to make it something of a cause célèbre among those at the
People's Educational Center. The gist of the story in the
original treatment they received on April 1, 1947 had
Abbott and Costello working as bumbling stewards on an
ocean liner where they get mixed up with secretive scientist named Dr. Fell who is transporting some mysterious
cargo from London to New York City. The boys eventually
discover that Dr. Fell runs a wax museum in New York and
his big mystery is the claim to be in secret possession of
actual bodies of Frankenstein's creature, the Wolf Man,

and Count Dracula. The crux of the plot revolves around Dr.
Fell having stolen the secret to re-animating life from
Baroness Von Frankenstein, with Count Dracula practically lit-
tle more than a minor supporting character.

Filed April 16, 1947

The title of today's lecture at the People's Educational Center
was taken directly from the writings of Vladimir Ilyich Lenin:
"Imperialism: The Highest Stage of Capitalism". It was delivered by a person identified only as Comrade Selby. Present at
the lecture was Robert Lees. The primary thrust of the lecture
could not have been made clearer: everyone in attendance
received an index card that they were told to keep in their
running folder with this written on it: "Communist Party members working in the movie industry must utilize mainstream
American movies for the purpose of indoctrination by rigidly
aligning to an exclusively theoretical, specifically economic
analysis of facts . . . to formulate the few necessary obser-
vations on politics with extreme caution, by hints, in an alle-
gorical language."
   Demonstration of this imperative was exhibited through the
screening of clips from several motion pictures, including
`Buck Privates Come Home.' Not coincidentally, this Abbott and
Costello comedy was co-written by Robert Lees and Fred Rinaldo.
The scene in question portrayed a party given for a General in
the Army whereas intermingling scenes disclose an enlisted man
on KP duty. It was clear that the juxtaposition of General and
Private was intended by Lees and Rinaldo to instill within the
audience an unnecessary recognition of class consciousness.
   Although the scene was not specifically brought up for discussion, the fact that such a patently subversive message in an
allegedly mindless bit of Hollywood entertainment wasn't
noticed by the authorities obviously emboldened the writing
team to introduce more of their basic communist doctrine about
the alleged decadence of the upper classes in America without
fear of any consequences.

Filed April 23, 1947

The title of today's lecture was derived from a quote spoken
by Count Dracula in Bram Stoker's novel: "This man belongs to
me!" Comrade Selby joyously enthralled his rapturous audience
with news that Lees and Rinaldo had reclaimed the vampire from
Adam Smith and Hamilton Deane and given him back to Bram
Stoker and Karl Marx. Selby then went on to write a series of
quotations taken from the works of Karl Marx, Friedrich Engels,
and Bram Stoker on the subject of vampirism as a metaphor for
capitalism. Each quotation was intended to serve as further
"evidence" that Universal Studios had corrupted the longstand-
ing critical interpretation of Dracula as the ultimate symbol
of the corrupt ideological characteristics inherent in the capitalist theory of economics. The quotes written by Selby on the
blackboard are verbatim:

> Capital is dead labor which, vampire-like, lives only by
> sucking living labour, and lives the more, the more
> labour it sucks.
>
> —Marx, *Das Kapital*
>
> The prolongation of the working-day beyond the limits of
> the natural day, into the night, only acts as a pallia-
> tive. It quenches only in a slight degree the vampire
> thirst for the living blood of labor.
>
> —Marx, *Das Kapital*
>
> It must be acknowledged that our worker comes out of the
> process of production other than he entered. In the mar-
> ket, as owner of the commodity "labor-power" he stood
> face to face with other owners of commodities, one owner
> against another owner. The contract by which he sold his
> labor-power to the capitalist proved in black and white,
> so to speak, that he was free to dispose of himself. But
> when the transaction was concluded, it was discovered
> that he was no "free agent," that the period of time for
> which he is free to sell his labor-power is the period of
> time for which he is forced to sell it, that in fact the
> vampire will not let go "while there remains a single
> muscle, sinew or drop of blood to be exploited."
>
> —Marx, *Das Kapital*

Necessity will force the working-men to abandon the remnants of a belief which, as they will more and more clearly perceive, serves only to make them weak and resigned to their fate, obedient and faithful to the vampire property-holding class.

—Engels, *The Condition of the Working Class in England*

The thrust of the lecture was a comparison of elements of the novel *Dracula* to the Communist interpretation of capitalism. Thirst for blood equals thirst for monetary profit. Vampires draining victims of blood in order to attain immortal life equals capitalists draining working class population to attain profit. Selby's explanation that Dracula's "This man belongs to me" puts in a nutshell the capitalist exploiter's delusion that owning the company means owning the workers drew sustained applause and cheers.

Background and Tactics Used by the Communists to Inject Communist Propaganda in the Motion Pictures

FEDERAL BUREAU OF INVESTIGATION
Form No. 1   File No. 100-138754-10196
THIS CASE ORIGINATED AT   Los Angeles

REPORT MADE AT Los Angeles	DATE WHEN MADE 6/14/1947	PERIOD FOR WHICH MADE 5/1/1947	REPORT MADE BY T=55 ███████

Title ~~THE BRAIN OF FRANKENSTEIN~~	CHARACTER OF CASE SECURITY MATTER: COMPIC part 10196

SYNOPSIS OF FACTS: CLASSIFIED BY Sr3C1/TMR	Confidential Informant # attended a party held at the home of Frank Tuttle, screenwriter and director, on May 1, 1947 ostensibly to discuss an important upcoming union vote. At some point during the evening, # decided to smoke a cigarette in the garden and walked outside to see actor

```
100-23438
     SCA: RH
Ddd: 33MPH
```

Howard Da Silva push actor John Garfield up against a tree as he harangued him about another matter. Before he could get close enough to hear what was being said, an arm reached out and pulled him back into the house through another doorway. He turned to find himself face to face with actor Sterling Hayden cautioning him in no uncertain terms about the inviolate protection of private matters at parties "such as these." The room into which Hayden pulled him was already the site of a discussion no less passionate but significantly more lighthearted in spirit than the private matter being discussed out in the garden.

/

According to our informant, those present during this discussion included, in addition to himself and Sterling Hayden, actor Lloyd Bridges, director Edward Dmytryk, singer/musician Burl Ives, director Elia Kazan, Frank Tuttle and an unidentified person that Hayden later identified as screenwriter Robert Lees but Kazan later referenced by the name Freddie (Rinaldo?).

The topic of discussion was the new screenplay that Lees and Rinaldo were working on. Although titled "The Brain of Frankenstein", that character and the monster who shares his name were hardly mentioned. The focus of the debate was the character of Dracula. The specific topic of conversation when our informant entered the room was about how Universal's 1931 production of *Dracula* was fostered by the so-called Red Scare of a decade earlier. Frank Tuttle, whose career in Hollywood traces back the longest of anyone in the room—to the late 1920s—provided firsthand examples of what he claimed to be evidence that the influx of investment money in the

early 1920s by big corporations like
DuPont, General Motors, and the Bank of
America caused the studios to produce far
more pro-business movies. This led to a
discussion of how a 1918 directive from
David Niles, serving in capacity as head of
both the Labor Dept. Motion Picture Section
and Chmn. of the Joint Committee of Motion
Picture Activities during the Wilson administration had the effect of fostering an
atmosphere of self-censorship by the studios. [NOTE: The letter sent by David Niles
to every motion picture studio included the
following excerpts: "request conference
with me prior to starting productions based
on Socialism, labor problems,
etc….Portraying a screen villain as a member of the IWW or the Bolsheviki is positively harmful whereas portraying the hero
as a strong, virile American and believer
of American institutions and ideals will do
much good . . . the motion picture industry
can do more to stabilize labor and help
bring about normal conditions than any
other agency . . . a number of films currently in production are being noted by the
Department, and there may be some sort of
Government supervision exercised before
they are marketed . . . valuable government
endorsements could result from cooperation
with the Labor Department while lack of
cooperation could open the door to federal
censorship."]

  Lees and Rinaldo seemed to be particularly well-acquainted with the details of
Niles's letter and also seemed intent on
exploiting its contents to justify their
contention that the so-called Red Scare
during the Wilson administration had an
ideological impact on Universal Studios'
1931 production of *Dracula*.

  Elia Kazan: The palookas in charge of
all the big companies snapped a cap at the
though that what happened in Russia in 1917

could happen here . . . some lug owns
General Motors buys a stake in a movie studio, you think it doesn't come with strings
. . . Dracula is the Chairman of the Board
of GM and US Steel all rolled into one.
Sucking the blood of out of union men.
That's what Renfield is, you know. He's a
square Joe who just wants to do his job,
but Dracula sucks the very life out of him.

Lloyd Bridges: Sacco and Vanzetti, the
Palmer Raids, anarchist bombings up and
down the country, it made everyone in the
country with money suspicious that anyone
from another country was just here to steal
from them . . . that's what Dracula became,
not so much a vampire as a sinister threat
from Europe . . . it was Lugosi's accent
that sealed the deal.

Burl Ives: [Ives mainly contributed by
singing folk songs in which he replaced the
original lyrics with new ones based on the
context of the conversation . . . "Froggy
Went a-Courtin" told a story about David
Niles courting Universal Studios producer
Carl Laemmle to make a movie in which a
corrupt union boss is revealed to be
Dracula who is creating a legion of vampire
union men trying to take over the studio .
. . "Home on the Range" became a song about
the Palmer Raids targeting Dracula for
deportation back to Transylvania.]

Edward Dmytryk: You know the only other
Dracula movie ever made before Universal
got the rights was a kraut picture called
"Nosferatu." Ugly as hell. The smartest
thing Browning did there was hire Lugosi.
That was all it took. One swing of the lum-
ber and Dracula went from a repulsive little ratface you wouldn't dare put on the
screen for more than ten seconds at a time
to a seductive foreigner that gave women
ants in their pants and brought back
stronger than ever the smell of blood
streaming from the throat of Tsar Nicholas.

Federal Bureau of Investigation
United States Department of Justice
Los Angeles, California
May 23, 1948

Director, FBI +! CHANGED TO APLL by SCA RH
RE: Abbott and Costello Meet Frankenstein
COMMUNIST SUBVERSION

Dear Sir:

THE MOTION PICTURE ALLIANCE FOR THE PRESERVATION OF AMERICAN
IDEALS is a staunchly pro-American organization populated by
such Hollywood luminaries as Walt Disney, Barbara Stanwyck,
John Wayne, Hedda Hopper, Gary Cooper, and FBI informant T-10,
Ronald Reagan. Another member in good standing is well-known
author Ayn Rand. In 1947, Rand testified before the House
Committee on Un-American Activities regarding Communist infiltration of the motion picture industry. She is admittedly an
anti-Communist and has previously co-operated with the Bureau's
request to review motion pictures as a result of her knowledge
of Communist propaganda tactics outlined in the pamphlet
published by the Alliance titled SCREEN GUIDE FOR AMERICANS.
  With the assistance of agents in the Bureau's Los Angeles
office, Rand was able to attend the first sneak preview of
"ABBOTT AND COSTELLO MEET FRANKENSTEIN" held at the Academy
Theater in Inglewood, California on May 18, 1948. A summary of
the highlights of pertinent information included in her review
is set out below. It should be noted that Rand's complete
review runs to twenty-two pages and features a great many
diversions and tangents on her self-described philosophy of
Objectivism as well as extended quotations from her
publications.

Testimony of Ayn Rand

Almost from the moment that the opening animated credits for
Abbott and Costello Meet Frankenstein drew to a close, I was
bombarded with a concrete affirmation of my own words: "the
purpose of the Communists in Hollywood is not the production of
political movies openly advocating Communism." If the Federal
Bureau of Investigation really wants to instruct its special

agents in the tactics of decoding subversive messages in non-political movies, then it could not likely find a more useful tool for these purposes than *Abbott and Costello Meet Frankenstein*.

To begin with, the film should more rightly titled *Abbott and Costello Meet Dracula* since that iconographic figure of literary horror is not just the most important character that the comedy duo meet, he is also the ideological center of gravity holding together what passes for a plot. Since that ideological center of gravity is portrayed as a bloodsucking figure of that most pernicious of communist myths—that capitalism is constructed upon the bedrock of belief that equates ownership of a business with absolute possession of the blood and soul of laborers.

I therefore feel compelled to remind all those who may read this analysis with, again, my own words: "the purpose of Communists working in the motion picture industry is to corrupt non-political movies by introducing small casual bits of propaganda into innocent stories and to make people absorb the basic premises of Collectivism by indirection and implication."

American moviegoers are smart enough to resist a dose of Communist propaganda delivered straight and without the sinister comfort of dilution. Things are different, though, with movies in which audiences don't expect a political message, like in a comedy or western or romance or horror film. When such movies are used as a foil to deliver a steady supply of subversion through hints and suggestions, even the strongest supporter of independent Americanism is subject to cracking like a rock battered by raindrops. Such is the potential danger posed by the most subversive element of this horror-comedy: the subtle yet utterly corrosive distortion of the character of Count Dracula.

The vampire met by Abbott and Costello is almost nothing like the Dracula that has been depicted on-screen before [not even—or perhaps, especially—portrayed by Bela Lugosi]. It is perhaps only because of this pre-existing familiarity that audience members may not immediately sense that Dracula has become a tool for Communist trickery. The aberrant portrayal of Dracula is subversive in its implications toward capitalism and represents the worst kind of pernicious communist propaganda. It seeks to arouse a false apprehension of class consciousness by generating insidious suspicion toward the motivation and purposes of businesspeople. To fully understand the utter depravity at the heart of this motion picture, keep in mind that it represents Dracula no longer as an agent of the supernatural, but as an agent of ideology. Unfortunately for movie

audiences receptive to dangerous messages, Dracula is not the
only businessman presented in such a slanderous manner.

The character of McDougal is introduced very early in the
picture as a boilerplate archetype designed to divert the audience from consciously perceiving Dracula as the film's authentic symbol of capitalist evil. This is done in such a clumsy
manner that we should perhaps actually be thankful that
Communists prefer crudely inserted proselytism over elegant
dramaturgy. Otherwise, their mischief might be significantly
less easy to spot. McDougal is the blustery owner of a House
of Horrors which quite clearly is intended to equate honestly
acquired wealth and free enterprise with such foolish associa-
tions as ghoulishness and preying upon the fears and anxieties
of Americans to achieve an honest profit.

Further undermining the status that McDougal should rightly
be awarded for his industrialism and contribution to our thriv-
ing economy is his boasting of making a great deal to cheaply
obtain the remains of the original Count Dracula and the body
of Frankenstein's monster. This boast is paired with an
unseemly undertone of sexual enticement to a young woman standing next to him, which only serves to indicate that he is
either foolish enough to have been tricked by the foreign agent
who sold him these two seemingly bogus items, or that he is
cunning enough to pass off what he knows can't actually be
authentic by feigning his own conviction.

Either way, McDougal is yet another representative in the
growing list of movie characters who in the real world would be
characterized by such virtuous traits as productive genius,
initiative, energy and the courage to dare. But in the hands of
motion pictures writing Soviet apparatchiks, he is likened to
gangsters, bank robbers, and looters. And to remove even the
faintest of doubts in the minds of their audience as regards
the true nature of McDougal in this clockwork propaganda
machine masquerading as a horror-comedy, the directors of
Abbott and Costello Meet Dracula don't even shy away from the
cheapest of showmanship: Near the end of the motion picture,
McDougal attends a masquerade ball—not in just any costume, no,
he dresses up as the devil, complete with horns. The businessman has eventually become a monster. This is, in turn, a
reflection of the movie's bolder proclamation that Dracula is
more monstrous as a capitalist than he ever was as a vampire.

*"This time the monster must have no will of his own . . .
no fiendish intellect to oppose his master."* This singular line
of dialogue spoken by Dracula in the movie is representative of
the reprehensible and utterly appalling premise of the entire
picture. If anyone should ever inquire why the Federal Bureau

of Investigation and the House of Representatives are "wasting" time and money scrutinizing non-political movies for examples of communist propaganda, simply reply that with this film Abbott and Costello have done something that even Karl Marx himself could not do: expose millions of Americans in an actually entertaining manner to an outline of the basic tenets of Communism's philosophy.

According to this worldview, the ideal worker within the capitalist system is little more than a soulless automaton incapable of making either moral or intellectual choices. He exists only to be conditioned into a sniveling, drooling, neurotic spiritual weakling. If McDougal is the model for those millions of local business owners who are merely blustering fools masquerading as the devil, then Dracula is the epitome of those captains of industry that capitalism can produce only at the expense of others and that gray herd of robots relieved of personal ambition, stripped of self-respect and so dispirited and hopeless that they can be easily manipulated to obey his every order.

At one point Dracula says "what we need today is young blood . . . and brains." Previous to Lees's and Rinaldo's incarnation of the vampire, Dracula has never expressed an interest in brains, further underlining just how far removed from this traditional vampiric origins the writers have moved the character. Perhaps this is some sort of inside joke for the Communists in the audience about the Marxian concept of the alienation of the worker, in addition to a clumsy plot device necessary to drive the bewildering narrative strain that clearly exists solely for the purpose of hammering home its simplistic, one-dimensional, and utterly depraved syllogism: all capitalists are evildoers and all evildoers are monsters, therefore all capitalists are monsters.

Surely, it is not by accident that the screenwriters never reveal exactly what evildoing Dracula plans once he has mastered Frankenstein's secrets of brain transplantation. Just one short scene touches upon this mystery. But it happens in such a passing way that all we know for sure is that it is "risky business" that promises to be "much more profitable" than criminal activities and requires a creature with "no fiendish intellect to oppose his master."

Final thought: Most distressing is the possibility that the writers actually intended Dracula to represent successful American businessmen—Businessmen trying to subjugate a Creature representing the growing segment of the populace being duped every day into accepting Communist propaganda.

```
AMSD           RECORDED - 18 1/0-
MMB: bjh
100-138754-101962
```

Excerpts from comment cards following sneak preview of "ABBOTT
AND COSTELLO MEET FRANKENSTEIN" held at Academy Theater in
Inglewood, California, May 18, 1948. (Only those excerpts
deemed appropriately relevant to the Bureau's investigation
have been included.)

". . . imbecilic . . . and offensive to the mind to be presented as entertainment in such troubled times"
"This is the type of picture which should only be a studio
preview. Charging admission is almost misrepresentation."

"I go to the movies so I can sit back, be entertained and
forget about the worries of the world for a couple of hours,
not so I can walk out a bundle of nerves and fearful of every
shadow that moves in the dark." Disagreement persists over the
exact meaning of this comment. Agents who interviewed audience
members remain convinced that all comments are directed toward
the actual content, however, a psychologist and a handwriting
expert brought in by the L.A. field office both concluded that
ALL negative comments on the cards exhibit clear signs of a
mind wrought with anxiety related to the communist threat. It
is my unofficial observation that nobody at the preview with
whom the Bureau communicated saw any signs of communist subversion. S.A. B.J.H.

RE: COMMUNIST INFILTRATION OF THE MOTION PICTURE INDUSTRY
L.A. File: 101962

DECLASSIFIED BY:
 John "Rip" Ripley
On: 1-15-96
```

# A Final Note

In his novel *Dracula*, Bram Stoker indicates that one of the few
effective means at the disposal of vampire slayers for bringing
the merciless serial killing spree of the creature to an end for
good is decapitation followed by stuffing the mouth of the dis-
```

embodied skull with garlic for good measure. If it's true that that those Americans expressing their Constitutional right to membership in the Communist Party (a right which was never at any time illegal, by the way) can accurately be described as hunted down by rabid stake-wielding anti-Communists, then it is also true that Robert Lees experienced the additional indignity described by Stoker.

Exactly fifty-three years, two months, and three days after actor Sterling Hayden figuratively drove a stake through the heart of Robert Lees by naming him as a member of the Communist Party to the House Committee on Un-American Activities, a homeless drifter broke into the home of the man who co-wrote *Abbott and Costello Meet Frankenstein* and, after a violent physical assault, quite literally decapitated the ninety-one-year-old unrepentant Communist.[1] Of course, the ultimate indignity suffered by Lees was perhaps living long enough to see Elia Kazan buried a little less than a year before with a Lifetime Achievement Oscar as his final reward for being the most famous namer of names from the Hollywood Blacklist era.[2]

---

[1] Editor's note: Yes, he really had his head cut off.

[2] Editor's note: Young and innocent readers may need to be told that this chapter combines real events with made up ones. We leave it to you to figure out which is which.

References

Arendt, Hannah. 1963. *Eichmann in Jerusalem*. Penguin.

———. 1970. *On Violence*. Harcourt, Brace Jovanovich.

———. 1973. *Origins of Totalitarianism*. Harcourt, Brace Jovanovich. 1973.

———. 1971. *Thinking*. Volume 1 of *The Life of the Mind*. Harcourt.

Aristotle. 2002. *Nicomachean Ethics*. Oxford University Press.

Auerbach, Nina. 1995. *Our Vampires, Ourselves*. University of Chicago Press.

Barthes, Roland. 1977. *Image, Music, Text*. Hill and Wang.

Becker, Ernest. 2007. *The Denial of Death*. Simon and Schuster.

Benjamin, Walter. 2009 [1936]. *The Work of Art in the Age of Mechanical Reproduction*. Classic Books America.

Bentham Jeremy. 2007 [1789]. *An Introduction to the Principles of Morals and Legislation*. Dover.

Butler, Judith. 1990. *Gender Trouble: Feminism and the Subversion of Identity*. Routledge.

———. 2011. Your Behavior Creates Your Gender. <http://bigthink.com/videos/your-behavior-creates-your-gender>.

Campbell, Joseph. 1968. *The Hero with a Thousand Faces*. Princeton University Press.

———. 1990. *The Hero's Journey: Joseph Campbell on His Life and Work*. Harper and Row.

Camus, Albert. 2008 [1942]. *The Stranger*. Cambridge University Press.

Cazotte, Jacques. 2011 [1991]. *The Devil in Love*. Dedalus.

Chalmers, David. 2010. *The Character of Consciousness*. Oxford University Press.

Daly, Carroll John. 1947. *The Legion of the Living Dead*. Popular Publications.

Dreyfus, Hubert L. 1978. *What Computers Can't Do: The Limits of Artificial Intelligence*. HarperCollins.

———. 1992. *What Computers Still Can't Do: A Critique of Artificial Reason*. MIT Press.

Elrod, P.N. 1993. *I Strahd: Memoirs of a Vampire*. Wizards of the Coast.

Engels, Friedrich. 1993 [1844]. *The Condition of the Working Class in England*. Oxford University Press.

Fischer, John Martin, and Mark Ravizza. *1998. Responsibility and Control: A Theory of Moral Responsibility*. Cambridge University Press.

Fodor, Jerry A. 1998. *Concepts: Where Cognitive Science Went Wrong*. Oxford University Press.

Freud, Sigmund. 1962. *Civilization and Its Discontents*. Norton.

Gallois, André. 1998. *Occasions of Identity*. Clarendon.

Greene, Richard, and K. Silem Mohammad, eds. 2010. *Zombies, Vampires, and Philosophy: New Life for the Undead*. Open Court.

Gunn, James. 2004. *The Immortals*. Gallery.

Hambly, Barbara. 1990. *Those Who Hunt the Night*. Del Rey.

Haslanger, Sally, and Roxanne Marie Kurtz. 2006. *Persistence: Contemporary Readings*. MIT Press.

Heidegger, Martin. 2008. *Being and Time*. Harper and Row.

Hohfeld, Wesley Newcomb. 2010. *Fundamental Legal Conceptions as Applied in Judicial Reasoning*. Lawbook Exchange.

Hume, David. 2000 [1739]. *A Treatise of Human Nature*. Oxford University Press.

Jackson, Ashley. 2013. *The British Empire: A Very Short Introduction*. Oxford University Press.

Jung, Carl Gustav, and Marie-Louise von Franz, eds. 1968. *Man and His Symbols*. Doubleday.

Kagan, Shelly. 2012. *Death*. Yale University Press.

Kant, Immanuel. 2002. *Groundwork for the Metaphysics of Morals*. Yale University Press.

Kierkegaard, Søren. 1986. *Fear and Trembling*. Penguin.

———. 1988. *Stages on Life's Way: Studies by Various Persons*. Princeton University Press.

———. 1992. *Either/Or: A Fragment of Life*. Penguin.

Locke, John. 1996. *An Essay concerning Human Understanding*. Hackett.

MacKenzie, Andrew. 1977. *Dracula Country: Travels and Folk Beliefs in Romania*. Barker.

Madison, Bob. 1997. *Dracula: The First Hundred Years*. Midnight Marquee.

Maimonides, Moses. 2004. *The Guide for the Perplexed*. Barnes and Noble.

Marx, Karl H. 1992. [1867]. *Capital: A Critique of Political Economy.* Volume 1. Penguin.

Melton, J. Gordon. 1998. *The Vampire Book: The Encyclopedia of the Undead.* Invisible Ink.

Mill, John Stuart. 2010. *Utilitarianism.* Broadview.

Nagel, Thomas. 1974. What Is It Like to Be a Bat? *Philosophical Review* 83:4. Reprinted in many places, including Nagel's *Mortal Questions*, and easily available free online.

———. 1991. *Mortal Questions.* Canto.

Nietzsche, Friedrich Wilhelm. 1914. *The Complete Works of Friedrich Nietzsche.* Volume 11, *Thus Spake Zarathustra.* Foulis.

———. 2003. *Beyond Good and Evil.* Penguin.

Plotinus. 1991. *The Enneads: Abridged Edition.* Penguin.

Polidori, John. 2008. *The Vampyre: And Other Tales of the Macabre.* Oxford University Press.

Ramsland, Katherine. 1998. *Piercing the Darkness: Undercover with Vampires in America Today.* HarperCollins.

Rice, Anne. 1976. *Interview with the Vampire.* Knopf.

———. 1985. *The Vampire Lestat.* Knopf.

Rice, Jeff. 1973. *The Night Stalker.* Pocket Books.

Saberhagen, Fred. 1980. *The Dracula Tape.* Ace.

———. 2002. *A Coldness in the Blood.* Tor.

Searle, John R. 1984. *Minds, Brains, and Science.* Harvard University Press.

———. 1992. *The Rediscovery of the Mind.* MIT Press.

Shelley, Mary. 2007 [1818]. *Frankenstein: Or, the Modern Prometheus.* Penguin.

Sider, Theodore. 2001. *Four-Dimensionalism.* Oxford University Press.

Sidgwick, Henry. 1981 [1874]. *The Methods of Ethics.* Hackett.

South, James B., ed. 2003. *Buffy the Vampire Slayer and Philosophy: Fear and Trembling in Sunnydale.* Open Court.

Stoker, Bram. 1994 [1897]. *Dracula.* Penguin.

———. 2002 [1897]. *Dracula.* Palgrave.

———. 2004 [1897]. *Dracula.* Barnes and Noble Classics.

———. Not dated [1897]. *Dracula.* <www.literature.org/authors/stoker-bram/dracula>.

———. Not dated [1897]. *Dracula.* Free eBooks, <www.planetebook.com/ebooks/Dracula.pdf>.

Strauss, Leo. 1988 [1952]. *Persecution and the Art of Writing.* University of Chicago Press.

Stroumsa, Sarah. 2009. *Maimonides in His World: Portrait of a Mediterranean Thinker.* Princeton University Press.

Swift, Jonathan. 2003 [1726]. *Gulliver's Travels.* Penguin.

Talmud. 2012. *The Soncino Babylonian Talmud: Sanhedrin*. Talmudic Books.

Twersky, Isadore, ed. 1972. *A Maimonides Reader*. Behrman House.

Williams, Bernard. 1981. *Moral Luck: Philosophical Papers 1973–1980*. Cambridge University Press.

Yarbro, Chelsea Quinn. 2002 [1978]. *Hotel Transylvania: A Novel of Forbidden Love*. Warner.

The New Crew of Light

JOHN ALTMANN is a philosophy student who operates his own online network known as Ferrum Intellectus on Issuu as well as Academia.edu, and who once wrote a thesis alongside Dracula on vampiric existentialism. The experience left him with two holes in his neck. He feels fine though, . . . totally fine.

ROBERT ARP is a philosopher who works for the US Army as a research analyst. Hey, What's the Kantian vampire's fundamental moral principle called? The Bat-egorical Imperative.

ADAM BARKMAN is an associate professor of philosophy at Redeemer University College, and the author and editor of more than half a dozen books, most recently *The Culture and Philosophy of Ridley Scott* and *Imitating the Saints*. One of Adam's proudest moments is when he took his two eldest kids to "Dracula's Castle" in Transylvania and watched them correctly wield their crosses, holy water (from Bulgaria), and toy crossbow.

COLE BOWMAN is an independent scholar and writer living in Portland, Oregon. While writing is her day job, her true passion brings her out at night to carry on Van Helsing's tradition. She contributed to this volume to flush out some of the bloodsuckers that lurk in philosophy departments the world over.

CARI CALLIS has always had an attraction to bad boys . . . and Dracula is only one in a long list of them. She lives with a wolf dog and a bat dog and teaches screenwriting to bloodthirsty students at Columbia College Chicago.

ARIANE DE WAAL is a lecturer and PhD candidate at Ruhr University Bochum, Germany. At the time of writing, she is pursuing research at Queen Mary University of London. Is she really, though? Rumor has it she arrived on a deserted ship containing nothing but fifty boxes of common earth . . .

MARY GREEN studies screenwriting in Oregon. In her spare time she is a Svengali who dominates, manipulates, and controls Ronald S. Green for malevolent purposes, transforming him into a great writer through a combination of hypnosis and the MLA.

RONALD S. GREEN teaches at Coastal Carolina University. To keep sane while being dominated, manipulated, and controlled by a Svengali, he and his two robot sidekicks provide a wisecracking commentary on various topics in pop culture and philosophy from front row seats in the Mystery Science Theater.

RICHARD GREENE is Professor of Philosophy at Weber State University, and is the Chair of the Intercollegiate Ethics Bowl's Executive Board. He's a fan of many a fine vampire, but most closely identifies with Count Blah from Greg the Bunny. Blah!

TIM JONES teaches Literature at the University of East Anglia and also works as an elected councilman for Norwich City Council. The latter role has absolutely nothing in common with sitting in a huge building overlooking the town and glutting yourself on the blood of its populace, despite what the press might have you think.

"Sleep all day long; run rampant at night; and live forever. Where do I sign up?", you might wonder. But JOHN V. KARAVITIS, CPA, MBA, knows that vampires have got it all wrong! Wanna live forever? No need to become one of the Undead. Just publish an essay in a Popular Culture and Philosophy book! *Immortalitas praestatur!*

CHRISTOPHER KETCHAM is a reformed academic who lives near Philly. He writes on social justice, philosophy and popular culture, and risk management where he has contributed to and edited two books. Having gone to school with the son of the great Dracula Scholar, Radu Florescu, his indoctrination to darkness came early . . . and never left . . . never left.

On moonless nights, GREG LITTMANN rises from his tomb to be associate professor of philosophy at SIUE, publishing on metaphysics, epistemology, philosophy of logic, and philosophy of professional philosophy. He has written numerous chapters, all in human blood, for books relating philosophy to popular culture, including volumes on *Dune, Frankenstein*, Sherlock Holmes, Roald Dahl, and Neil Gaiman. A silver crucifix is not an effective protection against Greg Littmann, unless you stab him with it, in which case it works pretty well.

JAMES EDWIN MAHON is Professor of Philosophy and Head of the Philosophy Department at Washington and Lee University. Like his countryman Bram Stoker, he is a graduate of Trinity College, Dublin. Unlike Woody Allen, he *does* want to achieve immortality through his work, rather than through not dying.

TRIP MCCROSSIN teaches in the Philosophy Department at Rutgers University, where he works on, among other things, the nature, history, and legacy of the Enlightenment. Why do his students find it odd, he wonders, on the first day of classes, to hear him say, "Welcome to my house. Come freely. Go safely; and leave something of the happiness you bring!"

SHAWN MCKINNEY teaches philosophy at Hillsborough Community College in Ruskin, Florida. He previously contributed to *Ender's Game and Philosophy: Genocide Is Child's Play*. Shawn enjoys vampire prose, movies, and comic books. His first exposure to Dracula was probably to the bunny rabbit version, Bunnicula.

NICOLAS MICHAUD teaches philosophy and English in Jacksonville Florida. His students have been spreading the rumor that he is a vampire. They may not be wrong. Too bad . . . for them . . . that they let his secret out.

JANELLE PÖTZSCH holds a PhD in philosophy and works at Ruhr University Bochum, Germany. She has contributed chapters to *Frankenstein and Philosophy: The Shocking Truth* and *Jurassic Park and Philosophy: The Truth Is Terrifying*. On lonely, moonless nights in the library she sometimes ponders whether she shouldn't leave her undead state as an academic philosopher and look for a real job. Vampire slayer, for instance.

NICOLE R. PRAMIK is a novelist and adjunct Humanities Instructor. She's been a contributor to *SpongeBob SquarePants and Philosophy: Soaking Up Secrets Under the Sea!* as well as *The Devil and Philosophy: The Nature of His Game*. She has at least one thing in common with Mina Harker—she believes the world is full of good men, even if there are monsters in it. But she's not telepathically linked to any vampire counts, at least, none she's aware of.

TIMOTHY SEXTON sucked the blood out of Arthur Conan Doyle, Alex Trebek, and Steven Spielberg in order to let the right idea in for his contributions to volumes about the philosophies of Sherlock Holmes, *Jeopardy!*, and *Jurassic Park*. For this, the Master conferred upon him the title (and cheaply priced domain) The Everything of Internet. And don't tell anyone, but he's the real-life model for the character of Spike in Buffy.

VIKTORIA STRUNK writes about serial killers and porcine indigestion when she is not busy bleeding red over her students' essays. She very much believes in vampires, ghosts, and other things that go bump in the night.

MICHAEL VERSTEEG has contributed to several books about pop culture and philosophy, including *The Philosophy of J.J. Abrams* and *The Devil and Philosophy: The Nature of His Game*. Oddly enough, his family has a history of the hereditary disease *porphyria,* also known as the *vampire's disease.* So every once in a while he might get a sudden uncontrollable craving for human blood . . . nothing too unusual.

JAMES WILLIS, III works at Indiana University and lives in the dark forests north of Bloomington, Indiana. He might be a vampire, but the discussion of what it means *to be* is far too complex. Let's just say he lives in the dark woods.

IVAN WOLFE has a PhD from the University of Texas at Austin and teaches at Arizona State University. He spends summers in Alaska, which makes it hard to actually do much, since it's light all the time.

Index